ECONOMICS:

AN INTERPRETATIVE SCIENCE OF HUMAN FLOURISHING

Carmelo Ferlito has persuasively and clearly demonstrated the relevance of the interpretive-hermeneutic tradition in the Austrian school of political economy, not only for economic policy but social scientific understanding more generally. The lessons of this publication should be imbibed by students, practitioners and especially academics, especially those in mainstream economic thought.

Dr. Bryan Cheang – *London School of Economics, United Kingdom*

This brilliant, impressive, and beautifully written book offers a powerful and incisive critique of the scientism and objectivism that afflict contemporary economics. Drawing on the hermeneutic tradition, a fallibilist conception of science, the Austrian School of Economics, and Schumpeter's theory of creative destruction, the author argues that economic dynamics cannot be captured by simplistic formal models or by mere correlations among statistical data. These dynamics ultimately arise from the ways in which agents creatively and unpredictably interpret the flow of experience, generating often unintended consequences. According to the author, the most urgent task is to re-humanize economics by restoring the indeterminism of action to the centre of analysis. In these passionate, erudite, and stimulating pages, younger scholars will discover a methodological and theoretical richness absent from mainstream textbooks, along with a clear and incisive account of their limitations.

Prof. Francesco Di Iorio – *University of Insubria, Italy, and Nankai University, China*

Drawing on a sustained engagement with the arguments developed across this volume, Carmelo Ferlito offers a remarkably coherent and original rethinking of economics as an interpretative science of human action. The book moves convincingly from methodological reflection to substantive debates on capital, cycles, money, and innovation, consistently restoring meaning, time, and agency to the centre of economic analysis. Firmly grounded in the Austrian tradition yet philosophically ambitious, this work speaks not only to economists, but to all readers concerned with the human foundations of social order and economic flourishing.

Dr. Andrea Passeri – *Taylor's University, Malaysia*

Center for Market Education

ECONOMICS:

AN INTERPRETATIVE SCIENCE OF HUMAN FLOURISHING

SELECTED ESSAYS BY

Carmelo Ferlito

With a Foreword by Fithra Faisal Hastiadi and
Prefaces by Sukasah Syahdan and Alvin Desfiandi

Monolateral

ISBN-13: 978-1-946374-34-9 (paperback)
ASIN: (e-book)

Typesetting and cover design by Amber BlueCat Creative
Cover images by Merlin Lightpainting, Nitin Arya

Monolateral
monolateral.com

Table of Contents

Foreword

There are moments in the life of a discipline when it must pause—not to calculate, not to forecast, but to remember why it exists. This book, *Economics: An Interpretative Science of Human Flourishing*, by Carmelo Ferlito, arrives precisely at such a moment—when economics risks becoming technically brilliant yet spiritually hollow, rich in equations yet poor in understanding.

For too long, we have treated the economy as if it were a machine: pull a lever, adjust an interest rate, tweak a variable, and expect predictable outcomes. Yet human societies are not engines of steel and code. They are living tapestries of hope, fear, creativity, memory, and meaning. Every transaction carries a story. Every price contains expectations. Every cycle reflects the fragile dance between knowledge and ignorance, optimism and error.

Carmelo Ferlito reminds us—gently yet firmly—that economics was never meant to be merely the science of numbers. It was born as a moral and interpretative inquiry into human action. Long before regression tables and optimization algorithms, economics sought to understand how people make choices in time, under uncertainty, guided by values, institutions, and imagination.

This book is an invitation to return to that deeper calling.

Across its pages, we encounter a vision of economics not as mechanical equilibrium, but as a dynamic process of discovery. Capital is not a pile of objects but a structure of meanings shaped by entrepreneurial interpretation. Markets are not static outcomes but conversations—imperfect, evolving, and profoundly human. Inflation is not just a statistic; it is a disruption of trust. Business cycles are not mere deviations but expressions of expectation, misjudgment, learning, and renewal.

At the heart of this work lies a simple yet radical proposition: understanding must come before measurement.

Data without meaning misleads. Models without humanity distort. Policy without humility risks becoming technocratic arrogance.

Drawing from the Austrian tradition and enriched by hermeneutical philosophy, Carmelo places human agency back at the center of economic life. Individuals are not passive responders to incentives but active interpreters of reality—constantly revising plans in the flow of real time.

Uncertainty is not a nuisance to be eliminated; it is the very condition that makes creativity, entrepreneurship, and progress possible.

And from this interpretative foundation emerges the book's ultimate concern: human flourishing. Flourishing is not reducible to GDP growth or price stability. It is about expanding real opportunities for people to pursue meaningful lives—within institutions that respect freedom, responsibility, and learning. Markets, when understood as processes of coordination and discovery, become moral ecosystems where trust, innovation, and cooperation can thrive.

What makes this contribution particularly powerful is that it is not written from the comfort of abstraction alone. Carmelo's intellectual journey is shaped by real-world experience—where volatility, time constraints, policy distortions, and entrepreneurial judgment are not theoretical curiosities but daily realities. Theory here is not ornament; it is a lens to understand life.

In an era increasingly dominated by algorithms, technocracy, and the illusion of perfect control, this book offers something far more valuable: wisdom.

It calls economists to be interpreters, not merely technicians.
It calls policymakers to be humble, not omniscient.
It calls students to seek meaning, not just methods.

Above all, it calls the discipline to remember that at the center of every economic model stands a human being—dreaming, choosing, failing, learning, and hoping.

If economics is to remain relevant in the twenty-first century, it must rediscover its soul.

This book is a courageous step in that direction.

May it inspire a new generation of economists to look beyond numbers, to listen to reality with openness, and to rebuild the science of economics as what it was always meant to be: a profound inquiry into human action, social coordination, and the conditions of flourishing.

Fithra Faisal Hastiadi
Spokesperson
Government Communication Agency
Republic of Indonesia

Prefaces

Over the past eight years, I have had the privilege of calling Carmelo Ferlito not only a colleague but a close friend. I first introduced him to Universitas Prasetiya Mulya in BSD City, where we now share the joy of teaching and, most recently, collaborated on the course *Evolution of Economic Thought*. Before Carmelo joined me in teaching this subject, I had earlier taught it in tandem with one of Indonesia's most prominent economists, Prof. Dr. Djisman Simanjuntak, then serving as Rector of Universitas Prasetiya Mulya. Recognizing Carmelo's deep expertise in the history of economic thought, I suggested to the head of Business and Economics at the university that we invite him to teach this subject with me—a decision that proved immensely rewarding.

This book, *Economics: An Interpretative Science of Human Flourishing*, is the fruit of more than a decade of his scholarly journey—a collection of essays that challenges the reduction of economics to mere measurement and prediction. Instead, it reclaims economics as a human science, rooted in meaning, creativity, and the complexity of lived experience.

In the coming pages, readers will encounter a vision of economics that prioritizes understanding before quantification, drawing inspiration from Austrian thinkers and hermeneutical philosophy. It is a work that speaks to our shared conviction: that economics, at its best, is not a mechanical pursuit of equilibrium but an interpretative endeavor aimed at human flourishing.

Sukasah Syahdan
Faculty Member
School of Business and Economics
Universitas Prasetiya Mulya

* * *

Economics is often taught as if it were a machine: adjust a lever, predict an outcome. Yet economies are not machines. They are living orders of human action shaped by meaning, expectations, error, learning, and institutions, unfolding in real time under uncertainty. When economics forgets this, it becomes technically impressive but interpretatively fragile.

This book, *Economics: An Interpretative Science of Human Flourishing*, argues for a demanding correction: economics must begin with understanding before it rushes to measurement. "Interpretative" does not mean unscientific; it means realistic. Data and models become informative only when grounded in a truthful account of human agency; how people form plans, revise them, discover knowledge, and coordinate (or fail to) through institutions and market processes.

Across topics such as money, inflation, capital, cycles, entrepreneurship, and innovation, Carmelo Ferlito develops a consistent view rooted in the Austrian tradition: markets are processes of discovery, prices are signals embedded in context, and profit and loss are feedback that disciplines plans. Entrepreneurship is therefore not a footnote to optimization, but a central force of coordination in an open-ended world.

The book's focus on human flourishing follows naturally. Flourishing is not reducible to a single statistic. It concerns the real opportunities people have to pursue meaningful lives, opportunities shaped by rules and institutions that stabilize expectations and widen the space for responsible choice.

These arguments carry weight because they are written by a scholar shaped by practice. Carmelo is an economist with substantial professional experience, including in the poultry industry, where time constraints, volatility, regulation, and supply chains make abstract shortcuts costly. That experience does not replace theory; it tests and sharpens it.

I have worked with Carmelo for almost seven years, since Kasah, my colleague at Universitas Prasetiya Mulya, first connected us. What has stood out is his rare seriousness about scholarship: careful reading, disciplined argument, and an insistence that economics remain honest about knowledge, time, and uncertainty. Carmelo serves as CEO of the Center for Market Education (CME) and is also a Faculty Member of

Universitas Prasetiya Mulya. In CME, he expanded my own economic knowledge by appointing me as one of his associates and drawing me into a community where ideas are treated as instruments of understanding, not ideological ornaments.

This book does not promise easy answers. It offers something more durable: a way of thinking that takes human agency seriously, treats time and uncertainty as fundamental, and judges institutions by whether they widen the space for responsible flourishing. In an era of rapid change and recurring policy certainty, that is not a niche approach. It is a necessary one.

Alvin Desfiandi
Head of Undergraduate Business Economics Program
School of Business and Economics
Universitas Prasetiya Mulya

Introduction

I never read [any other work of Hayek's], I simply found it incomprehensible[1, 2]

Robert Solow

Premise

Modern economics stands at a crossroads. For more than a century, it has pursued the ideal of precision, equating the advancement of knowledge with the refinement of mathematical and statistical instruments. This effort produced powerful tools and dazzling formal structures, yet it also impoverished the very spirit of inquiry that once made economics a moral and interpretative science. The crisis of economics today is not merely the failure to forecast recessions or to design effective policies; it is an intellectual and existential crisis — the eclipse of *understanding* by *measurement.*

What was once the "science of human action" has been reduced to a calculus of correlations. The living world of entrepreneurs, workers, and consumers has been translated into variables and coefficients, while the meaning of their actions — the reasons they act, the interpretations they form, the expectations they revise — has been pushed to the margins. The profession now measures what it no longer understands. It speaks in the grammar of data but has forgotten the language of meaning.

1. From *measurement* to *understanding*

The central ambition of this book is to contribute to the rebirth of economics as a science of understanding — *verstehen* — rather than

1 Birner (2002), p. 27. The full passage goes: «I did read Hayek as a student (...). I found it completely incomprehensible. I was assigned to read *Prices and Production* (...) [It was] not that I thought it was wrong so much as I did not understand it (...) I thought there's got to be something wrong with the man who could write that. And I never read [any other work of Hayek's]. I simply found it incomprehensible». I found the anecdote in White (2007, p. xxxii).

2 I chose to open the present essay collection with Solow's quote because I am aware that the way I present my research is, to say the least, somewhat out of fashion. I was trained as an economist before the widespread rise of econometrics and its near-complete dominance over the discipline—an evolution that has gradually diminished the role of economic theory in economic discourse.

Recognizing that my paper may speak a language different from what is now common not only in academic economics but also in policy discussions makes me all the more grateful to the Center for Market Education (CME). It has offered me a space to put into writing my unorthodox reflections, in the hope that they can enrich the debate and encourage new ways of thinking.

mere prediction. This perspective is not nostalgic. It does not call for abandoning rigor but for re-defining it. True rigor does not lie in the precision of models detached from life, but in the intellectual honesty of confronting complexity without reducing it to what can be quantified.

To understand is to interpret — to seek the meanings that individuals attribute to their actions and to the world they inhabit. Economic reality is not a set of physical events governed by immutable laws; it is a field of intentional behavior, shaped by human imagination, expectations, and learning. As the Austrian tradition has long emphasized, economic phenomena emerge from the interaction of *acting men and women* in historical time — a time filled with novelty, uncertainty, and discovery. Every market transaction, every investment decision, every entrepreneurial initiative is an act of interpretation: a response to perceived opportunities, risks, and meanings.

When measurement supplants understanding, the discipline loses its soul. Theories become detached from life; policies become exercises in social engineering; and economists, rather than interpreters of reality, become its bureaucrats. The dominance of econometrics and model-building has led to what F.A. von Hayek called "the pretense of knowledge": the illusion that social order can be planned and predicted through mathematical control. Yet, as history repeatedly reminds us, societies are not laboratories, and human beings are not particles. Their actions are meaningful, not mechanical.

2. Reason as *openness*: The Aristotelian foundation

The rediscovery of *understanding* must begin with a renewed conception of reason itself. The modern age has reduced reason to *rationality* — to calculation, optimization, and instrumental control. In this view, to be "rational" means to select the most efficient means for given ends. But Aristotle's *logos* was something far richer: reason as openness, as the capacity to be surprised by reality and to engage with it dialogically. True reason does not close the world within formulas; it keeps it open to inquiry. It is animated by *thaumazein* — the gaze of wonder — which acknowledges the mystery and plurality of being.

This Aristotelian spirit of openness stands at the heart of the interpretative vision proposed in this book. Understanding presupposes humility: the awareness that reality always exceeds our representations. Measurement, by contrast, presupposes closure: the belief that what cannot be quantified does not exist. The rebirth of economics will require recovering reason as openness — the readiness to learn from phenomena rather than to impose upon them the tyranny of models.

The act of understanding, therefore, is not passive contemplation but active interpretation. Economists, like entrepreneurs, are participants in a hermeneutical process: they seek meaning in the flux of time, interpreting not only others' actions but also their own conceptual frameworks. This double hermeneutic — individuals interpreting the world, and economists interpreting those interpretations — defines economics as a profoundly human science.

3. The structure of the book: A path toward rebirth

The essays collected in this volume reflect a long intellectual journey devoted to restoring meaning at the centre of economic thought. Each part of the book explores a different facet of that endeavour — from the re-definition of economics itself to the reinterpretation of capital, cycles, money, and innovation. Together they form a coherent attempt to revive economics as *hermeneutical humanism.*

Part I – Defining Economics

The opening part, *Defining Economics*, addresses the most fundamental question: what is economics about? The prevailing answer — the allocation of scarce means among competing ends — has imprisoned the discipline within a static and reductionist frame. It conceives of individuals as automatons who optimize under constraints, rather than as agents who interpret and create.

Against this mechanistic vision, the first chapter reclaims the idea that economics is, above all, a *science of meaning*. It argues that human action cannot be understood as the mechanical reaction to stimuli but as the expression of purpose, imagination, and interpretation. Every economic choice arises from a dialogue between the individual and the surrounding reality, mediated by expectations and shaped in real, historical time.

This re-definition re-connects economics with its classical and humanistic roots — from Menger and Mises to Hayek and Lachmann — and with a broader philosophical tradition stretching back to Aristotle. It is within this interpretative frame that all subsequent chapters must be read.

Part II – Capital and Business Cycles

Once the methodological foundation is laid, *Part II* explores the hermeneutical nature of capital and the cyclical rhythms of economic life. Here, capital is not a stock of measurable objects but a living network of interpretations. A "capital good" becomes such not by virtue of its physical properties but because entrepreneurs *see* it as suitable to achieve certain ends. Capital formation, therefore, is a hermeneutical process — the translation of expectations into plans, and of plans into actions.

In this context, prices are not static equilibria but signals within an interpretative conversation among entrepreneurs. They transmit information and meaning, guiding the transformation of potential capital into actual capital. Business cycles, in turn, are not pathological deviations from equilibrium but expressions of the temporal and interpretative nature of human action. Fluctuations arise because expectations and understandings are fallible; yet this very fallibility is the source of learning and renewal. The "natural" cycle and the "monetary" cycle, discussed in later chapters, reveal that economic life is rhythmic, not mechanical — a process of continuous coordination and re-coordination in real time.

Part III – Inflation and Monetary Policy

Part III turns to money, inflation, and the role of monetary policy. Here again, the central question is one of meaning. Money is not a mere instrument or neutral veil; it is a social institution sustained by shared expectations and trust. Inflation, too, is not a purely quantitative phenomenon but a disruption in the interpretative fabric of the market — a distortion in how agents perceive and respond to price signals.

The discussion culminates in a re-assessment of monetary policy's purpose. Beyond the technical target of price stability lies a deeper ethical and social question: how can monetary institutions foster sustainable growth and social welfare without undermining the interpretative processes that make markets self-coordinating? The argument is that the ultimate goal of monetary policy should not be control but *trust* — the creation of a stable environment in which expectations can form freely and creatively.

In this vision, central banks are not omniscient planners but participants in a wider process of social interpretation. Their legitimacy depends on acknowledging the limits of measurement and on fostering the conditions for decentralized understanding.

Part IV – Entrepreneurship, Innovation, and the Market Process

Finally, *Part IV* explores the role of entrepreneurship and innovation in sustaining the dynamic order of the market. Here, the Schumpeterian and Austrian legacies converge: innovation is the fruit of creative interpretation. The entrepreneur does not merely respond to data; he *sees* possibilities others overlook, re-interpreting the existing structure of capital and knowledge.

Competition, from this standpoint, is not a static race for efficiency but a discovery process through which new meanings, products, and processes emerge. Markets evolve not through mechanical adjustment but through the continual reinterpretation of what is possible.

The final chapter develops a *neo-Schumpeterian* approach that integrates products, processes, and policies (PPP). It shows how innovation is not confined to technology but extends to institutions and ideas — to the very way societies organize their interpretative energies. In this way, the market becomes a moral and epistemic order: a spontaneous coordination of meaning across dispersed individuals.

4. The hermeneutical turn

The unifying message of these essays is that economics must re-embrace its hermeneutical vocation. To interpret human action is to recognize that meaning precedes measurement, that understanding precedes prediction. The logic of markets is the logic of dialogue — of trial, error, and mutual learning. Prices, profits, and losses are communicative acts, not mechanical outputs.

This interpretative turn does not reject formal analysis; rather, it situates it within its proper philosophical context. Measurement remains necessary, but as a servant of understanding, not its master. Quantification without comprehension is sterile; comprehension without empirical grounding is blind. The task of the economist is to keep these two dimensions in creative tension — to read numbers as signs of meaning, and to interpret meaning without neglecting evidence.

Economics, viewed hermeneutically, is therefore an open system. It resists closure, determinism, and the illusion of final equilibrium.

The economy evolves in *real time* — the time of memory, expectation, and surprise — where novelty constantly emerges and coordination is always provisional. To study such a process requires an attitude of openness akin to that of the philosopher and the artist: a readiness to listen to reality rather than to dictate it.

5. Toward a rebirth of economics

The call for a rebirth of economics is not merely academic; it is civilizational. In an age of technocracy and algorithmic governance, societies risk forgetting that prosperity depends not only on efficiency but on meaning. When public policy becomes an exercise in data management, and when human beings are seen as predictable inputs rather than creative agents, the very fabric of freedom begins to erode.

Re-grounding economics in *verstehen* — in the capacity to interpret and to empathize — is therefore a moral imperative. It reminds us that markets are human institutions sustained by trust, imagination, and moral choice. It also reconnects economics with its classical roots in philosophy, where knowledge was inseparable from wisdom. Aristotle's reason as openness, Menger's subjectivism, Mises's human action, Hayek's theory of knowledge, Lachmann's hermeneutics, and Schumpeter's creative destruction all converge in this vision: *economics as an interpretative science of human flourishing*.

In this sense, the essays that follow are not simply technical contributions but steps toward an intellectual reawakening. They invite readers to look beyond the surface of data, to rediscover the drama of meaning that underlies every economic act. They argue that the future of the discipline lies not in ever more complex models, but in the courage to think again about what it means to understand.

Emphasizing economics as a hermeneutical discipline does not imply drifting into relativism or nihilism. On the contrary, it affirms that subjectivity is the necessary locus through which reality discloses its essence to human understanding. Following Emilio Betti's insight, interpretation is not an arbitrary creation of meaning but the rediscovery of the meaning already inscribed in reality. In this sense, hermeneutics becomes a bridge toward phenomenology: both share the same ontological aspiration to grasp the *Wesen* of things — to return, as Husserl would say, "to the things themselves". The interpretative act, far from dissolving objectivity, mediates the encounter between consciousness and being (*Sein*), allowing essences to be unveiled within historical experience. Thus, radical subjectivism, properly understood, is not an antithesis to phenomenology but its living precondition — the dynamic movement through which the human mind, in its interpretative freedom, participates in the revelation of truth. To view economics in this light is to recognize it as a phenomenological science of human action: a disciplined inquiry into the ways through which meaning, choice, and coordination reveal the intelligible order of reality.

Concluding reflection

The crisis of economics, then, is not a failure of intelligence but a failure of imagination. The obsession with measurement has blinded the discipline to the richness of human life. The way forward is not to abandon analysis but to re-humanize it — to bring back *understanding* as the heart of inquiry and *openness* as the spirit of reason.

If this book succeeds in showing that economics can be both rigorous and humane, interpretative and analytical, then it will have served its purpose. The rebirth of economics begins when we remember that every number has a story, every transaction a meaning, and every market a human face.

Final postil

I felt that this was the right moment to gather these essays and give them a sense of unity. Although they span more than eleven years of publication, they embody an intellectual journey that began twenty-five years ago — when, as a student at the University of Verona, I first heard the name *Schumpeter* in a course on the History of Economic Thought. That moment ignited a fascination that never faded.

Unable to pursue a full-time academic career, I have expressed my passion through the only way I could: by studying and writing within all the moments I was able to *steal* from my corporate commitments. Each essay represents a fragment of an ongoing effort to remain faithful to what most deeply moves me — the attempt to understand the ever-changing drama of human action and creativity.

Today, I sense that the most inventive stage of my intellectual reflection may be drawing to a close. The ideas contained in this book likely represent the essence of my personal legacy — the conceptual synthesis of a lifelong conversation with the thinkers who have inspired me and with the economic reality I have tried to interpret.

My greatest wish for the years ahead is to pass on this passion to younger minds — to nurture a new generation of curious spirits eager to rebuild economics on these foundations, with humility, imagination, and wonder.

PART I

DEFINING ECONOMICS

CHAPTER 1
Economics as a Science of Meaning[3]

Introduction

What is *Economics*? It appears that the community of economists has largely ceased to inquire into the scope and meaning of the discipline. This may be due to the belief that a broad consensus on the matter has already been established—rendering further reflection unnecessary—or to a waning interest in ontological questions among specialists. More plausibly, it is the result of both factors. Nevertheless, in view of the intellectual and practical crisis that contemporary economics is experiencing, as well as the renewed debate concerning its future trajectories, it seems appropriate to reconsider the question of what economics is. A heightened self-awareness in this regard can contribute to forming more accurate expectations concerning the tasks economists are able to perform and, equally, the limitations they necessarily face.

In this chapter, I propose a definition of economics grounded in an alternative approach to economic problems—an approach that, owing to its emphasis on meaning, has been termed 'radical subjectivism' (Storr, 2017). From this perspective, it becomes possible to elaborate a general theory of the economic system, one that aspires to provide coherent responses to economic questions within a comprehensive paradigm. Crucially, such a paradigm must incorporate two dimensions systematically neglected by mainstream economics: real individuals and real time.

1. An original approach to economics

The most frequently cited definition of economics is that proposed by Lionel Robbins (1932, p. 15), according to which economics «is the science which studies human behaviour as a relationship between ends and scarce means which have alternative uses». Robbins formulated this definition following a thorough examination of earlier approaches, setting it in deliberate contrast to them. Nevertheless, while Robbins' characterization subsequently evolved into a framework of static analysis centred on the hypothetical construct of *homo oeconomicus*—

3 This is an updated – and slightly revised – version of: C. Ferlito (2020), *Economics: Human Action and Its Meaning*, « CME EduPaper», 1, Kuala Lumpur, Center for Market Education.

arguably contrary to his original intentions (see Robbins, 1932, p. 89)[4]—the present discussion will pursue a different line of inquiry. In particular, reference will be made to the tradition of thought developed by economists of the so-called Austrian School of Economics (ASE)[5].

According to Ludwig von Mises[6] (1949, p. 233, emphasis added), the task of economics is «to investigate the market phenomena, that is, the determination of the mutual exchange ratios of the goods and services negotiated on markets, their origin in human action, and their effects upon later action». He further clarifies that it is not possible to distinguish between actions that are economic and those that are not, since every «action is motivated by the urge to remove a felt uneasiness. It does not matter for the science of action how people qualify this uneasiness from a physiological, psychological, or ethical point of view» (Mises, 1949, p. 233). For Mises (1949, p. 235), «a comprehensive theory of human action» is the necessary point of departure for the analysis of economics, namely, «the determination of money prices of goods and services exchanged on the market».

What, then, is human action? Mises explains that «[h]uman action is *purposeful behavior*. Or we may say: Action is *will* put into operation and transformed into an agency, is aimed at ends and goals, is the ego's *meaningful* response to stimuli and to the conditions of its environment, and is a person's conscious adjustment to the state of the universe that determines his life» (Mises, 1949, p. 11, emphasis added).

In the citation above, I have emphasized (with italics) four expressions: *purposeful behaviour*, *will*, *agency*, and *meaningful*. I will return to the last term later, while I now focus on the revolutionary implications of the first three. At first glance, it may seem self-evident that human action is purposeful behaviour; however, the implications of consciously acknowledging this fact are profound. First, economic analysis cannot

4 Robbins (1932, p. 90): «If this were commonly known, if it were generally realised that Economic Man is only an expository device—a first approximation used very cautiously at one stage in the development of arguments which, in their full development, neither employ any such assumption nor demand it in any way for a justification of their procedure—it is improbable that he would be such a universal bogey».

5 The Austrian School of Economics took off with the publication of Menger (1871). There is no lack of literature about its historical setting; see, among others, Ebeling (2016), Gloria-Palermo (1999), Holcombe (2014), Huerta de Soto (2000), Schulak and Unterköfler (2011), Vaughn (1994), Yu and Moon-Cheung Shiu (2011).

6 Ludwig von Mises (1881-1973) has been one of the ASE leading figures.

be reduced to the allocative problem (economizing). Every individual acts with a purpose, generally describable as moving toward a state that is subjectively perceived as superior to the present one. This implies that before economizing we must first choose our ends, which emerge from our interaction with reality. Such interaction—among individuals and between individuals and their surrounding world—initiates hermeneutical processes: interpretive acts necessary to identify the goals we consider worth pursuing. Subsequently, we engage in further hermeneutical processes to determine the means we believe suitable to achieve those goals.

Mises' *homo agens* (acting man) is aptly described by Israel Kirzner (1973, p. 33), who argues that, instead of focusing on economizing, «it will prove extremely helpful to emphasize the broader Misesian notion of *human action*. As developed by Mises, the concept of *homo agens* is capable of achieving all that can be accomplished through the notions of economizing and the drive for efficiency. Yet, unlike the concepts of allocation and economizing, the human-action framework does not confine the decision-maker (or the economic analysis of his decisions) to a structure of given ends and means. Human action, in Mises' sense, involves courses of action undertaken by the individual 'to remove uneasiness' and to make himself 'better off'. Being broader than the notion of economizing, the concept of human action does not limit analysis to the allocation problem arising from the juxtaposition of scarce means and multiple ends. Decisions, within the human-action framework, are not reached merely through mechanical computation of the solution to a maximization problem implicit in the configuration of given ends and means. Rather, they reflect not only the manipulation of given means to correspond faithfully with a hierarchy of given ends, but also *the very perception of the ends–means framework* within which allocation and economizing are to take place»[7].

Within this framework, conscious choices emerge from the interaction among individuals, each equipped with an active mind interpreting his or her situation. Mises also speaks of the will turning into agency—an expression that captures the dynamic nature of human action (indeed, the term 'action' itself necessarily implies dynamism). As we have seen, the identification of ends occurs through interaction with reality; hermeneutical (interpretative) processes guide individuals in selecting

7 See also Kirzner (1960).

the means they believe appropriate for achieving their desired ends. Yet ends and means must be coordinated through the formulation and subsequent implementation of a plan, and such implementation necessarily unfolds *in time*[8].

Before turning to the role of time within this framework, it is necessary to highlight a second important implication of conceiving human action as purposeful behaviour and as will transformed into agency. As Hülsmann (2000) and, later, Phaneuf and Ferlito (2014) explain, the concept of purposeful action—that is, the idea that we act with the aim of improving our condition (while aiming does not imply succeeding)—has profound implications for the understanding of rationality. Mises (1949a, pp. 18–19) makes this point explicit:

> [h]uman action is necessarily always rational. The term 'rational action' is therefore pleonastic and must be rejected as such. When applied to the ultimate ends of action, the terms rational and irrational are inappropriate and meaningless. The ultimate end of action is always the satisfaction of some desires of the acting man. Since nobody is in a position to substitute his own value judgments for those of the acting individual, it is vain to pass judgment on other people's aims and volitions. No man is qualified to declare what would make another man happier or less discontented. The critic either tells us what he believes he would aim at if he were in the place of his fellow; or, in dictatorial arrogance blithely disposing of his fellow's will and aspirations, declares what condition of this other man would better suit himself, the critic.

In short, Mises contends that, *ex ante*, all actions are rational, since the plans undertaken to achieve certain ends are consistent with the knowledge available to the actor at the moment of their implementation. No plan would ever be carried out if it were not considered suitable to the attainment of a particular end. However, the implementation of plans occurs *within time*, and the passage of time alters the informational context. This opens the possibility that a chosen course of action may turn out to be suboptimal relative to the intended end. Time, in fact, is the constant bearer of novelty and the principal medium through which information is transmitted.

It is precisely with respect to time that the Austrian School developed an original and indispensable approach. As Meacci and Ferlito (2018)

8 Kirzner (1973) applied such a framework to entrepreneurial theory. See Ferlito (2016, 2018) for an application to capital theory.

explain, Hicks (1976) introduced the distinction between the *economics of time* and *economics in time*. This distinction can still be employed to classify models into those in which time is treated as a mere container in which the production process unfolds, and those in which time is conceived as an active ingredient of the process itself. My preference is for the latter perspective—economics *in* time—which emphasizes human action, expectations, uncertainty, and fluctuations.

As Meacci (2006) notes, different conceptions of time in economics have given rise to distinct paradigms: the General Equilibrium Theory (GET paradigm) and the Economics of Uncertainty and Expectations (EUE paradigm)[9]. This distinction is rooted in the attempts of Shackle (1965)[10] and Robinson (1974)[11] to move beyond the "spatialized" conception of time used by neoclassical economics, toward a more realistic and dynamic understanding of time. O'Driscoll and Rizzo (1985) distinguish between *Newtonian time* and *real time*, linking the latter to the inevitable ignorance that characterizes human action[12]. In my view, the proper context for sound economics is historical time, which embodies novelty and uncertainty. What O'Driscoll and Rizzo describe as real time represents an evolution of Robinson's historical

9 The following table, from Meacci (2006, pp. 3-4), clarifies Robinson's distinction between logical and historical time, as summarized in Harris (2005, pp. 81-108). Regarding the link between Robinson's approach and the Austrian vision on time see also Lucarelli (2018).

	Logical Time	Historical Time
Directionality of time	Reversibility	Irreversibility
Time intensity of action	Instantaneous	Discreteness, lags; inertia
Expectations	Self-realizing, correct foresight	Falsifiable, future unknowable
Information/Knowledge	Complete, free, symmetric	Imperfect, costly, local learning
Capital goods	Substitutability	Specificity, lumpiness
Investment	Elastic	Inertia, driven by animal spirits
Technical change	Disembodied	Embodied, path-dependent
Money/finance	Barter, passive money, complete futures markets	Active money, liquidity preference, incomplete markets

10 Time of mechanism versus time of uncertainty, or expectational time.

11 Logical time versus historical time.

12 See also Yu (2012).

time and Shackle's expectational time. Mainstream economics, by contrast, operates in a framework of logical time—what O'Driscoll and Rizzo (1985, p. 82) define as Newtonian time—a spatialized conception of time in which its passage is represented by "movements" along a line, whether as discrete intervals or continuous points. In both cases, time is assimilated to space, and what holds for the latter is assumed to apply to the former.

O'Driscoll and Rizzo (1985, pp. 82–85) identify three characteristics of Newtonian time: homogeneity, mathematical continuity, and causal inertia. Homogeneity implies that temporal moments are mere points in space, without anything occurring between them; time is therefore fundamentally static. Mathematical continuity means that time is simply a sequence of moments, but no endogenous change can occur within them; all changes must be exogenous. Causal inertia implies that nothing happens within the flow of time itself—there is no learning, no alteration of knowledge, and no adjustment of expectations. The system is assumed already to contain all the elements required for its functioning. Clearly, such a conception fails to capture the unpredictable and dynamic nature of human action.

By contrast, what matters for our analysis is real time: a «dynamically continuous flow of novel experiences. [...] We cannot experience the passage of time except as a flow: something new must happen, or real time will cease to be» (O'Driscoll and Rizzo, 1985, p. 89). Real time, as they describe it (pp. 89–91), is characterized by dynamic continuity, heterogeneity, and causal efficacy. Dynamic continuity links past, present, and future through memory and expectations, such that no present can exist without recollection of the past and anticipation of the future. Heterogeneity means that the individual's perception of reality changes from moment to moment: past events become memories that shape the present and alter expectations of the future. This shifting perception generates causal efficacy, since the flow of time modifies knowledge, awareness, and information, thereby expanding the creative potential of human action. Crucially, this is possible only because of the acquisitions made earlier in time.

In a Newtonian framework, by contrast, nothing happens between the formation of expectations and the execution of plans: time is reduced to a fiction, a mere marker distinguishing one static situation from another. Reality, however, operates differently.

When real or historical time is incorporated into the analytical framework, the picture changes radically. We move from a scenario in which nothing occurs between two objective events to one in which novelty is continuously unfolding. The interaction between human beings and reality generates hermeneutical processes through which individuals form their expectations. These expectations in turn shape ends and the corresponding means; human action thus consists in implementing plans believed to be appropriate to achieve the chosen ends. Yet, from the very moment plans are set in motion, individuals enter into processes of mutual interaction and engagement with their environment. This interaction becomes a discovery process, through which economic actors acquire vital information about one another, their expectations, ends–means frameworks, and plans. In short, information is transmitted. A perpetual flow of novelty emerges, compelling actors to revise continually their expectations and the plans derived from them.

Finally, we must not overlook Mises' reminder that human action is also «the ego's meaningful response to stimuli and to the conditions of its environment». Action cannot be detached from the meaning it holds for the subject who performs it.

2. A science of *meaning*

Following Storr (2017), we can therefore emphasize that to be «an [...] economist is to be concerned with meaning. If we hope to understand human action, we must pay attention to the meanings that individuals attach to their own actions, to the actions of others, to the various choices they consider, and to the possible outcomes of those choices. Ours is, at its root, a science of meaning».

If economics is to be defined as the science of human action, and if human action is understood as purposeful behaviour, it follows that the task of the economist is to interpret such actions and to seek their meaning, since every action is intrinsically connected with the ultimate end it seeks to achieve.

A study of human action, therefore, requires engagement with the meanings that individuals attribute to their actions. Mises (1949a, p. 92, emphasis added) makes this point unambiguously: economics «is not about things and tangible material objects ... [on the contrary] it is about men [sic], their *meanings*, and their actions. Goods, commodities, and wealth, and all the other notions of conduct, are not elements of nature; they are elements of human *meaning* and conduct. He who wants to deal with them must not look at the external world; he must search for them in the meaning of acting men».

By introducing the category of meaning, we enter the realm of interpretation—or *verstehen* (understanding)[13]—which is central to the analysis of human action (Antiseri, 2011, p. 7). This represents the most significant innovation introduced by the German economist Ludwig Lachmann[14] and his followers, particularly Don Lavoie, and leads toward what McCloskey (2017) refers to as *humanomics*[15]. *Interpretation* processes must, in fact, be understood as the essential subjective link connecting different objective facts and events.

Human actions are objective facts; they constitute responses to other objective facts and thus form part of reality. However, the way in which such responses are defined is entirely subjective—the outcome of interpretative processes that may be described as hermeneutical actions. As Bellet and Durieu (2004, p. 236) explain, «the relationship between objective economic variables or 'business situations' and expectations depends on the interpretation which the agents give to the former». This is what Lachmann referred to as the subjectivism of active minds. Such a perspective does not deny the objective character of reality; rather, it emphasizes that the nature of the response to objective elements is profoundly subjective and ontologically hermeneutical.

It is now evident that subjective hermeneutical processes form the indispensable link between objective facts. Without the interpretative moment, reality could not take shape, as no action could be determined. As noted earlier, Lachmann developed this approach from insights first suggested by Mises. Storr (2017) reminds us that the centrality of meaning, understanding, and interpretation is already present in the works of both Mises and Hayek:

---

13 As explained by Di Iorio (2015, p. 178), «[v]erstehen [is] the idea that the ultimate causes of social phenomena must be sought in the meanings individuals attach to their actions and which result from mental interpretative processes».

14 Lachmann (1986, p. 3) reminded us that Austrian research main aim «ever since Menger, has been to *understand*, and not merely give formal express to, what men do in markets».

15 Following Wilson, McCloskey (2017) suggests that «economists might better walk on both feet. Yes, to be sure: let us also walk on the behaviourist, positivist, quantitative foot [...] But then let us walk also on the other cognitive, hermeneutic, qualitative foot».

> As Mises (1998, 26) argued in his magnum opus *Human Action*, 'we cannot approach our subject if we disregard the meaning which acting man attaches to [his] situation.' And, as Mises (1998, 51) also explained, 'the task of the sciences of human action is the comprehension of the meaning and relevance of human action.'
>
> Hayek echoed Mises' position. In *The Counter-Revolution of Science*, Hayek (1952, 31) wrote that 'unless we can understand what the acting people mean by their actions any attempt to explain them ... is bound to fail.' If we hope to explain social phenomena, if we hope to make sense of the world, we must be concerned with what people think and feel, with their assessments and valuations, with the way that they see the world and their place within it, and with the importance they place on particular relationships, particular rules, particular places and things, as opposed to others.

What does it mean to say that economists deal with meaning? Their central task is to seek an understanding of purposeful human action, and thereby of «the emergence of social phenomena, [...] the opinions and beliefs that guide individual decision making» (Storr, 2017). As Storr (2017) reminds us, Hayek (1952, p. 27) explained that «the things are what the acting people think they are," and that "the facts of the social sciences are merely opinions, views held by the people whose actions we study» (p. 28).

This approach—rooted in Menger, Mises, and Hayek, and further developed by Lachmann—is known as radical subjectivism. Adopting such a perspective entails practicing economics in a way fundamentally distinct from the 'mainstream'. It means, for example, «defining benefits in terms of private valuations, and defining costs in terms of individuals' perceptions of their foregone opportunities; recognizing that people's personal interpretations of their past and present, as well as their private expectations about the future, shape their actions; and understanding that the rules guiding people's actions are those they believe to be in force (and not necessarily those written on parchment)» (Storr, 2017).

What does this imply for the practice of economics? First, replacing *homo oeconomicus* with *homo agens* and Newtonian time with real time requires an awareness that economics must remain connected to reality. Formal rigor cannot be pursued at the expense of a deeper understanding of actual phenomena. As Hayek (1974, pp. 43–44) observed: «I confess that I prefer true but imperfect knowledge, even if it leaves much undetermined and unpredictable, to a pretense of exact knowledge that is likely to be false».

This also implies that economics cannot be deterministic; it cannot be based on «the idea that everything that happens must happen as it does and could not have happened any other way» (Fullbrook, 2016, p. 1). If economics were deterministic, it would cease to be a science of human action and would instead become a science of human reaction—a consequence of adopting the fictional model of *homo oeconomicus*. As Madi (2018, p. 202) explains, «an approach to the hermeneutic process rejects the determinism of natural laws and the primacy of Newtonian time. As a result, the use of the expression ontological uncertainty [...] reveals that the pretensions of absolute certainty are abandoned, since real economic relations are not strictly causal and governed by a system of absolute laws. In fact, ontological uncertainty corresponds to a real-world view in which economic experience presents novelty in the flow of time».

Human experience shows that different individuals respond differently when confronted with the same situation, and even the same individual may respond differently when the situation reoccurs under different conditions of time and place. Time and place matter. Reality is not determined by reactions whose content is fixed *a priori* by the situation encountered. Rather, the future is shaped by how people interpret their circumstances; the actions that follow such interpretive processes generate both intended and unintended consequences. As Storr (2017) emphasizes, life is characterized by open-endedness: we all face choices shaped by the specific content of information and knowledge available to us—unique for each individual—within a particular context of time and space. A direct implication is that macro phenomena cannot be properly understood without reference to their microfoundations, as Horwitz (2000) has masterfully demonstrated in relation to various aspects of economic theory and policy.

It is therefore clear that, while market participants are constantly engaged in interpretive processes as they seek to understand reality, economists must undertake a different kind of hermeneutical activity: the interpretation of the meaning of human actions in the market and of the unintended consequences that extend beyond the intentions of individual actors. Understanding, therefore, is not limited to how market participants act. Their actions undoubtedly involve hermeneutical processes, but, as Prychitko (2018, pp. 162–163) explains, we must also account for economists' interpretations and the visions that emerge from them.

> But the hermeneutical act that we economists engage in does not reduce meaning to original intentions or plans of the actors alone. We see something that goes beyond the actors' views of the matter. That is the Gadamerian element that I cannot find in Lachmann's discussion [...] there is more to the story than simply a purchase plan and sale plan have successfully occurred. And so, of course, we may also draw further lessons (meaning) from this simple purchase at the grocery store that the actual participants do not see – the goods are moving toward higher-valued uses, the overall market is becoming better coordinated by placing the items on sale, and so on. The 'mere' acts of buying and selling (strictly recognizing only the plans of the participants) are part of a process with a more central lesson – meaning – that we emphasize to our students: the unintended coordination of the market order. We wish for our students to take our theoretical interpretation seriously. The economist's lesson, while recognizing 'the plan' of each actor, has something more to say, has something greater to focus on, has a deeper 'meaning,' in fact a meaning that even the individual participants might not understand themselves. The buyer merely speaks of having bought groceries on his way home from work. The seller merely speaks of cutting her price to move some unsold inventory. We speak of a process of greater market coordination and spontaneous economic order.

In this regard, following Emilio Betti's hermeneutical vision, interpretation should not be understood as attributing or donating meaning to an object—as it may have been conceived by Heidegger, Gadamer, or Bultmann—but rather as rediscovering the meaning already inherent within the object itself. Thus, in the act of interpretation, meaning is not something to be secretly infused into the object, but something to be drawn out and revealed from it (Reale and Antiseri, 2010, pp. 194-195).

While hermeneutics is here associated with radical subjectivism, it does not necessarily lead to nihilism or the denial of objective meaning. In fact, following Emilio Betti's hermeneutical approach, interpretation is not a mere act of imposing subjective meaning upon an object, but rather a disciplined effort to extract the meaning already embedded within it. This perspective enables hermeneutics to be reconciled with Husserl's phenomenology, which seeks to return "to the things themselves" and to grasp their very essence (*das Wesen*). Betti's understanding of interpretation as the rediscovery of inherent meaning provides the bridge between the subjective act of understanding and the objective reality that presents itself to consciousness. Thus, hermeneutics, far from collapsing into relativism or nihilism, becomes a methodological pathway toward uncovering the essential structures of reality—an interpretative journey that begins in subjectivity but is oriented toward the revelation of truth as it resides in the things themselves.

This approach to economics runs counter to the prevailing academic method, yet growing discontent with mainstream economics is creating greater space for heterodox perspectives, including the one discussed here.

Conclusions

In this chapter, by placing human action as purposeful behaviour at the core of economic analysis and following the tradition of the Austrian School of Economics, I have expanded the traditional scope of economics—typically limited to economizing and equilibrium—to include not only decisions made within a given means–ends framework, but also the very definition of such a framework. In doing so, I have emphasized the role of active minds interacting with the surrounding reality within the realm of real time. This perspective leads to a non-deterministic approach, grounded in the recognition of the dispersed and ever-changing nature of the knowledge held by individuals. The future, therefore, must be understood as radically open-ended.

From this standpoint, economics must be conceived as a science of meaning, since «an economics without meaning is incapable of understanding economic growth, business cycles, or many other of our profane mysteries» (McCloskey, 2017). This is the case not only because the individuals under examination are continuously engaged in interpretative processes regarding the world around them, but also because economists themselves must interpret the meaning of the actions they study in order to comprehend their broader, unintended consequences.

Exposed to these ideas, economics students will come to appreciate the possibility of conducting research within a general framework applicable to all forms of human action—the very foundation of both micro- and macroeconomic theorizing. Such a framework, moreover, proves capable of capturing the nature and meaning of reality, rather than reducing it to fictionalized models.

Appendix: On the relationship between economics and history[16]

The relationship between historical facts and pure theory lies at the heart of the first major controversy involving the Austrian School—the *Methodenstreit* with the German Historical School, a dispute that Schumpeter (1954, p. 782) famously described as a «history of wasted energies».

Although Carl Menger (the founder of the Austrian school) never intended to exclude history from the study of economic theory—in fact, his notion of "exact theory" presupposed a strong connection with the real world—the *Methodenstreit* gave rise to the enduring misconception that Austrian economists viewed economics and history as dichotomous disciplines rather than as distinct but complementary ones. As Lavoie and Storr (2011) point out, the word *distinction* denotes a non-conflictual relationship, whereas *dichotomy* implies a rigid and antagonistic separation.

Unfortunately, a degree of ambiguity in Ludwig von Mises's methodological writings helped to reinforce this myth. As Lavoie and Storr (2011, p. 215) note, *Human Action* appears to portray history and theory as strictly opposed. Mises maintained that history deals with concrete and particular facts, whereas praxeology «is a theoretical and systematic, not a historical, science. Its scope is human action as such, irrespective of all environmental, accidental, and individual circumstances of the concrete acts. Its cognition is purely formal and general... Its statements and propositions are not derived from experience. They are, like those of logic and mathematics, a priori» (Mises 1949, p. 32).

Taken literally, such statements suggest that Mises believed history could never influence theory. Yet, as Lavoie and Storr (2011, p. 215) ask, did «Mises really need to draw an indelible line between conception and understanding in this way?». The authors argue that Mises felt intellectually compelled to emphasize what looked like a dichotomy between *thymology*—defined by Mises (1957, p. 266) as «knowledge of the social environment in which a man lives and acts or, with historians,

16 The contents in this section were first presented in C. Ferlito (2023), *History and Economic Theorizing*, in D. Howden and P. Bagus (Eds.), *The Emergence of a Tradition: Essays in Honor of Jesús Huerta de Soto*, Volume I: *Money and the Market Process*, London, Palgrave Macmillan, 2023, pp. 113-121.

of a foreign milieu about which he has learned by studying special sources»—and praxeology, because economic theory at the time was under siege from positivists, historicists, and other critics.

In other passages of *Human Action*, however, Mises clarified his position. As he wrote (1949, p. 65), «The end of science is to know reality. [...] Therefore praxeology restricts its inquiries to the study of acting under those conditions and presuppositions which are given in reality. [...] Experience merely directs our curiosity toward certain problems and diverts it from others. It tells us what we should explore, but it does not tell us how we could proceed in our search for knowledge». He further insisted that economics is «devoted to the comprehension of reality» and not detached from it (Mises, 1949, p. 66).

Here we find an affinity with Schumpeter's emphasis on the role of *vision* in economic theorizing. I have long believed that exploring this affinity could greatly enrich the Austrian tradition. Schumpeter argued that before beginning any analysis, «we should first have to visualize a distinct set of coherent phenomena as a worthwhile object of our analytic efforts. In other words, analytic effort is of necessity preceded by a preanalytic cognitive act that supplies the raw material for the analytic effort» (Schumpeter 1954, pp. 38–39). He called this preanalytic act *Vision*.

The economist, then, is not an external observer detached from reality. He or she lives within specific temporal and spatial conditions, and the *vision* that guides analysis arises from interaction with and observation of that reality. Analytical work transforms vision into concepts and frameworks—but this process also refines the vision itself. As Schumpeter (1954, p. 40) explained, «[f]actual work and 'theoretical' work, in an endless relation of give and take, naturally testing one another and setting new tasks for each other, will eventually produce scientific models... to which increasingly more rigorous standards of consistency and adequacy will be applied».

Mises faced an intellectual environment in which theory was under attack from historicism and positivism. By contrast, today's challenge is nearly the opposite: a proliferation of theories that are increasingly detached from reality. Much of contemporary economics seems driven by an urge—sometimes conscious, sometimes not—to escape the need for Schumpeterian vision. The pursuit of "pure" economics has distanced researchers from the world they inhabit. Ironically, this occurs at a time when the discipline cannot be accused of being insufficiently empirical. Data collection and econometric manipulation have largely replaced what was once called theorizing.

As a result, analytical work has become severed from its precondition—vision—and therefore from theory itself. It is time for economists to pause, look beyond their models, and let their direct observation of the world once again shape their vision—without which the abstractions on the blackboard lose meaning.

This, ultimately, brings us back to Mises and to the broader Austrian programme: an economic science aimed at understanding reality. Ludwig Lachmann, reviving Max Weber's research programme, placed this aspiration within the hermeneutical framework of *Verstehen* (Lachmann, 1971), in which *thymology* and *praxeology* are distinct yet complementary dimensions of the study of human action.

The introduction of *Verstehen*—as discussed earlier in this chapter—helps to construct an economic science where historical facts and pure theory form a unified approach to the study of "human meanings" (Lavoie and Storr, 2011, p. 232). Schumpeterian vision serves as the bridge that connects these two realms within the economist's interpretive process.

Even Arthur Spiethoff, the last major representative of the German Historical School, sought reconciliation through his *Economic Gestalt Theory*, based on *real types*—the isolation of specific spatio-temporal phenomena that characterize a unique economic style (Spiethoff 1952, 1953, 1970).

This synthesis reaches its fullest expression in Don Lavoie (2011), who argued that interpretation and the search for meaning are inseparable from the facts to which meaning is attached. As he put it (2011, p. 122), «History moulds the direction of theoretical investigation, while theory is used as the interpretative framework with which the specific historical narratives can be told». History thus becomes the supplier of the facts, events, and interactions upon which the economist applies an interpretive lens.

Our conception of "what can happen" shapes how we examine the evidence as we ask "what did happen". Conversely, the answers to "what did happen" influence which of the infinitely many possible "what can happen" questions the economist deems worth pursuing. In Mises's account—echoing Gadamer's hermeneutics—history must always be guided by presuppositions derived from theory, including the *a priori* reflection on the lifeworld (Lavoie 2011, p. 122).

In conclusion, the *Methodenstreit* created a lasting misunderstanding about the relationship between economics and history within the Austrian School. Some of Mises's radical methodological statements helped entrench the notion of a dichotomy rather than a distinction between *thymology* and *praxeology*. Yet Mises never argued that theory should be detached from historical reality.

On the contrary, by insisting that theory must engage with real facts, Mises mirrored Schumpeter's view that *vision*—informed by the observation of reality and by introspection—is indispensable to praxeology. Following Lachmann's hermeneutical programme, Don Lavoie and Virgil Storr later showed that the category of *understanding* reconciles the two great branches of the social sciences in a unified endeavour to comprehend human meaning.

References

Antiseri, D. (2011), *Contro Rothbard. Elogio dell'ermeneutica*, Soveria Mannelli, Rubbettino.

Bellet, M. and Durieu, J. (2014), *Lundberg and Lachmann on Expectations*, in M. Bellet et al. (Eds.), *Evolution of the Market Process: Austrian and Swedish Economics*, London and New York, Routledge.

Di Iorio, F. (2015), *Cognitive Autonomy and Methodological Individualism: The Interpretative Foundations of Social Life*, New York, Springer.

Ebeling, R.M. (2016), *Austrian Economics & Public Policy. Restoring Freedom and Prosperity*, Fairfax, The Future of Freedom Foundation.

Ferlito, C. (2016), *Hermeneutics of Capital. A Post-Austrian Theory for a Kaleidic World*, Hauppauge, Novinka.

Ferlito, C. (2018), *For a New Capital Theory: A Hermeneutical Approach*, «StoriaLibera», IV, 7, pp. 11-51.

Fullbrook, E. (2016), *Narrative Fixation in Economics*, Bristol, World Economics Association.

Gloria-Palermo, S. (1999), *The Evolution of Austrian Economics. From Menger to Lachmann*, London and New York, Routledge.

Harris, D.J. (2005), *Robinson on 'History versus Equilibrium*, in B. Gibson (Ed.), *Joan Robinson's Economics. A Centennial Celebration*, Cheltenham and Northampton, Edward Elgar.

Hayek, F.A. von (1952), *The Counter-Revolution of Science: Studies on the Abuse of Reason*, London, The Free Press of Glencoe, 1964.

Hayek, F.A. von (1974), *The Pretence of Knowledge*, in F.A. von Hayek, *A Free-Market Monetary System*, Auburn, Ludwig von Mises Institute, 2008, pp. 29-56.

Hicks, J. (1976), *Some questions of time in economics*, in A.M. Tang, et al. (Eds.), *Evolution, welfare, and time in economics*, Lexington, MA, Lexington Books, pp. 135-151.

Holcombe, R.G. (2014), *Advanced Introduction to The Austrian School of Economics*, Cheltenham and Northampton, Edward Elgar.

Horwitz, S. (2000), *Microfoundations and Macroeconomics. An Austrian Perspective*, London and New York, Routledge.

Huerta de Soto, J. (2000), *The Austrian School. Market Order and Entrepreneurial Creativity*, Cheltenham and Northampton, Edward Elgar, 2008.

Hülsmann, J.G. (2000), *A Realist Approach to Equilibrium Analysis*, «The Quarterly Journal of Austrian Economics», 3, 4, pp. 3-51.

Kirzner, I.M. (1973), *Competition and Entrepreneurship*, Chicago, The University of Chicago Press.

Kirzner, I.M. (1960), *The Economic Point of View. An Essay in the History of Economic Thought*, Kansas City, Sheed & Ward, 1976.

Lachmann, L.M. (1971), *The Legacy of Max Weber*, Berkeley, Glendessary Press.

Lachmann, L.M. (1986), *The Market as an Economic Process*, Oxford and New York, Basil Blackwell.

Lavoie, D. (2011), *The interpretive dimension of economics: Science, hermeneutics, and praxeology*, «The Review of Austrian Economics», 24, pp. 91-128.

Lavoie, D. and Storr, V.H. (2011), *Distinction or dichotomy: Rethinking the line between thymology and praxeology*, «The Review of Austrian Economics», 24, pp. 213-233.

Lucarelli, S. (2018), *For a New Capital Theory. A Comment to Carmelo Ferlito's Hermeneutical Approach*, «StoriaLibera», IV, 7, pp. 167-173.

Madi, M.A.C. (2018), *Ferlito's "For a New Capital Theory: Hemeneutical Approach". A comment*, «StoriaLibera», IV, 7, pp. 201-202.

McCloskey, D.N. (2017), *Lachmann practiced humanomics, beyond the dogma of behaviorism*, «The Review of Austrian Economics», DOI: 10.1007/s11138-017-0404-1.

Meacci, F. (2006), *Uncertainty and Expectations in Shackle's Theory of Capital and Interest*, MPRA paper 11700, Munich Personal RePEc Archive.

Meacci, F. and Ferlito, C. (2018), *The Classical Roots of the Austrian Theory of Capital and Entrepreneurship*, «The Review of Austrian Economics», 31, 3, pp. 315-339, DOI: 10.1007/s11138-017-0407-y.

Menger, C. (1871), *Principle of Economics*, Auburn, AL, Ludwig von Mises Institute, 2007.

Mises, L. von (1949), *Human Action. A Treatise on Economics*, Auburn, Ludwig von Mises Institute, 1998.

Mises, L. von (1957), *Theory and History: An Interpretation of Social and Economic Evolution*, Auburn, Ludwig von Mises Institute, 2007.

O'Driscoll, G.P., and Rizzo, M.J. (1985), *The Economics of Time and Ignorance*, London and New York, Routledge, 2002.

Phaneuf, E. and Ferlito, C. (2014), *On Human Rationality and Government Control*, «Procesos de Mercado: Revista Europea de Economía Política», 11, 2, pp. 159-176.

Prychitko, D.L. (2018), *Levels of Interpretation in a Hermeneutical Economic Theory: Comment on Ferlito*, «StoriaLibera», IV, 7, pp. 157-165.

Reale, G. and Antiseri, D. (2010), *Storia della filosofia*, Vol. 10: *Fenomenologia, esistenzialismo, filosofia analitica e nuove teologie*, Milan, Bompiani.

Robbins, L. (1932), *An Essay on the Nature and Significance of Economic Science*, London, MacMillan.

Robinson, J. (1974), *History versus Equilibrium*, in J. Robinson, *Collected Economic Papers*, Oxford, Basil Blackwell, 1979, pp. 48-58.

Shackle, G.L.S. (1965), *A Scheme of Economic Theory*, Cambridge, UK, Cambridge University Press.

Schulak, E.M. and Unterköfler, H. (2011) *The Austrian School of Economics. A History of Its Ideas, Ambassadors, and Institutions*, Ludwig von Mises Institute, Auburn, AL.

Schumpeter, J.A. (1954), *History of Economic Analysis*, London and New York, Routledge, 2006.

Spiethoff, A. (1952), *The "Historical" Character of Economic Theories*, «The Journal of Economic History», 12, 2, pp. 131-139.

Spiethoff, A. (1953), *Pure Theory and Economic Gestalt Theory: Ideal Types and Real Types*, in F.C. Lane and J.C. Riemersma (Eds.), *Enterprise and Secular Change*, London, George Allen and Unwin, pp. 444-463.

Spiethoff, A. (1970), *Economic Styles*, «The Journal of Economic History», 30, 3, pp. 640-652.

Storr, V.H. (2017), *Ludwig Lachmann's peculiar status within Austrian economics*, «The Review of Austrian Economics», DOI: 10.1007/s11138-017-0403-2.

Vaughn, K.I. (1994), *Austrian Economics in America. The Migration of a Tradition*, Cambridge, UK, Cambridge University Press, 1998.

Yu, F.-L.T. (2012), *Two perspectives of time in economics: the neoclassical school (Newtonian) versus the Austrian school (Bergsonian)*, «International Journal of Pluralism and Economics Education», 3, 1, pp. 91-103.

Yu, F.-L.T., and Moon-Cheung Shiu, G. (2011), *A new look at the Austrian School of Economics: review and prospects*, «International Journal of Pluralism and Economics Education», 2, 2, pp. 145-161.

PART II

CAPITAL AND BUSINESS CYCLES

CHAPTER 2
The Hermeneutical Nature of Capital[17]

1. Hermeneutical processes in time: The framework

Ludwig M. Lachmann (1906–1990) was a German economist who studied under Friedrich A. Hayek at the London School of Economics during the 1930s[18]. He later taught economics in South Africa and New York, and, together with Israel Kirzner and Murray N. Rothbard, became one of the key figures in the revival of Austrian economics between 1974 and 1976 (Blundell, 2014; Vaughn, 1994).

Lachmann's work focused on the role of expectations and on the impossibility of the economic system ever reaching a final equilibrium—despite the continuous presence of equilibrating forces. In developing these ideas, he founded what came to be known as the "radical subjectivist" stream within the Austrian School, distinguished by its shift from preferences to expectations and by the introduction of hermeneutics into economic analysis (Lachmann, 1990).

As Prychitko (1995a) observed, «Lachmann attempted to reconstruct the individualist phenomenology of the Austrian School. He called for a hermeneutical-interpretative project capable of studying and understanding the coordinating roles of social and economic institutions. Lachmann was the first economist I am aware of to suggest that hermeneutics could be profitably applied to economics, particularly within the Austrian tradition».

Building on the Lachmannian tradition, it is now necessary to clarify what I mean by the application of hermeneutics to economics in general and to capital theory in particular. Without question, the Austrian School of Economics (ASE) has taught us that human action lies at the heart of economic analysis—a vision descending directly from Menger's

17 This is an updated and revised version of C. Ferlito (2018), *For a New Capital Theory: A Hermeneutical Approach*, «StoriaLibera. Rivista di scienze storiche e sociali», 4, 7, pp. 11-61. In particular, the sections on the measurement of capital and on entrepreneurial profit have been completely rewritten. Moreover, a new section has been added discussing how the theory presented here may offer a potential solution to the Cambridge Capital Controversy. Some repetitions with Chapter 1 may be noticed; to preserve the original substance of the essays, these have been intentionally retained, as they reflect the shared intellectual foundations from which both contributions emerged.

18 For a biographical sketch see Mittermeier (1992) and Moss (2000).

(1871) *subjective revolution* and reaching its full expression in Mises, who famously stated that economics «is not about things and tangible material objects», but rather «about men, their meanings and actions. Goods, commodities, and wealth, and all the other notions of conduct are not elements of nature; they are elements of human meaning and conduct. He who wants to deal with them must not look at the external world; he must search for them in the meaning of acting men» (Mises, 1949, p. 92).

By introducing the category of meaning, we enter the realm of *interpretation*—or *verstehen* (understanding)[19]—which is central to the analysis of human action (Antiseri, 2011, p. 7) and represents the major innovation introduced by Lachmann and his followers[20]. Interpretation is the subjective bridge connecting objective facts and events. Human actions are indeed objective facts, as are the circumstances to which they respond. However, the way in which such responses are formulated is entirely subjective—the outcome of interpretative processes that we may call *hermeneutical actions*.

As Bellet and Durieu (2004, p. 236) explain, «the relationship between objective economic variables or 'business situations' and expectations depends on the interpretation which agents give to the former». This is what Lachmann called the *subjectivism of active minds*. Such a perspective does not deny the objective character of reality, but it emphasizes that responses to objective conditions are always mediated by subjective, hermeneutical processes.

An example may help to illustrate this point. An earthquake is an objective event. Yet can we say that its economic consequences are

19 «Verstehen, i.e., the idea that the ultimate causes of social phenomena must be sought in the meanings individuals attach to their actions and which result from mental interpretative processes» (Di Iorio, 2015b, p. 178).

20 According to Prychitko (1994), Lachmann introduced a sort of objectivistic hermeneutics, rooted in the Weberian concept of *verstehen* and focused on the analysis of individual plans in the context of evolving institutions (Lachmann, 1971). Prychitko (1994) argued that such a vision is not as radical as Gadamer's and Ricoeur's phenomenological hermeneutics; he explained the differences between the two approaches at length. However, Antiseri (2011) and Di Iorio (2015a) do not agree with this categorization. According to Di Iorio, Gadamer defended an objective conception of truth (similar to the Weberian one), stressing that the validity of an interpretation is never arbitrary nor subjective, and during the last years of his life he pointed out several common features between his vision and the Popper's. Following Popper, Dario Antiseri explained that fallibility and hermeneutics are different words to describe the same kind of knowledge theory.

determined by the earthquake itself? If the answer were "yes", we would have to assume—as many econometric models implicitly do—that every earthquake produces a predictable set of economic outcomes, independent of time, place, or human perception. This view reflects the mechanization of reality, reducing human behavior to a set of predetermined reactions.

In contrast, if we recognize the interpretative nature of human action, the answer must be "no". The consequences of an earthquake depend on the meanings and expectations that individuals and communities attach to it. For instance, people might interpret the disaster as a challenge to rebuild their city using better engineering and safety standards, thereby fostering research, investment, and progress. Alternatively, they might interpret it as a divine punishment, resigning themselves to fate and ceasing all productive effort.

In both cases, the same objective event leads to radically different economic outcomes, depending on the hermeneutical processes that follow. These interpretations unfold within specific spatial and temporal contexts and are influenced—but never determined—by them. The final, observable outcomes are always the result of subjective processes of evaluation and interpretation, not of mechanical causation.

In this sense, to apply hermeneutics to economics means to restore the human dimension of action—to recognize that economic phenomena are not mere reactions to stimuli but expressions of meaning, purpose, and understanding within historical time.

It is now clear that subjective hermeneutical processes form the essential link between objective facts. Without interpretation, reality could never fully take shape, for no action could be conceived or decided upon. This understanding also sheds light on the fundamental weakness of modern economics—its obsession with *economizing* and *maximizing* functions.

However, true economic analysis must account not only for how individuals allocate resources, but for how they interpret, define, and revise their goals and means in light of changing expectations and understandings. Action is not mechanical optimization—it is an interpretative, creative, and meaning-oriented process.

While the infamous *economizing man* can only react in a predetermined way to a fixed set of ends and means, a true *homo agens* is capable of identifying which ends to pursue and which means are available to achieve them. This is possible because, as Ludvig von Mises observed, human beings «can imagine the future—even a nonexistent, unknowable future» (Kirzner, 1992, p. 25). In contrast, economizing behaviour fails to account for the process through which ends and means are actually identified and constructed.

It is precisely here that the hermeneutical processes described earlier come into play. How are ends and means defined in the first place? As Lachmann emphasized, one of the most significant achievements of modern subjectivism is the shift from preferences to expectations. Any analysis of human action that neglects expectations remains incomplete, for action always takes place within a context in which interpretative (hermeneutical) processes generate expectations about the future.

Human minds establish their goals and corresponding means according to the expectations they regard as suitable for achieving those goals. Action, therefore, consists in the implementation of plans and the employment of means to attain the ends defined by expectations—expectations that themselves arise from an ongoing process of interpretation shaped by the interaction between individuals and their surrounding reality[21].

To understand human behaviour, then, we must interpret actions as plans in motion—the concrete expression of how individuals envision, interpret, and act upon the future (Koppl, 1998, p. 63).

The implementation of plans necessarily occurs within time. As Menger (1871)[22] clearly observed, the «idea of (originary) causality [...] is inseparable from the idea of time. A process of change involves a beginning and a becoming, and these are only conceivable as processes in time».

To proceed, it is essential to introduce an appropriate concept of time, which will be crucial for the subsequent analysis of capital. There are, in fact, two distinct ways of conceiving time in economic theory—corresponding to what John Hicks described as the *economics of time* and the *economics in time*[23]. These two perspectives can be summarized

21 This is what is usually labelled as the purposefulness of human action. See Cowan and Rizzo (1996, p. 333-335) and Phaneuf and Ferlito (2014).

22 Quoted in Cowan and Rizzo (1996, p. 329).

23 See the detailed discussion in Chapter 1 and the references listed therein.

as follows: in the first, time functions as an ingredient of the economic process, while in the second, it serves as the container within which the process unfolds.

Modern Austrian economists have largely built upon the Hicksian foundation, developing an *economics in time* that emphasizes human action, expectations, and uncertainty. This approach recognizes that economic life does not occur in abstract or mechanical time but in historical time, where plans are formed, revised, and realized through the interpretative interaction of human beings with a continually evolving reality.

As Meacci (2006) clearly explain, different conceptions of time have given rise to distinct paradigms in economics: the General Equilibrium Theory (GET) paradigm and the Economics of Uncertainty and Expectations (EUE) paradigm. This distinction builds on the efforts of Shackle and Robinson to move beyond the spatialized notion of time used in neoclassical economics and to return to a more realistic understanding of temporal processes.

O'Driscoll and Rizzo (1985) further developed this idea by distinguishing between *real time* and *Newtonian time*, linking the former to the inevitable ignorance that characterizes human action. From Hayek onward, Austrian economists have clearly operated within the framework of *historical time*—a conception that recognizes time as a source of novelty and uncertainty. What O'Driscoll and Rizzo call *real time* can be viewed as a further development of Robinson's (1974, pp.48-58) *historical time*[24] and Shackle's (1965) *expectational time*[25].

Mainstream economics, by contrast, builds its theoretical constructions within the framework of *logical time*—what O'Driscoll and Rizzo (1985, p. 82) referred to as *Newtonian* or *spatialized time*. In this conception, «its passage is represented or symbolized by 'movements' along a line. Different dates are then portrayed as a succession of line segments (discrete time) or points (continuous time). In either case, time is fully analogized to space, and what is true of the latter becomes true of the former».

According to O'Driscoll and Rizzo (1985, pp. 82-85), time conceived in this way possesses three key features: homogeneity, mathematical

24 Logical time versus historical time.

25 Time of mechanism versus time of uncertainty, or expectational time.

continuity, and causal inertia. Homogeneity implies that temporal moments are merely spatial points or positions in time, meaning that nothing can occur between them—time is thus fundamentally static. Mathematical continuity suggests that time is a smooth sequence of moments, but one in which no endogenous change can take place; every change must be exogenous. Finally, causal inertia means that nothing happens *within* the flow of time—there is no learning, no evolution of knowledge, no adjustment of expectations. The system must already contain all the elements necessary for its functioning.

Such a conception of time may be appropriate for describing physical phenomena, where every action is met with a predictable reaction, but it is inadequate for representing the dynamic, uncertain, and creative nature of human action. Economic life unfolds in real, historical time—where change, discovery, and learning are not anomalies, but the very essence of the process itself.

What concerns us, by contrast, is the notion of *real time*—a «dynamically continuous flow of novel experiences. [...] We cannot experience the passage of time except as a flow: something new must happen, or real time will cease to be» (O'Driscoll and Rizzo, 1985, p. 89). As O'Driscoll and Rizzo (1985, pp. 89-91) explain, the characteristics of real time are the exact opposites of those associated with Newtonian time: they are dynamic continuity, heterogeneity, and causal efficacy.

Dynamic continuity implies that time is composed of interrelated moments—past, present, and future—linked through the perceptions of the individual. One cannot imagine a present that is not shaped by memory of the past and expectations of the future. Consequently, all moments in the flow of time are interconnected and mutually influential.

Heterogeneity means that in each successive moment, an individual's perception of reality may—and indeed does—change. The past, once experienced, becomes memory; this memory enriches the present and alters the way the future is perceived. Perceptions therefore evolve continuously, making each moment in time qualitatively distinct from the one that preceded it.

From heterogeneity follows causal efficacy. As time flows, it transforms knowledge, awareness, and information, thereby expanding the creative potential of human action. Such evolution is possible only because it builds upon what has already been acquired—because every new moment rests on the interpretative achievements of those that came before. In real time, change is not an anomaly but the very essence of experience and action.

It is therefore evident that, within a framework of logical or Newtonian time, nothing truly happens between the moment expectations are formed and the moment plans are executed. Time serves only as a convenient fiction to separate two distinct states, without allowing for any intervening disturbances or deviations that might alter the course of action.

Reality, however, functions quite differently. Once *real* or *historical time* is introduced into the analytical framework, the entire picture changes. We move from a static scenario—where nothing happens between two objective events—to one in which everything is continuously happening. As previously discussed, the interaction between human beings and their environment gives rise to hermeneutical processes through which individuals form expectations. These expectations, in turn, define their goals and the means deemed appropriate to achieve them. Human action thus consists of implementing plans that are believed to be suitable for attaining those ends with the available means.

Yet, the very moment plans begin to be implemented, individuals enter a process of continuous interaction—with one another and with the surrounding reality. This interaction becomes a process of discovery, revealing new and previously unknown information about other actors, their expectations, goals, and plans. In this sense, information transmission becomes a fundamental element of the analytical scheme.

Mainstream economics typically operates under the assumptions of *perfect knowledge* and *perfect foresight*, where information is fixed once and for all. By contrast, when we introduce human action unfolding in historical time, we enter a world of imperfect and ever-changing knowledge. Since information is continuously generated and exchanged, the content of knowledge constantly evolves, requiring that hermeneutical processes remain dynamically active. The novelty and uncertainty arising from this ongoing flow of information compel individuals to engage in continuous interpretation, leading to revisions of their expectations, ends, means, and plans.

What emerges from this vision is Shackle's (1972, pp. 76-79) notion of the *kaleidic society*—«a society in which sooner or later unexpected change is bound to upset existing patterns, a society interspersing its moments or intervals of order, assurance, and beauty with sudden disintegration and a cascade into a new pattern» (Lachmann, 1976a, p. 74). At the root of this cyclical process of disintegration and renewal lies the unceasing stream of hermeneutical activity through which individuals confront the continuous emergence of novelty brought about by human action unfolding in real time.

2. Hermeneutics of capital

2.1. Defining capital

Austrian Capital Theory (ACT) is commonly associated with Böhm-Bawerk (1884, 1889). However, later generations of Austrian economists observed that his formulation diverged from the original Mengerian subjectivist approach and remained entangled within neo-Ricardian constraints[26].

Ludwig Lachmann (1976b, p. 27) explicitly judged the Austrian Capital Theory inadequate for inclusion in the Austrian paradigm. Following Lachmann's insights and trying to link themselves back with Menger, later generations of Austrian economists tried to overcome Böhm-Bawerk's contradictions and develop a subjectivist view of capital. However, what I believe to be still missing in the context of Austrian Capital Theory is a clear definition of what capital is in physical terms and in value.

My aim here is to fill that gap by defining capital both in physical and in value terms, starting from the very roots of the Austrian School. Following Menger (1871, p. 53), we can describe as *useful* those things «that can be placed in a causal connection with the satisfaction of human needs». If «we both recognize this causal connection, and have the power actually to direct the useful things to the satisfaction of our needs, we call them goods».

Menger clearly identified four conditions that must be simultaneously present for a thing to acquire the status of a *good*:

1. The existence of a human need;
2. Properties that render the thing capable of being brought into a causal connection with the satisfaction of that need;

26 For a more detailed discussion of the Austrian debate on capital theory, see Ferlito (2015, 2018).

3. Human knowledge of this causal connection; and
4. Command over the thing sufficient to direct it toward the satisfaction of the need.

These four points highlight the subjective and hermeneutical nature of goods. If a thing does not correspond to a subjective need, it cannot be considered a good—it simply remains a thing. Prerequisite (1) can therefore be identified with *expectations*. It should be followed by prerequisite (3), which represents the choice of the ends–means framework defined by those expectations.

From my perspective, prerequisite (3) is also hermeneutical in nature: the potential of a thing to satisfy a need is not primarily an objective property; rather, the thing is *initially* believed to be suitable for satisfying a given need. The human mind subjectively interprets the object, imagining its capacity to meet the need in question. Only at this point does prerequisite (2) come into play: things reveal their ability to satisfy needs through a discovery process—the empirical testing of the preceding hermeneutical judgment.

Prerequisite (4) represents the implementation of a plan and cannot be separated from prerequisite (2). Once expectations are formed and a certain ends–means framework is believed to be consistent with them, the framework is tested through action, revealing over time whether our hermeneutical intuitions were correct or in need of revision.

Thus, for a thing to become a *good*, it must first be *conceived* as suitable for satisfying a need, and subsequently this suitability must be *tested* in reality. The initial hermeneutical process can be confirmed or denied: subjective interpretation must always be validated by factual reality. One is free, for example, to imagine a watch as suitable for cutting a steak—but the practical test of this hypothesis would promptly disappoint such expectations. Subjective and objective aspects of reality therefore complement one another.

It must be noted that this testing process is never at rest. In fact, a thing could lose, or acquire, goods status if circumstances change. The important elements remain unchanged: expectations, interpreting some means as suitable to achieve ends, testing the intuition through a plan implementation, and revising plans as a consequence of information acquired during plan implementation. Now, how to distinguish between goods and capital goods? I believe that the Mengerian distinction between higher- and lower-order goods is not enough. Similarly, Lachmann's heterogeneous stock of material resources does not help, as it seems to be recursive: what are material resources, then? Lachmann (1956, p. XV) added confusion in arguing that certain *goods* «are capital not by virtue of their physical properties but by virtue of their economic functions. Something is capital because the market, the consensus of entrepreneurial minds, regards it as capable of yielding an income». While I can agree with the first part of the statement, the second part, linking capital and income, sees Lachmann dangerously sliding onto a Böhm-Bawerkian or neo-Ricardian trap.

As mentioned, the Mengerian distinction between higher- and lower-order goods also seems to be inadequate. In fact, is it really possible to distinguish when a good is directly serving a need and when it is only participating in a process to get a lower order good? Consider a machine, for example. Common sense would judge it as at a capital good and Menger would be on the same page, imagining the machine to contribute to producing something that would satisfy more direct needs. But, at the same time, the very same machine is also serving a direct need, that is the entrepreneurial need to produce things. It could be argued that first-order goods are directly consumed and cannot be used a second time, while higher-order goods can serve their purposes several times—their consumption is spread over time. However, the possibility of a one-time use juxtaposed with multiple-time usage seems incapable of grasping the ontological essence of capital goods.

My distinction, thus, begins with Menger and attempts to move beyond his view. The basic distinction between consumption goods and capital goods is that the latter enter production processes. As I shall clarify later, from this perspective labour must also be considered as a capital good. The second characteristic of capital goods, deriving from the first, is that they cannot serve their mission by themselves but only in combination with other capital goods. It is true, however, as pointed out by Lachmann, that such goods are *capital goods* by virtue of an economic function and not because of certain physical characteristics. It means that they need to be *thought* of as suitable to enter a production process in combination with other goods, and generate a certain result.

My definition for *capital goods*, therefore, is as follows: *capital goods are goods that, in a specific moment in time, are* thought *to be suitable for generating a certain output when combined with other goods in a production process unfolding over time.* It will be the unfolding of the production process that will confirm their suitability as capital goods.

More specifically, I distinguish two categories of capital goods:

1) *Potential capital goods*: They are what I defined above, *stricto sensu.* Potential capital goods are goods that, in a specific moment in time, are thought to be suitable for generating a certain output when combined with other goods in a production process unfolding in time.

2) *Actual capital goods*: Goods that, in a specific moment in time, after being thought of as suitable for generating a certain output when combined with other goods in a production process unfolding in time, are actually implemented in such a production process.

The physical definition of capital should reflect the distinction outlined above. From a physical standpoint, we may say that, at any given moment, *potential capital* consists of the set of *potential capital goods*—that is, goods that are expected to be combined into production processes because they are, at that moment, *believed* to be suitable for implementing plans aimed at achieving ends derived from expectations.

Actual capital, on the other hand, refers to the set of goods that, at a given moment, are *actual capital goods*—goods that are already combined within production processes to realize the intended ends.

In both cases, capital is therefore not merely a collection of goods, nor simply a collection of productive combinations of goods. Rather, it represents a *set of consciously organized productive combinations* of goods, deliberately implemented because they are perceived as the logical outcome of plans initiated with the intention of fulfilling expectations.

Such a distinction is inspired by Edith Stein (1931). For Edith Stein, every being (*ens*) carries within itself a *potentia*—a directedness toward form and completion—which becomes *actus* when its essence is actualized in existence. Potency is not mere possibility but *ordered openness*: the intrinsic orientation of being toward realization. In this sense, potential capital corresponds to the interpretative orientation of entrepreneurial mind—its openness to the future through expectation and imaginative projection. Actual capital represents the realization of this openness—the concretization of meaning into operative form within time and market reality.

At first glance, there may appear to be no difference between *potential* and *actual* capital. However, the first distinction lies in the different points in time at which these two entities come into being. *Potential capital* refers to the stage at which the ends–means framework—following the formation of expectations—is conceived in the mind of the economic actor (the *hermeneutical moment*). *Actual capital*, by contrast, emerges when the plans deemed consistent with that framework are put into action (the *operational* or *implementation moment*).

A further distinction can also be made. During the hermeneutical moment, certain things may be identified as potential capital goods even though they are not actually available to the individual for various reasons. Consequently, a subsequent hermeneutical process may be required, at a later stage, to identify suitable alternatives. Thus, the formation of *actual capital*—that is, the implementation stage—may occur only after several successive hermeneutical moments have taken place.

It should now be clear what I mean by the *hermeneutics of capital*. The identification of capital goods is, first and foremost, a hermeneutical process in which active minds engage with objects after expectations have already been formed. Capital cannot exist without expectations, precisely because it is a quality attributed to objects through the subjective interpretive process undertaken by individuals seeking to fulfil those expectations. The implementation of plans serves as the bridge between potential and actual capital.

With this clarification in place, all the typical features of capital identified by Austrian economics can be applied to both potential and actual capital. Above all, capital is a *heterogeneous* set of goods that acquire their character as capital only by virtue of being used *in combination* within a production process. Viewing capital as a stock or as a homogeneous aggregate is therefore impossible—a misconception that lies at the root of many difficulties encountered when attempting to define capital in monetary terms.

Consequently, the most suitable vantage point for observing capital is not the abstract, macroeconomic perspective typical of the neoclassical and Keynesian traditions. As Lachmann (1976c, p. 310) pointed out, the appropriate locus is the *firm*—understood as the environment in which subjective, entrepreneurial, and interpretative processes take place.

2.2. The bridge between *potential* and *actual* capital: price theory

In the previous section, we have established a fundamental distinction between potential and actual capital, framing capital formation as a *hermeneutical* and *subjective* process rooted in the interpretation and implementation of expectations. Potential capital represents the stage at which the entrepreneur, guided by expectations, identifies certain goods as *suitable* for achieving specific ends within an imagined production plan. It is a phase of mental construction—the *hermeneutical moment*—in which subjective judgment anticipates productive utility. Actual capital, by contrast, emerges when these goods are *actually* deployed within production, transforming interpretive expectations into concrete operations—the *implementation moment*. The passage from potential to actual capital, therefore, is the transformation from *potency* to *act*, from subjective anticipation to realized coordination.

The key mechanism governing this passage is price theory. Prices act as the informational bridge between imagination and execution, providing the signals through which entrepreneurs test, validate, or revise their expectations. In Austrian economics, price theory explains how dispersed knowledge is transmitted through market interactions, allowing entrepreneurs to compare alternative uses of resources and evaluate the feasibility of their plans. Prices thus embody the collective outcome of subjective valuations and opportunity costs, aligning individual interpretations with objective market realities. Entrepreneurial choice—deciding which potential capital becomes actual—is therefore guided by the continuous interpretation of price signals. Through prices, expectations are disciplined by scarcity, preferences, and competition, turning subjective visions into coordinated, market-tested acts of production.

Stein's (1931) ontology emphasizes that the passage from potency to act is not automatic but mediated by *spiritual acts*—interpretation, judgment, decision—through which meaning takes form. This mediation corresponds, in our hermeneutical economics, to the *entrepreneurial discovery process* governed by price signals. Price theory becomes the epistemic bridge between the imagined (*potentia*) and the realized (*actus*): entrepreneurs interpret price movements to test and actualize their anticipations, turning hermeneutical potential into operative coordination.

In other words, entrepreneurs, guided by these price signals, continually adjust their plans—deciding which potential combinations of goods are worth transforming into actual capital. Rising prices indicate profitable opportunities and attract resources toward new uses, while falling prices signal that expectations were mistaken or that resources are being wasted.

In this way, the price mechanism coordinates decentralized plans, translating subjective expectations into objective action. It is through the interpretation of price movements that entrepreneurs navigate uncertainty, discover errors, and reallocate resources—thus ensuring the continuous evolution of the capital structure from *potentiality* to *actuality*.

Figure 2.1 depicts the hermeneutical bridge where expectations (potential capital) become validated combinations (actual capital) through entrepreneurial discovery, price signals, and market feedback—then loop back via reinterpretation.

Figure 2.1: Interpretative transformation (potential → actual capital).

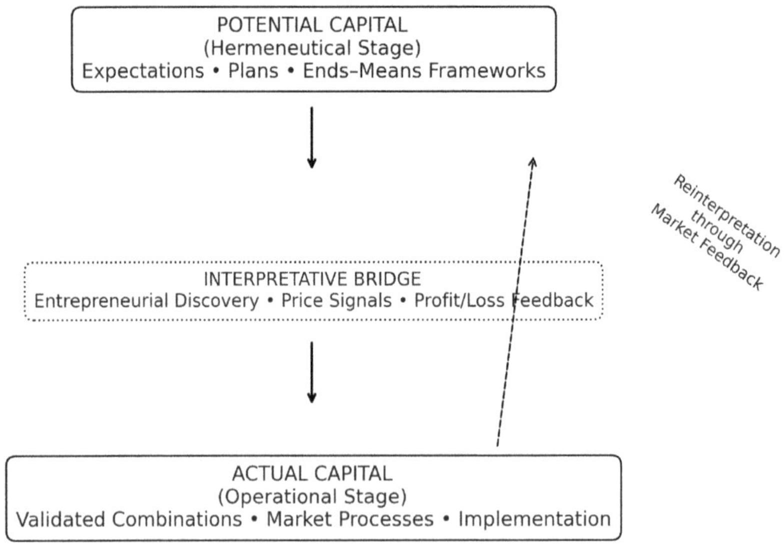

Prices, therefore, can be understood as the objective synthesis of subjective interpretations. Each individual market participant approaches exchange with their own hermeneutical horizon—interpreting needs, scarcities, and opportunities through personal expectations and experiences. Yet, when these subjective valuations encounter one another through the act of exchange, a process of mutual testing and adjustment occurs (market interaction). The price that emerges from this process is not merely a numerical outcome but the phenomenological manifestation of intersubjective meaning—a synthesis forged through the market's interpretative dialogue. In this sense, prices are the objectified results of countless hermeneutical acts: they condense dispersed expectations into a visible signal that reflects, in a provisional and dynamic equilibrium, the lived interpretations of market actors. The market test—where anticipations meet reality—transforms the plurality of subjective evaluations into an objective social fact, allowing coordination to emerge from interpretative diversity, transforming hermeneutics into phenomenology.

2.3. Capital value

It is now time to try to understand if and how capital can be measured, that is, if it is possible to find a quantitative measure for capital and capital goods. As acknowledged by Lachamnn (1941) and Lewin (1997), in fact, the heterogeneous nature of capital goods creates several problems when attempting to reach a meaningful measurement for the value of capital goods. Several options are also presented and analyzed by Kirzner (1966).

Another question to address is whether measuring capital has any meaningful purpose. Why should we be concerned with determining the value of capital goods? Ultimately, what truly matters is the value of the *output* generated by those goods, understood as described above. Measuring capital becomes relevant mainly for scholars who define the rate of profit as the return on capital, interpreting investment profitability as dependent on the employment of capital goods that can be objectively aggregated and quantified. By contrast, I regard profit as the difference between the price at which a good is sold and the total costs required to produce it. Profit, therefore, is inherently *microeconomic* in nature—a dimension largely ignored by aggregate approaches.

Nevertheless, some attempt at definition can still be made. What cannot be meaningfully measured is the *value* of individual capital goods. Of course, each capital good has a market price—an objective expression of subjective evaluation processes. Yet equating the value of a capital good with its market price is meaningless within the framework developed here. As we have seen, certain things acquire the status of capital goods only when they are *conceived* as suitable for achieving an end in combination with other goods within an intertemporal production process. Therefore, what holds analytical meaning is not the value of isolated goods, but the value of *capital*—whether potential or actual—understood as the *productive combination* of specific goods.

It is now useful to recall our definition of capital—both potential and actual. At any given moment, *potential capital* refers to the set of potential capital goods, meaning those goods that are expected to be combined into production processes because they are, at that point in time, believed to be suitable for implementing plans aimed at achieving ends derived from expectations. *Actual capital*, on the other hand, consists of the set of goods that, in a given moment, are *actual capital goods*—that is, goods already combined within production processes to attain the desired ends. In both cases, capital represents a consciously organized set of productive combinations of goods, deliberately implemented because they are regarded as the logical outcome of plans initiated with the intention of fulfilling expectations.

What we are looking for, thus, is the value of each productive combination at different moments in time. However, such formulas cannot be "mechanical" like in neoclassical capital theory, because here capital emerges from *expectations*, *plans*, and *interpretation* rather than from objective aggregations of physical goods. The goal, therefore, is not to *measure* capital ex post like in mainstream models, but to *model* how it forms and transforms through entrepreneurial interpretation and market validation.

Let's define the following variables

- E_t: set of expectations at t
- $\mathcal{G}$: set of all available goods
- $\psi_i(E_t)$: subjective perception (hermeneutical interpretation) of good i as suitable for production given expectations E_t
- $\pi_i(t)$: market price of good i at time t
- $q_i(t)$: quantity of good i available or planned for use
- $\phi_i(t)$: actual contribution of good i to production (revealed ex post)
- $\alpha_i(t)$: weight or relevance assigned by the entrepreneur to good i in the production plan

Potential capital

Potential capital reflects the *expected* productive combination of goods, still in the hermeneutical (mental) stage (Function 2.1):

$$K_P(t) = \sum_{i \in \mathcal{G}} \alpha_i(t)\, \psi_i(E_t)\, \pi_i(t)\, q_i(t)$$

where:

- $\psi_i(E_t) \in [0,1]$ measures the *subjective belief* that good *i* will be effective in achieving the planned end (a kind of *expectational coefficient*);
- $\pi_i(t)\, q_i(t)$ gives the market valuation of the resource;
- $\alpha_i(t)$ weights each good according to its perceived strategic role in the production combination.

Interpretation: Potential capital is the value of resources believed to be productive given current expectations and price signals. It is a *plan-based,* not *output-based,* construct.

Actual capital

Actual capital represents those goods that are effectively integrated into production processes and *tested by market validation* (Function 2.2):

$$K_A(t) = \sum_{i \in \mathcal{G}_A} \phi_i(t)\, \pi_i(t)\, q_i(t)$$

where:

- $\mathcal{G}_A \subseteq \mathcal{G}$ is the subset of goods actually employed in production;
- $\phi_i(t) \in [0,1]$ measures the *realized effectiveness* of each good in contributing to production (the ex-post productivity coefficient).

Interpretation: Actual capital is the market-valued set of goods whose usefulness has been validated through the implementation of plans.

From potential to actual capital: the transformation function

The transformation from potential to actual capital can be expressed as a *realization operator* acting on expectations (Function 2.3):

$$K_A(t + \Delta t) = \Omega[K_P(t), \mathcal{P}(t + \Delta t)]$$

where $\mathcal{P}(t + \Delta t)$ is the vector of new market prices and Ω represents the entrepreneurial discovery process — the continual testing and revision of expectations through price signals and profit/loss feedback.

The simplest dynamic version could be written as (Function 2.4):

$$K_A(t + \Delta t) = K_P(t) \cdot \rho(t)$$

where $\rho(t) \in [0,1]$ is a *realization ratio* — the fraction of planned (potential) capital that successfully becomes actual capital. This ratio depends on (Function 2.5):

$$\rho(t) = f(\Delta P, \Delta D, \Pi_t)$$

where:

- ΔP: changes in relative prices;
- ΔD: changes in demand or preferences;
- Π_t: profit/loss feedback indicating entrepreneurial accuracy.

Capital valuation and adjustment

Over time, entrepreneurs continuously re-evaluate potential capital based on new information (Functions 2.6 and 2.7):

$$K_P(t + 1) = K_P(t) + \Delta E_t + \Delta \pi_t$$

$$K_A(t + 1) = K_A(t) + \rho(t)[K_P(t) - K_A(t)]$$

This dynamic expresses Austrian capital as a flow of interpretations corrected by market experience, rather than as a static stock.

Link to price theory and entrepreneurial choice

Price theory governs this entire dynamic because prices act as the *epistemic bridge* between subjective plans and objective validation (Function 2.8):

$$\frac{\partial K_A}{\partial \pi_i} > 0 \quad \text{and} \quad \frac{\partial \rho}{\partial \Pi_t} > 0$$

Entrepreneurs read price changes ($\Delta \pi_i$) as signals of coordination or discoordination. Profit and loss (Π_t) feed back into the realization ratio ρ, determining whether expectations were correct. Thus, prices are the dynamic variable transforming subjective potential capital into realized, objective actual capital.

Figure 2.2 captures the circular flow of meaning: Expectation → Interpretation → Validation → Re-interpretation, governed by feedback variables (Δp, Δd, π/ℓ) shaping the realization ratio ρ.

Figure 2.2: Hermeneutical cycle of capital formation.

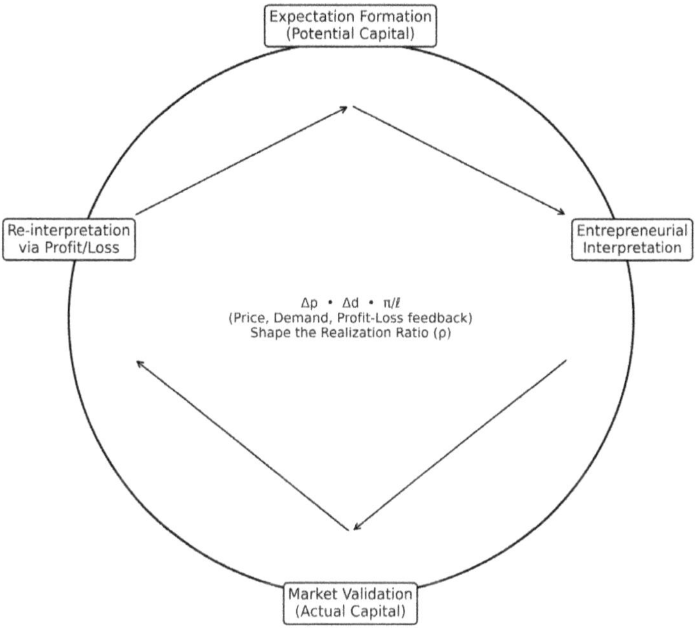

2.4. Capital structure and the production process

After having focused on the analysis of capital goods and capital value with exclusive reference to individual expectations, we can now ask whether it is possible to move from the micro to the macro level in order to formulate an appropriate definition of capital as it pertains to the economy as a whole. Some attempts in this direction were indeed made by Austrian economists.

As we have previously noted, one of the defining features of Austrian capital theory lies precisely in its refusal to treat capital as a macroeconomic aggregate. In line with the Mengerian tradition, the Austrians preferred to refer to the various forms of capital goods, recognizing the inherently heterogeneous nature (Lachmann, 1956, p. 2) of a set of goods that cannot meaningfully be combined into a single aggregate entity (Foss, 2012).

As is well known, in order to overcome these obstacles and develop a structural perspective on capital, some Austrian economists built upon the concept of the *period of production* or *length of the production process* (Hayek, 1941, p. 70). Yet, as Hayek himself acknowledged, it is difficult to conceive of the production period or process length in aggregate terms, precisely because of the heterogeneous nature of capital.

To address this difficulty, Hayek (1931, p. 39) introduced the well-known *Hayek's triangle*. In this model, the base of the right-angled triangle represents the production period, while the height measures the value of the final consumption goods produced during that process. The various vertical distances between the hypotenuse and the time axis represent the values of goods at different stages of production. Consequently, the hypotenuse illustrates the value added through time and the application of additional inputs.

The aim of this representation was to depict the intertemporal structure of capital through fundamental Austrian concepts such as the *production period* and *roundabout production*. However, it appears that such a model does not fully capture the essence of capital as defined here.

Before attempting to define capital at the level of the entire economic system, and in line with the traditional Austrian approach, it is useful to first refer to the notion of *capital structure*.

We can define the *potential capital structure* as the set of all combinations that, at a given moment, are considered suitable for fulfilling expectations once implemented in production processes. Similarly, the *actual capital structure* consists of the set of combinations of actual capital goods that are currently being implemented according to plans designed to meet those expectations.

These definitions follow directly from the earlier ones, yet they likely fall short of offering a deeper understanding of the specific configuration or form that the structure itself takes.

This structure, which is determined by expectations and production plans, can hardly be viewed as stable over time. It is therefore evident that the neoclassical function of production, in which there is no process but simply the relationship between output and the combination of capital and labour, is unable to grasp the essence of the production process as the combination, over time, of capital goods.

> [T]he neoclassical constant-returns production function [...] does not describe production as a process, i.e., as an ordered sequence of operations. It is more like a recipe for bouillabaisse where all the ingredients are dumped in a pot, (K, L), heated up, f(*), and the output, X, is ready. This abstraction from the sequencing of tasks, it will be suggested, is largely responsible for the well-known fact that neoclassical production theory gives us no clue to how production is actually organized (Leijonhufvud, 1986, pp. 203-204).

The neoclassical production function, moreover, marks the contrast between capital and labour as two distinct and often conflicting factors of production. Such a distinction penetrated economic theory so deeply that it is widely accepted as describing the 'capitalistic mode of production' through the so-called aggregate production function (Solow, 1956, p. 66 and 1957, p. 312):

$$q = f(\mathrm{K}, \mathrm{L})$$

This formula is perhaps one of the most familiar in all of microeconomics—every student encounters it early in their studies. It is, of course, true that a certain output results from the combination of capital goods, as described above, together with human intervention, which is conventionally denoted as *L*.

Setting aside the usual debates about the measurability of *K* and *L*, and recalling my definition of *actual capital*, I would argue that *L* is neither opposed nor merely complementary to *K*; rather, *L* is included within *K*. When I defined *actual capital* as the set of goods implemented together in production processes, in real time, to generate an output consistent with expectations, labour was naturally encompassed among the goods chosen to form that capital combination.

It follows, therefore, that labour should be conceived as an integral component of both *potential* and *actual capital*. In this sense, the notion of labour must be understood broadly: it includes the manual activities of factory workers, the administrative tasks of white-collar employees, and the organizational and managerial functions carried out by executives and directors.

I will try now to present an alternative production function which is consistent with the argument developed so far. Building on the potential vs. actual capital framework, here is an Austrian, price-theoretic alternative to Solow's $Y = F(K, L)$. It rejects an aggregate, homogeneous "K" and makes output hinge on (i) entrepreneurial plans, (ii) market prices, and (iii) realized coordination.

<u>A recap</u>

- Potential capital (plan-based) (Function 2.1):

$$K_P(t) = \sum_{i \in \mathcal{G}} \alpha_i(t)\, \psi_i(E_t)\, \pi_i(t)\, q_i(t)$$

- Actual capital (implemented, market-tested) (Function 2.2):

$$K_A(t) = \sum_{i \in \mathcal{G}_A} \phi_i(t)\, \pi_i(t)\, q_i(t)$$

- Realization ratio (coordination index) (Function 2.9):

$$\rho(t) = \frac{K_A(t)}{\sum_i \psi_i(E_t)\, \pi_i(t)\, q_i(t)} \in [0, 1]$$

Here, ψ_i (expectational suitability) and ϕ_i (realized effectiveness) are subjective/ex post coefficients; α_i are plan saliences; π_i are prices; q_i are quantities. Labour can be treated as one of the goods i.

<u>A Plan-validated complementarity (PVC) production function</u>

Let $x_i(t) \coloneqq \phi_i(t)\, \pi_i(t)\, q_i(t)$ denote effective capital services from good i. Entrepreneurs choose a set of *recipes/bundles* $\mathcal{B}(t) = \{B_1, \dots, B_m\}$, each bundle B_b being a complementary subset of goods required together (Austrian heterogeneity + bottlenecks). Define per-bundle intensity $\theta_b(t) \geq 0$ (the extent to which the recipe is implemented) and weights $w_b(t)$ (economic significance/scale).

Production aggregates across implemented bundles, with within-bundle complementarity captured by a Leontief (bottleneck) operator and economy-wide coordination captured by $\rho(t)$ (Function 2.10):

$$Y(t) = \rho(t) \sum_{b=1}^{m} w_b(t) \min_{i \in B_b} \{\, x_i(t) \,\}\, \theta_b(t)$$

Why this opposes Solow:

- No single homogeneous K ; we use a vector of heterogeneous goods $\{x_i\}$.
- Complementarities and bottlenecks (via $\min$) matter—one weak link caps output.
- Expectations, prices, and profit/loss enter directly (through ψ, ϕ, π), not as a black-box "Total Factor Productivity" (TFP).
- The coordination index ρ is a structural driver of realized output, not an error term.

Entrepreneurial selection and price theory inside the function

Bundles $\{B_b\}$, their intensities θ_b, and weights w_b are chosen by entrepreneurs via price signals and profit/loss. For a bundle B_b producing output sold at price $p_b(t)$, with input coefficients a_{bi}, a simple adaptive rule is (Function 2.11):

$$\theta_b(t+1) = \theta_b(t) + \eta \left[p_b(t) \min_{i \in B_b}\{x_i(t)\} - \sum_{i \in B_b} \pi_i(t)\, a_{bi} \right]_+$$

("$[z]_+$" denotes the positive part). Profitable bundles scale up; unprofitable ones shrink. Prices $\{\pi_i, p_b\}$ discipline expectations and reallocate resources, updating α, ψ, ϕ and hence K_P, K_A, ρ.

Summary metrics

We can write a compact evolution:

- Realized output (Function 2.12):

$$Y(t) = \rho(t) \sum_b w_b(t) \min_{i \in B_b}\{x_i(t)\}\, \theta_b(t)$$

- Feedback and coordination (Function 2.13):

$$\rho(t+1) = \rho(t) + \kappa\, \Pi_t \quad \text{with} \quad \Pi_t \approx \Delta K_A - \Delta K_P$$

(Profits/losses improve/worsen coordination as plans are validated/rejected).

Expectational updating (illustrative) (Function 2.14):

$$\psi_i(t+1) = \psi_i(t) + \gamma \frac{\partial \Pi_t}{\partial x_i}, \qquad \phi_i(t+1) = \phi_i(t) + \delta \frac{\partial Y(t)}{\partial x_i}$$

(Entrepreneurs revise beliefs ψ and effectiveness ϕ based on price-profit signals).

Interpretation

Output is what price-guided entrepreneurs actually coordinate: plans (K_P) priced by markets become implemented combinations (K_A), filtered through complementarity and validated by profit/loss into Y via ρ. This puts price theory and entrepreneurial choice at the heart of production, in explicit contrast to Solow's aggregate K and residual TFP.

The production structure

When relating the production function to time and expectations, the structure of capital cannot be regarded as stable or fixed. The multitude of goods combinations continuously formed, dissolved, or reconfigured over time means that *something is always changing somewhere*. Each combination interacts with others—some as complements, others as substitutes—and certain goods may lose their suitability, thus ceasing to qualify as capital altogether. As Lachmann observed, the capital structure of society is an *aggregate of capital combinations*, but these combinations are not additive except in the theoretical condition of general equilibrium. In practice, complementarity is twofold: within each combination, it is *planned*, the result of entrepreneurial choice and intentional coordination; across combinations, it is *unplanned*, emerging spontaneously from the operation of the market process as entrepreneurs respond to price signals and profit opportunities.

The form that the capital structure takes at any moment is determined by *production plans*, each representing a particular configuration of goods. The relative proportions in which goods enter these plans—the *capital coefficients*—reveal the degree of complementarity among them. In equilibrium, these coefficients would define the structure's proportions; in reality, constant disequilibrium makes them fluid, continuously revised as entrepreneurs test expectations against market feedback and new information.

In this dynamic setting, the capital structure is not a fixed "stock" but a *living process of coordination*, perpetually reshaped by shifting expectations and changing prices. At any instant, one may observe a specific arrangement of capital goods, but this arrangement is merely a transient cross-section of an ongoing evolutionary process. The kaleidoscopic metaphor remains apt: as soon as the structure appears to take shape, it begins to transform again. The production structure, therefore, should be seen as a *kaleidic and ever-changing configuration of capital combinations*—expanding, contracting, and reconfiguring in response to entrepreneurial interpretation and the guidance of price signals. It exists, but never in a stable form; it evolves continuously as the hermeneutical process of expectation formation unfolds within the market.

Figure 2.3 represents capital as a *living network* of planned and unplanned complementarities among combinations, dynamically reshaped by entrepreneurial interpretation—your "kaleidoscopic" metaphor in visual form.

Figure 2.3: Kaleidic capital structure.

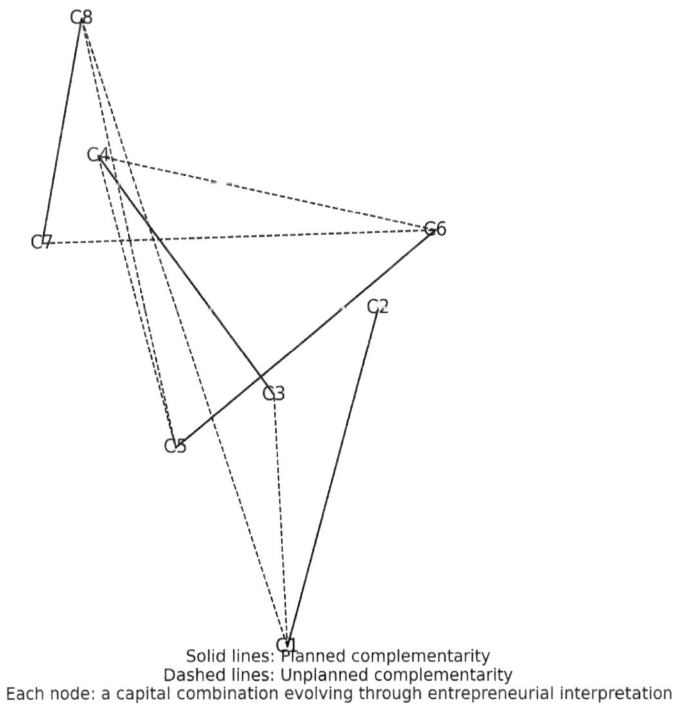

3. Entrepreneurial profit

As should be clear from our discussion thus far, profit can arise only within the realm of *expectational* or *historical* time (Shackle, 1972, Chapter 32). It is within historical time—where novelty and uncertainty are continuously generated—that profit opportunities emerge and can be seized through entrepreneurial alertness. If uncertainty did not exist, "there would be no profit. All production plans in such a world would be successful" (Lewin, 1997, p. 117).

In a framework governed by *logical time,* the concept of *waiting* is sufficient to express Böhm-Bawerk's idea of interest as the "marginal productivity of waiting" (Wicksell, 1893, pp. 21–22). However, only the ontological uncertainty inherent in *historical time* makes it possible to understand profit as the necessary outcome of a context characterized by limited knowledge—both of other actors' present conditions and of the future state of the economic system.

By disregarding the microfoundations of macroaggregates, Ricardo, Marx, the neo-Ricardians, Keynes, and even Böhm-Bawerk—according to Lachmann—treated capital as a homogeneous entity. This assumption enabled them to define a uniform rate of profit directly linked to the return on capital. Thus, while Böhm-Bawerk and Hayek (1941, p. 354) remained aligned with the classical tradition in connecting capital to the rate of profit, later generations of Austrian economists broke from this view, instead associating profit with entrepreneurial activity.

Lachmann (1973, p. 26) argued that profit should first and foremost be understood as the difference between the price at which a commodity is sold and its cost to the seller. The ability to sell goods at prices exceeding their production costs is the very essence of entrepreneurial activity. Consequently, profit can only arise in a *disequilibrium* situation, since in equilibrium all profit opportunities would already have been exhausted.

This conception of profit as the outcome of entrepreneurial activity was most clearly articulated by Kirzner (1973, p. 48). Likewise, Schumpeter (1911, p. 128) defined profit as a surplus over costs—the difference between receipts and outlays generated through entrepreneurial action—adding that interest on capital constitutes a separate remuneration, not part of profit *stricto sensu.*

Profit, therefore, bears no relation to the supposed *productivity of capital.* Indeed, such productivity could be defined only if capital itself could meaningfully be treated as an aggregate. For the same reason, the classical and neoclassical discussions surrounding the *rate of return* lose their significance, as they ultimately rest on the untenable assumption that capital can be expressed as a homogeneous aggregate.

As we have seen, the value of capital can only be defined at a specific moment in time and with reference to particular combinations of goods implemented to produce a given output. In my view, the value of capital changes continuously over time, being determined by the expected value of the output, the interest rate, and time itself. Profit, therefore, can be understood only from a microeconomic perspective—as the outcome of entrepreneurial activity.

According to the neo-Austrian definition, which I share, profit—being the result of entrepreneurial action—can also assume a negative value. In a market economy, every firm or entrepreneur acts with the intention of maximizing profit; yet the motivation to achieve positive profit and the actual success in doing so are two different things. The very nature of the market process makes it impossible for all plans to succeed (Lachmann, 1973, p. 26).

Equilibrium exists only *ex ante*, when plans are consistent with expectations and with the limited information available. *Ex post*, however, it may be revealed that a given plan was inadequate to achieve its intended goal—malinvestments can and do occur.

Hence, there is «no such thing as a rate of profit; there are only rates of profit which may differ widely» (Lachmann, 1973, p. 26). Each rate of profit corresponds, like capital itself, to a specific output and to the particular combination of goods employed to obtain it. Consequently, it is impossible to define a uniform or aggregate rate of profit for the economic system as a whole.

Staying faithful to my plan-vs-implementation framework, entrepreneurial profit should be defined at the level of plans (ex-ante) and implementations (ex post), with price theory transmitting the test of coordination.

<u>A recap</u>

- Goods $i \in \mathcal{G}$; bundles/recipes $B_b \subset \mathcal{G}$ (complementary sets).
- Physical effective services of input i: $s_i(t) = \phi_i(t)\, q_i(t)$ (ex post); planned services $\hat{s}_i(t) = \psi_i(t)\, q_i(t)$ (ex ante).

- Input prices $\pi_i(t)$; output (bundle) prices $p_b(t)$.
- Bundle intensity (scale) $\theta_b(t) \geq 0$.
- Complementarity within bundle b: use a Leontief (or low-elasticity CES) aggregator (Function 2.15),

$$f_b\big(\{s_i\}_{i\in B_b}\big) = \min_{i\in B_b}\left\{\frac{s_i(t)}{a_{bi}}\right\} \quad \text{(Leontief)},$$

where $a_{bi} > 0$ are input coefficients.

- Economy-wide coordination index (realization ratio) $\rho(t) \in [0,1]$ from our framework.

Then realized output of bundle b (Function 2.16):

$$y_b(t) = \rho(t)\,\theta_b(t)\,f_b\big(\{s_i(t)\}_{i\in B_b}\big).$$

<u>Ex-ante (planned) entrepreneurial profit</u>

Using plans and expected prices (Function 2.17):

$$\hat{\pi}(t) = \sum_b p_b^e(t)\,\theta_b(t)\,f_b\big(\{\hat{s}_i(t)\}\big) - \sum_i \pi_i^e(t)\,q_i(t) - \hat{C}_{\text{time}}(t) - \hat{C}_{\text{overheads}}(t)$$

where $\hat{s}_i(t) = \psi_i(t)\,q_i(t)$ are *expectational* (hermeneutical) services and the superscript e denotes expected prices. This is the potential (plan-based) profit tied to K_P.

<u>Ex-post (realized) entrepreneurial profit</u>

(Function 2.18):

$$\pi(t) = \underbrace{\sum_b p_b(t)\,y_b(t)}_{\text{revenue}} - \underbrace{\sum_i \pi_i(t)\,q_i(t)}_{\text{explicit input costs}} - \underbrace{C_{\text{time}}(t) - C_{\text{overheads}}(t)}_{\text{time/finance \& overheads}}$$

where typically $C_{\text{time}}(t)$ embeds time preference/finance (e.g., discounting or carrying cost along a multi-period process), and $C_{\text{overheads}}(t)$ includes fixed/organizational costs. Substituting $y_b(t)$ gives (Function 2.19):

$$\pi(t) = \sum_b p_b(t)\,\rho(t)\,\theta_b(t)\,f_b(\{s_i(t)\}) - \sum_i \pi_i(t) q_i(t) - C_{\text{time}}(t) - C_{\text{overheads}}(t).$$

Interpretation. Profit is the market test of whether *actual* combinations (driven by ϕ, θ, ρ) were superior to their opportunity cost in the price system $\{\pi_i, p_b\}$.

Profit as a discovery/coordination decomposition

The realized-minus-planned profit surprise is the sum of price errors, quantity/efficiency errors, and coordination (Function 2.20):

$$\pi(t) - \hat{\pi}(t-1) = \underbrace{\sum_b (p_b - p_b^e)\, y_b}_{\text{output price surprise}} + \underbrace{\sum_b p_b^e\, (y_b - \hat{y}_b)}_{\text{realization/efficiency surprise}} - \underbrace{\sum_i (\pi_i - \pi_i^e) q_i}_{\text{input price surprise}} - \underbrace{\sum_i \pi_i^e\, (q_i - \hat{q}_i)}_{\text{input quantity surprise}} - \Delta C_{\text{time,overheads}},$$

with $\hat{y}_b = \theta_b f_b(\{\hat{s}_i\})$. The realization term captures ρ and ϕ effects: plans becoming (more/less) feasible/productive than anticipated.

Selection rule (price-guided scaling of bundles)

A simple marginal rule for each bundle b (Function 2.21):

$$\frac{\partial \pi(t)}{\partial \theta_b} = p_b(t)\, \rho(t)\, f_b(\{s_i\}) - \underbrace{\sum_{i \in B_b} \pi_i(t)\, \frac{\partial q_i}{\partial \theta_b}}_{\text{marginal input cost}} \gtrless 0.$$

Entrepreneurs expand θ_b if the price-weighted marginal product (filtered by coordination ρ) cxcccds marginal input cost at market prices. With Leontief, the marginal product is pinned to the *bottleneck* input, making the price of that input decisive.

Link to our capital measures

Use your earlier constructs:

- $K_P(t) = \sum_i \alpha_i\, \psi_i\, \pi_i\, q_i$ (plan value of *potential* capital),
- $K_A(t) = \sum_i \phi_i\, \pi_i\, q_i$ (value of *actual* capital services),
- $\rho(t) = \dfrac{K_A(t)}{\sum_i \psi_i\, \pi_i\, q_i}.$

Then a compact profit identity that highlights coordination is (Function 2.22):

$$\pi(t) = \sum_b p_b(t)\,\theta_b(t)\,f_b(\{s_i(t)\})\,\rho(t) - \left[K_A(t) + C_{\text{time}}(t) + C_{\text{overheads}}(t)\right]$$

(Here K_A proxies the value of actually employed inputs).

<u>Time and interest (multi-period extension)</u>

For genuinely intertemporal plans, discount cash flows of each bundle b (Function 2.23):

$$\pi = \sum_b \left(\sum_{\tau=0}^{T_b} \frac{p_b(\tau)\,y_b(\tau)}{(1+r)^\tau} - \sum_{\tau=0}^{T_b} \frac{\sum_{i\in B_b} \pi_i(\tau)\,q_i(\tau)}{(1+r)^\tau} \right) - \text{overheads},$$

with $y_b(\tau) = \rho(\tau)\,\theta_b(\tau)\,f_b(\{s_i(\tau)\})$. The interest rate r (market intertemporal price) ties our capital structure to time preference and opportunity cost.

<u>A summary</u>

Entrepreneurial profit is the price-valued surplus of *implemented*, complementary recipes over their opportunity costs, with the gap between plans and realizations governed by ρ (coordination), ψ vs. ϕ (beliefs vs. effectiveness), and the evolving price vector that disciplines selection (θ_b) across bundles.

<u>Profit as a disequilibrium phenomenon</u>

Within a Ricardian framework, it would be unacceptable to acknowledge that no single rate of profit can be defined for the entire economic system, given the inherently micro nature of entrepreneurial action and the heterogeneity of capital. Even two identical machines may yield different results if used in different ways or under varying conditions of time and space. Profit is not determined merely by the physical characteristics of capital, but rather by the specific *combinations* in which capital is employed. Capital can generate profit only when utilized in a particular manner—when the entrepreneurial function is actively engaged in continuously reshaping and reorganizing the capital structure (Lachmann, 1956, pp. 3–13). For this reason, it is impossible to speak meaningfully of a uniform rate of profit (Lachmann, 1973, p. 27) or of a marginal productivity of capital.

As previously discussed, and following Shackle's emphasis on *expectational time* as the setting in which uncertainty gives rise to profit, Lachmann (1973, p. 31) and the neo-Austrian school more broadly regard profit as an inherently and ontologically *disequilibrium phenomenon*. Since profit arises from the difference between selling prices and production costs, it cannot exist in a state of equilibrium. In the competitive pursuit of profit, entrepreneurial activity tends to activate equilibrating forces; yet profit persists precisely insofar as equilibrium does not prevail. In a *kaleidic world*—that is, within historical time—coordination tendencies are indeed present, but they never fully dominate, as equilibrium itself is continuously in flux.

The entrepreneurial function, in its pursuit of profit, drives the market from a state of disequilibrium along a path of coordination toward equilibrium (Kirzner, 1973, pp. 69–75). Human action always begins in disequilibrium, a condition marked by market ignorance. It is through market interaction that knowledge is exchanged and acquired, prompting revisions of individual plans. Entrepreneurial alertness enables these adjustments to occur and thus serves as an equilibrating force by reducing ignorance and aligning plans toward greater mutual consistency.

The equilibrating process, therefore, consists precisely in the progressive acquisition of better and more accurate information about the plans of different market participants (Kirzner, 1963, p. 38). Profit opportunities exist—and can be discovered by entrepreneurial alertness—only in conditions of disequilibrium (Kirzner, 1992, p. 5). In this sense, alertness fosters discovery, and discovery performs an equilibrating role by diminishing market ignorance.

However, contrary to Kirzner, Lachmann (1973, p. 32) maintained that such equilibrating forces can never fully prevail in a market economy—and that this very fact gives meaning to the competitive process. Profit continues to exist because disequilibrium is a permanent feature of the economic system, always present in at least some of its sectors.

Lachmann (1973, p. 32) drew two conclusions from his analysis on the nature of profit:

> First, the ever-elusive and fugitive price-cost differences which are the source of all profits can have no place in the long-term equilibrium world to which the two rival schools [Cambridge and neo-classical schools] are both committed. *An equilibrium rate of profit is thus a contradiction in terms.* Secondly, profits are pre-eminently a micro-economic phenomenon. Their basis is to be found primarily in the ever-changing pattern of price-cost differences in a thousand different markets. Without understanding this micro-foundation of the phenomenon we cannot understand its essence. We certainly should not be able to formulate a general theory of profits without it. A macro-economic theory of profit can therefore make little sense.

According to Lachmann (1973, pp. 33–35), the Ricardian perspective implicit in Böhm-Bawerk's theory of capital prevents us from grasping the true nature of profit, which resides in the micro-level forces of market competition. Böhm-Bawerk, in his analysis of profit and capital, introduced innovative ideas but remained tied to the aggregative framework of the classical economists—an approach from which the neo-Austrians decisively departed. They developed instead a microeconomic understanding of profit as the outcome of entrepreneurial action. When speaking of wealth and capital, one might say that Böhm-Bawerk, like Marx, elaborated on certain insights of Adam Smith, though they pursued them in very different directions.

The post–Böhm-Bawerk Austrian economists took a fundamentally different path, clearly identifying profit as the result of entrepreneurial activity. Profit, in this view, arises from distinct economic initiatives and can assume either positive or negative values. The element of time—introducing continual change into the economic landscape—is central to understanding the perpetual nature of profit in the neo-Austrian framework. As time unfolds, the information available to market participants evolves, and thus the tendency toward equilibrium operates within a context where equilibrium itself is constantly shifting. The kaleidoscopic character of economic life ensures that profit opportunities are always present, waiting to be discovered by entrepreneurial alertness.

In conclusion, the neo-Austrians—by developing their analysis within the framework of historical time—emphasize the role of entrepreneurial action over time as the enduring source of profit. This perspective, however, moves beyond Böhm-Bawerk's original concern with the justification of the interest rate within the framework of logical time.

4. Solving the Cambridge Capital Controversy

4.1. The Cambridge Capital Controversy: A debate on the foundations of capital theory

The Cambridge Capital Controversy[27], which unfolded between the 1950s and 1970s, was one of the most profound and philosophically charged debates in economic theory. It pitted economists based in Cambridge, England (notably Joan Robinson, Piero Sraffa, and Nicholas Kaldor), against their counterparts in Cambridge, Massachusetts (particularly Paul Samuelson and Robert Solow). At stake was not merely a technical disagreement over the measurement of capital, but a deeper challenge to the foundations of neoclassical production theory, distribution, and the marginalist vision of equilibrium.

At the heart of the debate was the concept of capital. Neoclassical economists in the American Cambridge treated capital as a measurable, homogeneous factor of production—comparable to labour—whose marginal productivity determined its remuneration, i.e., the rate of profit or interest. In this view, aggregate capital could be represented as a single quantity K, independent of the distribution of income, allowing production functions such as the Cobb–Douglas to describe the relationship between inputs and output.

Economists in the British Cambridge questioned this logic. Joan Robinson, followed by Piero Sraffa in his *Production of Commodities by Means of Commodities* (1960), argued that capital cannot be measured independently of prices and income distribution. The value of capital goods depends on the rate of profit, but in turn, the rate of profit depends on the valuation of capital—a circular reasoning that undermines the coherence of the neoclassical model. In other words, one cannot first measure the "quantity of capital" and then derive the profit rate from it, because the valuation of capital goods presupposes a profit rate in the first place.

This insight led to the phenomena of reswitching and capital-reversing, identified by Sraffa's followers. These refer to cases where a particular production technique—previously abandoned for being less profitable at a certain interest rate—becomes more profitable again when interest rates change. Such reversals violate the neoclassical assumption of a

27 See Harcourt (1972) and Birner (2002).

monotonic relationship between the rate of profit and the “capital intensity” of production. The implication is radical: there is no smooth, one-to-one substitution between capital and labor, and thus, no well-defined downward-sloping demand curve for capital.

The implications of the British argument went beyond capital theory. If capital cannot be aggregated or measured independently of income distribution, then the marginal productivity theory of distribution collapses, and with it the idea that competitive markets naturally lead to an equilibrium allocation of income based on productivity. The critique also cast doubt on the validity of aggregate production functions widely used in macroeconomics, as these rest on precisely the assumptions the controversy had shown to be flawed.

Paul Samuelson, representing the American side, eventually conceded in 1966 that the logical validity of the British critique was undeniable—famously acknowledging that «reswitching is a perverse but possible case». Yet, he argued that such phenomena were rare and of limited practical significance for applied economics. In contrast, the Cambridge (UK) school insisted that even if rare, the possibility of such paradoxes revealed a fundamental inconsistency in the marginalist framework.

In retrospect, the controversy did not produce a clear “winner”. The neoclassical paradigm survived, largely because of its empirical flexibility and its usefulness for modeling and policy. However, the Cambridge Capital Controversy profoundly altered the philosophical and methodological landscape of economics. It exposed the limits of aggregative reasoning, revived interest in classical and Sraffian approaches to value and distribution, and laid the groundwork for post-Keynesian and heterodox alternatives.

Ultimately, the debate was less about capital itself than about the nature of economic explanation—whether economics should be built upon abstract equilibrium models or grounded in historical and structural realities. In this sense, the Cambridge Capital Controversy remains a landmark episode in the ongoing dialogue between mathematical formalism and the deeper economic logic of production, distribution, and value.

4.2. Solving the Cambridge Capital Controversy

The Cambridge Capital Controversy arose because both sides—neoclassical and neo-Ricardian—shared the same implicit assumption:

that capital is a quantifiable entity with an objective physical or aggregate existence. The disagreement concerned *how* to measure it, not *whether* it could be meaningfully measured in the first place. Both approaches presupposed the possibility of identifying a measurable "quantity of capital", independent from the interpretative and temporal processes through which capital actually comes into being.

The hermeneutical definition of capital developed in this chapter overcomes that impasse by reframing the ontological nature of capital. Capital is not a physical stock, nor an aggregate of produced means of production; it is a subjective and interpretative relation between means and ends, continuously reconstructed through human expectations, plans, and actions in time. In other words, capital exists only insofar as economic agents *interpret* certain goods as capable of fulfilling certain purposes. It is therefore an emergent property of human understanding, not an objective factor comparable to labour or land.

This hermeneutical approach allows us to disarm the logical contradictions identified by Joan Robinson and Piero Sraffa. Since capital as an aggregate is not an objectively measurable magnitude, its value cannot be determined independently of the expectations, temporal preferences, and interpretive frameworks of economic agents. The supposed circularity between capital valuation and the rate of profit dissolves: the two are not linked through mechanical causality, but through hermeneutical coherence. Profit exists only as a reflection of entrepreneurial expectations and temporal valuations, not the marginal productivity of an objectively measurable capital stock.

By distinguishing between potential and actual capital—corresponding respectively to the moments of expectation formation and plan implementation—the theory explicitly embeds capital within historical time and interpretative action. This destroys the static framework within which the Cambridge controversy was fought. Once we accept that capital combinations are unique, context-dependent, and constantly reinterpreted through time, it becomes meaningless to seek an aggregate measure of "the quantity of capital". The only meaningful magnitude is the value attributed to specific capital combinations at particular moments, based on subjective expectations about their ability to generate output in the future.

Thus, the hermeneutical definition of capital resolves the Cambridge Capital Controversy by transcendence. It shows that the controversy was rooted in a misplaced search for an objective measure of something that is ontologically subjective. Capital cannot be measured as a stock because it is a process of interpretation unfolding in time, not a set of physical objects.

In this sense, both Sraffa and Samuelson were right within their own frameworks, but both were asking the wrong question. The real issue is not whether capital can be measured consistently across techniques, but whether it can be measured at all as an independent entity. Once capital is redefined as a hermeneutical relation—a mental and temporal construct that connects expectations, plans, and production processes—the question of measurement ceases to make sense. The controversy, therefore, is not solved *within* the neoclassical–Ricardian paradigm but *dissolved* by adopting a genuinely subjectivist and time-bound conception of economic reality.

Conclusions

This chapter has attempted to redefine the concept of capital by moving beyond both its classical and neoclassical formulations and grounding it instead in a hermeneutical framework. The argument developed here stems from a fundamental methodological conviction: economics, as a science of human action, cannot be reduced to the manipulation of objective magnitudes or mechanical relations. Capital, like any other economic category, exists only within the interpretative horizon of acting individuals—within the temporal and meaningful structure of human plans.

Reading potential and actual capital through Stein's metaphysics invites a phenomenological deepening of Austrian capital theory. Capital ceases to be a mere technical category and becomes a structure of becoming—an ontological rhythm of interpretation and realization. Potential capital is thus analogous to *form in potency* (the meaningful horizon of possibilities), while actual capital embodies *form in act* (the fulfilment of those possibilities through praxis).

In this light, capital formation is an ontological drama, not simply an economic process: it is the continual actualization of meaning through human action in historical time, precisely as Stein conceived of being as dynamic fulfilment—*Sein als Akt*.

By introducing the distinction between potential and actual capital, the chapter has clarified that capital is not a physical stock but a process of *interpretation and implementation* that unfolds in time. Potential capital represents the hermeneutical moment, in which expectations and ends–means frameworks are formed; actual capital corresponds to the operational moment, in which those expectations are tested through action. The value of capital, therefore, is never an intrinsic or measurable quantity—it is always a subjective evaluation derived from expectations about future outcomes.

This vision allows us to overcome the theoretical impasse that has haunted capital theory since Böhm-Bawerk, and that ultimately gave rise to the Cambridge Capital Controversy. By disentangling capital from its physical nature and interpreting it as an emergent, interpretative relation, we free the concept from the circularities of value and distribution that trapped both Ricardian and neoclassical approaches. Capital is not a "factor of production" comparable to labour, but a *category of meaning* that captures how human beings relate to time, uncertainty, and the transformation of reality through purposive action.

The hermeneutical re-foundation of capital also restores its organic link with entrepreneurship and profit. In a context of real time and uncertainty, profit arises not from the productivity of an aggregate capital stock, but from the success or failure of entrepreneurial interpretations—the constant reshaping of plans and combinations in the face of novelty. In this perspective, capital and profit are not separate categories but two expressions of the same creative and interpretative process through which human beings engage with the future.

Finally, the hermeneutical approach re-establishes the unity between ontology and methodology in economic theory. To speak of capital is to speak of human action in time; to analyze economic dynamics is to interpret the unfolding of meaning within history. This does not weaken the analytical power of economics but strengthens it, by aligning it with the true nature of its object: not a system of quantities, but a living process of understanding, coordination, and discovery.

In conclusion, capital should no longer be conceived as a measurable thing or a homogeneous stock, but as a hermeneutical relation—a dynamic, subjective, and time-bound process through which human minds interpret the world and transform it through action. By embracing this ontological and methodological redefinition, we not only reconcile the long-standing contradictions of capital theory but also open the way for a renewed, genuinely human economics: one that understands production, value, and profit as the outcomes of meaning in motion.

Thus, by connecting *potential and actual capital* with Stein's *potency and act*, we can interpret our hermeneutical economics as a phenomenology of creative realization. The entrepreneur's interpretative act mirrors the metaphysical movement by which being comes to presence: from openness (*Potenz*), through understanding, to fulfilment (*Akt*). Capital, in this sense, becomes a living analogy of being itself—a hermeneutical unfolding of potential meaning into actual form within the temporal and social order.

References

Antiseri, D. (2011), *Contro Rothbard. Elogio dell'ermeneutica*, Soviera Mannelli, Rubbettino.

Bellet, M. and Durieu, J. (2004), *Lundberg and Lachmann on expectations*, in M. Bellet, S. Gloria-Palermo and A. Zouache (Eds.), *Evolution of the Market Process. Austrian and Swedish economics*, London and New York, Routledge, pp. 230-252.

Birner, J. (2002), *The Cambridge Controversies in Capital Theory. A study in the logic of theory development*, London and New York, Routledge.

Blundell, J. (2014), *IHS and the Rebirth of Austrian Economics: Some Reflections on 1974–1976*, «The Quarterly Journal of Austrian Economics», 17, 1, pp. 92-107.

Böhm-Bawerk, E. von (1884), *Capital and Interest. A Critical History of Economical Theory*, London and New York, Macmillan and Co., 1890.

Böhm-Bawerk, E. von (1889), *The Positive Theory of Capital*, New York, G.E. Stechert, 1930.

Cowan, R. and Rizzo, M.J. (1996), *The Genetic-Causal Tradition and Modern Economic Theory*, in S. Gloria-Palermo (Ed.), *Modern Austrian Economics. Archaeology of a Revival*, Volume I: *A Multi-Directional Revival*, London, Pickering & Chatto, 2002, pp. 315-360.

Di Iorio, F. (2015a), *Cognitive Autonomy and Methodological. Individualism. The Interpretative Foundations of Social Life*, Cham, Springer International Publishing.

Di Iorio, F. (2015b), *Hayek and the hermeneutics of mind*, «Social Science Information», 54, 2, pp. 177-191.

Ferlito, C. (2015), *Ludwig M. Lachmann Against the Cambridge School*, «Journal of Reviews on Global Economics», 4, 2015, pp. 251-267.

Ferlito, C. (2018), *For a New Capital Theory: A Hermeneutical Approach*, «StoriaLibera. Rivista di scienze storiche e sociali», 4, 7, 2018, pp. 11-61.

Foss, N.J. (2012), *The Continuing Relevance of Austrian Capital Theory*, «The Quarterly Journal of Austrian Economics», 15, 2, pp. 151-171.

Harcourt, G.C. (1972), *Some Cambridge controversies in the theory of capital*, Cambridge, Cambridge University Press.

Hayek, F.A. von (1931), *Prices and Production*, New York, Kelley, 1967.

Hayek, F.A. von (1941), *The Pure Theory of Capital*, Chicago, The University of Chicago Press, 1952.

Kirzner, I.M. (1963), *Market Theory and the Price System*, Princeton, D. van Nostrand.

Kirzner, I.M. (1966), *An essay on capital*, in I.M. Kirzner, *Essays on Capital and Interest: An Austrian Perspective*, Cheltenham, Edward Elgar, 1996, pp 13-122.

Kirzner, I.M. (1973), *Competition and Entrepreneurship*, Chicago, University of Chicago Press.

Kirzner, I.M. (1992), *The Meaning of Market Process. Essays in the development of Modern Austrian Economics*, London and New York, Routledge.

Koppl, R. (1998), *Lachmann on the Subjectivism of Active Minds*, in, R. Koppl and G. Mongiovi (Eds.) (1998), pp. 61-79.

Koppl, R. and Mongiovi, G. (Eds.) (1998), *Subjectivism and Economic Analysis. Essays in memory of Ludwig M. Lachmann*, London and New York, Routledge, 2003.

Lachmann, L.M. (1941), *On the Measurement of Capital*, in D. Lavoie (Ed.), *Expectations and the Meaning of Institutions. Essays in economics by Ludwig Lachmann*, London and New York, Routledge, 1994, pp. 87-101.

Lachmann, L.M. (1956), *Capital and Its Structure*, Kansas City, Sheed Andrews and McMeel, 1978.

Lachmann, L.M. (1971), *The Legacy of Max Weber*. Berkeley, The Glendessary Press.

Lachmann, L.M. (1973), *Macro-economic Thinking and the Market Economy. An essay on the neglect of the micro-foundations and its consequences*, London, The Institute of Economic Affairs.

Lachmann, L.M. (1976a), *From Mises to Shackle: An Essay on Austrian Economics and the Kaleidic Society*, «Journal of Economic Literature», 14, 1, pp. 54-62.

Lachmann, L.M. (1976b), *Austrian Economics in the Present Crisis of Economic Thought*, in W.E. Grinder (Ed.), *Capital, Expectations, and the Market Process*, Kansas City, Sheed Andrews And McMeel Inc., 1977, pp. 25-41.

Lachmann, L.M. (1976c), *On Austrian Capital Theory*, in S. Gloria-Palermo (Ed.), *Modern Austrian Economics. Archaeology of a Revival*, Volume I: *A Multi-Directional Revival*, London, Pickering & Chatto, 2002, pp. 305-313.

Lachmann, L.M. (1990), *Austrian Economics: A Hermeneutic Approach*, in D. Lavoie (Ed.), *Economics and Hermeneutics*, London and New York, Routledge, 1990, pp. 132-144.

Leijonhufvud, A. (1986), *Capitalism and the Factory System*, in R.N. Langlois, *Economic as a Process: Essays in the New Institutional Economics*, New York, Cambridge University Press, 203-223.

Lewin, P. (1997), *Capital in Disequilibrium: A re-examination of the capital theory of Ludwig M. Lachmann*, unpublished draft, http://www.utdallas.edu/~plewin/hopentrv.pdf.

Meacci, F. (2006), *Uncertainty and Expectations in Shackle's Theory of Capital and Interest*, MPRA Paper 11700, Munich, Munich Personal RePEc Archive, http://mpra.ub.uni-muenchen.de/11700/.

Menger, C. (1871), *Principle of Economics*, Auburn, Ludwig von Mises Institute, 2007.

Mises, L. von (1949), *Human Action. A Treatise on Economics*, Auburn, Ludwig von Mises Institute, 1998.

Mittermaier, K.H.M. (1992), *Ludwig Lachmann (1906-1990), A Biographical Sketch*, in S. Gloria-Palermo (Ed.), *Modern Austrian Economics. Archaeology of a Revival*, Volume I: *A Multi-Directional Revival*, London, Pickering & Chatto, 2002, pp. 252-269.

Moss, L.S. (Ed.) (2000), *Ludwig M. Lachmann (1906-1990): Scholar, Teacher, and Austrian School Critic of Late Classical Formalism in Economics*, «American Journal of Economics and Sociology», 59, 3, pp. 367-417.

O'Driscoll, G.P. and Rizzo, M.J. (1985), *The Economics of Time and Ignorance*, London and New York, Routledge, 2002.

Phaneuf, E. and Ferlito, C. (2014), *On Human Rationality and Government Control*, «Procesos de Mercado: Revista Europea de Economía Política», XI, 2, pp. 137-181.

Prychitko, D.L. (1994), *Ludwig Lachmann and the Interpretative Turn in Economics: A Critical Inquiry into the Hermeneutics of the Plan*, in *Advances in Austrian Economics*, Volume I, London, JAI Press, pp. 303-319.

Prychitko, D.L. (1995a), *Introduction: Why hermeneutics?*, in D.L. Prychitko (Ed.) (1995b), pp. 1-5.

Prychitko, D.L. (Ed.) (1995b), *Individuals, Institutions, Interpretations. Hermeneutics Applied to Economics*, Aldershot and Brookfield, Avebury.

Robinson, J. (1974), *History versus Equilibrium*, in J. Robinson, *Collected Economic Papers*, Volume V, Oxford, Basil Blackwell, 1979, pp. 48-58.

Schumpeter, J.A. (1911), *The Theory of Economic Development. An Inquiry into Profits, Capital, Credit, Interest and Business Cycle*, New Brunswick and London, Transaction Publishers, 1983.

Shackle, G.L.S. (1965), *A Scheme of Economic Theory*, Cambridge, Cambridge University Press.

Shackle, G.L.S. (1972), *Epistemics and Economics: A critique of economic doctrines*, New Brunswick and London, Transaction Publishers, 2009.

Solow, R.M. (1956), *A Contribution to the Theory of Economic Growth*, «Quarterly Journal of Economics», 70, 1, pp. 65-94.

Solow, R.M. (1957), *Technical Change and the Aggregate Production Function*, «Review of Economics and Statistics», 39, 3, pp. 312-320.

Stein, E. (1931), *Potency and Act: Studies Toward a Philosophy of Being*, Washington, Institute of Carmelite Studies, 2009.

Vaughn, K. (1994), *Austrian economics in American. The migration of a tradition*, Cambridge, Cambridge University Press, 1998.

Wicksell, K. (1893), *Value, Capital and Rent*, London, George Allen & Unwin, 1954.

CHAPTER 3

Natural and Monetary Business Cycles[28]

Introduction: On the inevitability of economic fluctuations

The economic crisis that erupted in 2007 prompted Austrian economists to revive the Austrian Business Cycle Theory (ABCT) and to highlight the distortions caused by government intervention in general and by central banks in particular[29]. Perhaps the most striking feature of the post-crisis economic debate is that, while the neoclassical mainstream has struggled, older heterodox schools have sought to reassert themselves and have gained growing attention. In this light, it has become clear that the Hayek–Keynes debate is far from obsolete: the disciples of these two great economists remain very much engaged in the intellectual arena.

The first point I wish to emphasize is that economic crises do not signify the demise of the free market system; rather, they attest to its vitality. In previous works (Ferlito, 2013, p. 30; Ferlito, 2014), I argued that economic development cannot exist without fluctuations[30]. In line with this view, I have suggested that the cycle represents the genuine form of economic development (Ferlito, 2011, p. 96). Marx was the first to recognize this dynamic (Rothbard, 1969, p. 13), and a similar understanding can be found in Schumpeter's work, influenced by Spiethoff (1925, p. 112), who concluded that «the cyclical upswings and downswings are the evolutionary forms of the highly developed capitalist economy and their antithetic stimuli condition its progress». Schumpeter, in turn, influenced his student Paolo Sylos Labini (1954, pp. 12–14; 1984, pp. 37, 89), while related perspectives can also be traced in Lachmann (1956, pp. 110–112). Recognition of cyclicality as a defining

28 This is an updated and radically revised version of my work on the natural cycle which began with C. Ferlito (2014), *The Natural Cycle: Why Economic Fluctuations are Inevitable. A Schumpeterian Extension of the Austrian Business Cycle Theory*, «Journal of Reviews on Global Economics», 3, pp. 200-219. The paper has been thoroughly revised, and new sections have been added examining its relationship to Minsky's Financial Instability Hypothesis and on the measurement of economic activity and business cycles.

29 Among the others, see Prychitko (2010), Salerno (2012), Hülsmann (2013), Ferlito (2013) and Koppl (2014).

30 Huerta de Soto (1998, p. 468) pointed out that «[o]ne of the more curious points on which a certain agreement exists [between Marxian and Austrian analysis] relates precisely to the theory of the crises and recessions which systematically ravage the capitalist system».

feature of modern economic development also emerges in the writings of Marco Fanno (1931, pp. 248–249).

Building on the testimony of these economists, I will present the motivations that have led me to similar conclusions. At the core of my analysis lies the emphasis on expectations, time preferences, and innovation mechanisms. The framework developed here draws upon the Austrian Business Cycle Theory. However, I argue that Mises's thesis—that crises occur only when monetary authorities intervene in the money supply—requires revision. While the Austrian tradition distinguishes between sustainable and unsustainable booms, with crises arising only in the latter case, I maintain that depressions always follow booms, differing only in their intensity and duration. To advance this argument, I will take Hayek's perspective as my point of departure and integrate it with essential insights from Schumpeter and Lachmann.

1. Methodological intermezzo: Why mainstream economics fails in cycles forecasting

I believe that modern macroeconomics has failed to understand the true nature of economic fluctuations because it remains confined within a static paradigm—that of general equilibrium—sustained by econometric forecasting. Yet crises, by their very nature, cannot be meaningfully explained from within an equilibrium framework.

The first step, then, is to clarify the object of investigation. Method follows from the object, not the other way around. This does not mean yielding to an indistinct methodological relativism, but rather acknowledging that reality presents itself as complex, multifaceted, and dynamic. The business cycle, in particular, is not a static or mechanical event; it is a dynamic process. As with all economic theory, it must be anchored to reality, to living human beings acting within concrete contexts of time and space. As argued in Chapter 1, the centre of economic analysis must therefore be human action. Studying human behaviour is profoundly different from studying physical or chemical processes, or the natural sciences in general.

From this perspective, it becomes evident that the proper way to approach economic dynamics is through a subjective lens. The first fact to acknowledge about individual action is that it is always guided by a principle of purpose. Economists, therefore, are confronted with elements that are not abstract or hypothetical, but qualitative and concrete: people and the reality they inhabit. Analysis must begin with these realities, allowing itself to be surprised and inspired by them rather than attempting to cage them within rigid formal structures. The essence of the economist's task lies in observation—careful, attentive observation of reality. It is through such observation that we can identify recurring tendencies that mark human action.

One such tendency is the purposive character of human action. This does not mean, as in the rationalist formulations of general equilibrium theory, that individuals maximize units of utility according to mathematical models. Reality does not work that way. What can be observed, however, is that people act with the aim of achieving goals. In doing so, they enter into relationships with their environment, with other people, with material objects, and with society in all its complexity. The dynamics of enterprise—of striving, experimenting, and adapting—emerge from this search for goals. Economists may certainly study these dynamics, but they should do so without the illusion that behaviour can be planned in advance or compressed into strict functional models.

Explanations are possible, but they must be qualitative, not mechanistic. This requires using the right conceptual tools—tools suited to capturing processes, intentions, and uncertainty.

In conclusion, the work of the economist becomes meaningful only when the pursuit of rigid functional relations is replaced by a deeper aspiration: to understand how reality actually unfolds. This requires abandoning constructivist temptations and the pseudo-scientific fascination with perfect planning, and instead embracing the richness, complexity, and open-endedness of human action.

2. The traditional version of the ABCT: A summary

The most influential version of the Austrian Business Cycle Theory is that developed by Ludwig von Mises (1912, 1936, 1949). In its simplest form, the theory identifies the overexpansion of credit as the primary cause of cyclical fluctuations. This expansion may take the form of artificially low interest rates or the direct creation of money and its substitutes. Cheap credit encourages projects and investments that would not normally be considered viable, giving rise to an economy built on false signals.

Mises explained that when banks issue fiduciary media—such as notes and deposits not backed by reserves—they are able to extend credit well beyond the limits of their actual resources. This artificially lowers interest rates, stimulating economic activity and making previously unprofitable projects appear profitable. The resulting boom increases demand for labour and production materials, pushing up wages and prices. However, the process is unsustainable: while money supply expands, the real availability of resources does not.

If banks persist in credit expansion to sustain the boom, inflation accelerates, eventually leading to a collapse of confidence. As soon as the public realizes that price increases will not abate, a rush to spend money sets in, further destabilizing the system. On the other hand, if banks halt credit expansion earlier, the artificial profitability created by low interest rates is quickly exposed. Enterprises that were viable only under these artificial conditions face losses or bankruptcy, prices fall, and the economy enters a crisis and depression. Recovery requires liquidation of malinvestments and the accumulation of new savings, so that capital can be redirected toward genuinely sustainable uses.

This interpretation of crises is diametrically opposed to the Keynesian view, which attributes downturns to insufficient consumption and prescribes stimulating demand to restore growth. In the Austrian framework, however, recovery depends on renewed saving rather than consumption. Even monetarist approaches that rely on manipulating interest rates are regarded as ineffective. Further reductions in rates, as often attempted by central banks during recessions, worsen distortions rather than fostering recovery.

Mises observed that once a downturn begins, credit contracts, interest rates rise sharply due to panic, and then fall again during the depression. Yet low rates in such conditions do not revive economic activity; cash balances accumulate, but stagnation persists. Attempts to engineer recovery by artificially lowering rates through new credit expansion may create temporary relief, but inevitably lead to a deeper and more prolonged decline. For the Austrian school, economic stability can only be achieved by allowing prices, wages, and interest rates to be determined by the free play of market forces, without interference.

In essence, the Austrian theory maintains that cycles are not the result of market failure but of state-supported credit expansion. As Rothbard (1969, p. 37) emphasized, depressions do not end because banks and governments eventually abandon expansionary policies, but because such policies are continually sustained. Credit expansion misleads entrepreneurs by lowering interest rates artificially, generating widespread malinvestment. At the same time, inflation creates the illusion of higher income for consumers, prompting them to increase spending on consumption goods at the expense of capital formation. The outcome is a structure of production misaligned with real preferences and resource constraints, which must ultimately collapse in crisis.

3. Toward a new vision: From the *Monetary Cycle* to the *Natural Cycle*

Later developments of the Austrian Business Cycle Theory introduced a distinction between sustainable and unsustainable booms. In both cases, the focus lies on changes in the intertemporal structure of preferences—whether on the side of consumers/savers or investors—that lead to shifts in the natural interest rate and, consequently, in the intertemporal structure of production.

A sustainable boom occurs when no monetary manipulation is involved and economic agents are free to coordinate their temporal preferences through the price signal conveyed by the natural interest rate[31]. In this case, the interest rate functions properly as a mechanism of information transmission, aligning savings and investment decisions. Such a boom is not followed by a bust.

By contrast, in an unsustainable boom, the monetary interest rate imposed by central banks prevents the natural rate from playing its coordinating role. The resulting misalignment in the structure of preferences persists, and the expansion inevitably ends in crisis.

Drawing on some of Hayek's insights, however, I will argue that this distinction should be reconsidered. Crises should not be seen as the

31 Hayek (1933, p. 145) stated that «an equilibrium rate of interest would then be one which assured correspondence between the intentions of the consumers and the intentions of the entrepreneurs. And with a constant rate of saving this would be the rate of interest arrived at on a market where the supply of money, capital was of exactly the same amount as current savings». In turn, Garrison (2006, pp. 58-59) explained that «the natural rate [is] the rate that reflects the time preferences of market participants and allocates resources among the temporally defined stages of production. [...] In summary terms, the natural rate is seen as an equilibrium rate. It is the rate that tells the truth about the availability of resources for meeting present and future consumer demands, allowing production plans to be kept in line with the preferred pattern of consumption. By implication, an unnatural, or artificial, rate of interest is a rate that reflects some extra-market influence and that creates a disconnect between intertemporal consumption preferences and intertermporal production plans».

exclusive outcome of unsustainable, credit-driven booms, but as the natural consequence of booms in general. What is needed, therefore, is not a dichotomy between sustainable and unsustainable booms, but a recognition of two types of cycles:

1. *Monetary cycles*, corresponding to the Austrian view of unsustainable boom–bust patterns driven by credit expansion.

2. *Natural cycles*, which begin as sustainable booms but culminate in liquidation crises.

In both cases, the process originates in changes to the intertemporal structure of preferences. The two cycle stages can be described as follows:

Table 3.1: Monetary Cycle vs Natural Cycle.

	Monetary Cycle	Natural Cycle
Stage 1	Boom, ignited by a modification of the intertemporal structure of preferences. Price mechanism information transmission role blocked by monetary authority action.	Boom, ignited by a modification of the intertemporal structure of preferences. No monetary authority.
Stage 2	Secondary boom: Schumpeterian and imitation and speculation processes.	Secondary boom: Schumpeterian and imitation and speculation processes.
Stage 3	Crisis: liquidation of the secondary boom.	Crisis: liquidation of the secondary boom.
Stage 4	Depression: liquidation of most of the initiative initiated with stage 1.	

I shall now turn to a description of these cycles, with particular attention to the natural cycle, which I regard as the most important theoretical innovation proposed here.

3.1. The *Monetary Cycle*

Economic fluctuations originate in shifts within the intertemporal structure of preferences. At any given moment, individuals' relative valuation of present and future goods is expressed through a structure of time preferences, summarized by the *natural interest rate*. This rate acts as the pivotal link between the subjective world of choice and the objective organization of production: it conveys how strongly agents prefer present satisfaction over future returns.

In Hayek's terms (1929, p. 123), stability depends on the consistency between the production structure and the prevailing system of preferences. That system, in turn, evolves through the expectations of market participants who, guided by their anticipations, continuously revise and coordinate plans in the market process. Under free-market conditions, such coordination occurs spontaneously as agents adjust their plans in light of new information, ensuring—albeit imperfectly—that the realization of one's own purposes takes account of others' actions.

Mises introduced a crucial asymmetry into this picture. When a central authority sets a *monetary rate of interest*, this rate—being public, visible, and authoritative—tends to dominate the *natural rate* as the guiding signal for entrepreneurs. It thus interrupts the discovery process that ordinarily links time preferences to the organization of production. The monetary rate becomes the key reference for profit expectations, plan formation, and ultimately for the allocation of resources.

When the monetary rate diverges from the natural one, it communicates misleading information. A rate below the natural level, for instance, signals the false availability of additional savings, prompting entrepreneurs to extend production plans into longer time horizons. Yet these plans lack real support from genuine savings. A tension emerges between investors—encouraged to adopt a future-oriented stance—and consumers, whose preferences remain anchored in the present. The resulting disequilibrium expresses a unilateral shift in intertemporal preferences.

In a purely market setting, such unilateral shifts are transparent: the natural rate transmits them across agents, allowing coordinated adaptation. But once monetary policy interferes, the natural signal is muted. The market's coordinating mechanism is short-circuited, and the production structure drifts away from the real configuration of preferences.

Hayek (1929, pp. 147–168) noted that a monetary rate below the natural one may arise in two ways. The first is deliberate intervention: central banks reduce rates to stimulate expansion, misleading entrepreneurs into assuming that more capital is available than truly exists. The second originates endogenously, through rising profit expectations. Optimistic entrepreneurs—reacting to technological innovations, new markets, or fortuitous shocks—demand more funds for long-term projects, pushing the *natural* rate upward. If banks fail to raise the *monetary* rate accordingly, excess credit creation again emerges, even without explicit policy manipulation. In both cases, expectations are reshaped unilaterally: the structure of production lengthens without the counterpart of additional saving, and equilibrium is lost.

In both versions, expectations play the central role. Whether driven by monetary expansion or by entrepreneurial optimism, expectations determine the direction of investment and the time structure of production. Entrepreneurs, perceiving profit opportunities, become more future-oriented and undertake longer, more roundabout processes. Some innovate genuinely; others imitate or speculate. Once imitation spreads, optimism transforms into collective euphoria—Schumpeter's "secondary wave"—sustaining the boom beyond its real foundations.

As the boom unfolds, the new demand for raw materials and labour raises input prices and wages. Rising wages expand consumer demand just when the supply of consumption goods has been curtailed by the reallocation of resources to higher-order stages. Prices in consumer industries rise, purchasing power falls, and the system faces mounting inflationary pressure. Credit expansion must then continue merely to maintain ongoing projects. Yet as prices accelerate, interest rates eventually rise, profit margins shrink, and investment plans become unsustainable. Capital goods industries find themselves overextended: part of the productive apparatus—though physically intact—cannot be used profitably. Apparent abundance reveals a *scarcity of capital* (Hayek 1933, p. 149).

This paradox captures the essence of the crisis. The problem is not insufficient consumption but an intertemporal mismatch: production has been organized on the assumption of greater saving than consumers were willing to provide. The expansionary phase diverts resources from consumer goods to investment goods; the contraction reverses the process as resources are pulled back to satisfy immediate wants.

The crisis thus represents the market's attempt to restore coherence between time preferences and the production structure.

Hayek (1931, p. 67) illustrated this through his famous island metaphor: an economy that has exhausted its food supplies before completing a great machine must suspend work on it and return to producing daily necessities. Likewise, after an artificial expansion, the economy must reorient production toward current consumption before long-term projects can resume on sustainable grounds.

In sum, fluctuations emerge whenever expectations—monetary or entrepreneurial—push the structure of production beyond the real limits imposed by genuine saving. The subsequent correction, though painful, re-establishes the correspondence between intertemporal preferences and productive organization, closing the cycle that links credit, expectations, and capital scarcity.

3.2. From the sustainable boom to the ***Natural Cycle***

The previous section builds on the traditional Austrian explanation of business cycles, which provides an indispensable foundation, highlighting how monetary distortions mislead entrepreneurs and set in motion sequences of malinvestment and correction. Yet, while this framework captures the dynamics of the *monetary* disturbance, it remains incomplete if interpreted as the sole source of cyclical change. Even in the absence of credit expansion, the economy would continue to oscillate, for it is animated by the interpretative and temporal nature of human action itself. To grasp this deeper, endogenous rhythm of expansion and contraction—rooted in the very logic of discovery, uncertainty, and capital reconfiguration—we must move beyond the monetary narrative and turn to what may be called the *Natural Cycle*.

According to the traditional formulation of the Austrian Business Cycle Theory, economic development would unfold in a sustainable manner if, during periods of heightened optimism, market participants were left free to interact, learn, and have their choices tested by the market process itself. In the absence of interference from a monetary rate artificially imposed by central authorities, individuals would discover—through the very act of exchange—the degree to which their expectations align with those of others. Over time, such interactions would foster an increasing coherence among the plans of different agents, allowing coordination to emerge spontaneously.

Within this framework, the natural rate of interest—though not directly measurable—continuously arises from the interplay of time preferences across the economy. It serves as the interpretative link between present and future, guiding the formation of a production structure consistent with the prevailing intertemporal valuations of individuals. Every adjustment in that structure reflects a dynamic response to evolving expectations and preferences. For example, if entrepreneurial optimism raises profit expectations and pushes the natural rate upward, the reconfiguration of production would proceed only as consumers themselves adopt a more future-oriented stance. Yet such adjustments rarely occur in perfect synchrony: the increase in investment demand typically exceeds the growth in voluntary savings, so the natural rate tends to stabilise at a level lower than the initial surge inspired by entrepreneurial enthusiasm.

In a market unencumbered by monetary manipulation, this interpretative mechanism—embodied in the interaction between demand and supply—operates as a genuine process of discovery. Through prices and interest rates, individuals continuously interpret and reinterpret the signals emerging from the market, aligning their plans through trial, error, and adaptation. In such a framework, where no central authority dictates the cost of credit, the only prevailing rate is the *natural* one: a reflection of dispersed expectations and the temporal structure of human choice. It is this self-organising process that allows the economy to evolve coherently within the boundaries set by real preferences and knowledge.

Consider now what happens when time preferences shift unilaterally—say, when consumers become more future-oriented and the propensity to save increases. An immediate tension emerges between consumers, who wish to defer consumption, and investors, who may initially remain focused on shorter-term returns. Yet this very alteration in preferences sets in motion a self-correcting process. The rise in savings pushes the equilibrium rate of interest downward, signalling that society is now prepared to allocate a larger share of resources to future production. Entrepreneurs interpret this signal as an invitation to re-plan: they lengthen production processes, adopt more roundabout methods, and engage in projects that would have been unprofitable under the previous constellation of preferences. In other words, the lower rate communicates new meaning to market participants — that additional real resources have become available for long-term investment, and that these investments are funded precisely by the savings voluntarily set aside by consumers.

The new equilibrium rate thus performs a crucial coordinating role. It allows entrepreneurs to realign their expectations with those of consumers and to adjust their strategies accordingly. Acting as an informational and interpretative signal, it informs producers that fresh resources exist and that new ventures can be undertaken profitably. The entrepreneurial instinct—Schumpeterian in nature and already highlighted by Spiethoff—becomes decisive in this readjustment, guiding expectations toward a renewed harmony between the plans of entrepreneurs and the time preferences of consumers.

In a market free from central-bank interference, the natural rate of interest—emerging as the spontaneous outcome of supply and demand rather than the product of administrative decree—serves as the sole coordinating signal. Profit expectations encouraged by the lower rate are not frustrated, for they find their counterpart in the behaviour of consumers who have voluntarily postponed present consumption. The result is a *sustainable expansion*: growth proceeds coherently because plans, expectations, and resources evolve in mutual consistency.

This process, however, does not imply perfect foresight or frictionless adaptation. Adjustment unfolds in real time, through trial and error, and expectations are continually revised as new information emerges. Market participants learn from their mistakes and reorganize their plans in light of evolving circumstances. Adaptation, therefore, is never complete but remains an open-ended dynamic. Stability in such a system does not arise from stillness but from continuous movement guided by truthful signals. Only when the natural rate—generated by the uncoerced interaction of saving and investment—retains its primacy can this process function effectively. Once external distortions impose conflicting signals, plans are misdirected, preferences fall out of alignment, and the intertemporal coordination of the economy is undermined.

In short, sustainable growth materializes when collective shifts in time preferences are transmitted faithfully through an undistorted price system. The interest rate, freely formed in the market, expresses the evolving balance between present and future orientations, allowing entrepreneurs and consumers alike to interpret one another's intentions. Through this ongoing conversation of expectations, the economy traces a coherent, though never static, path of development.

In all the cases examined so far, we have observed that an expansionary phase emerges whenever the intertemporal structure of preferences shifts forward—whenever economic agents become, in some sense, more future-oriented. Such changes may originate either on the consumer side, through increased saving, or on the entrepreneurial side, through heightened profit expectations. What matters, however, is not the direction of causality but the interpretative alignment that follows: both forms of adjustment give rise to a lengthening of the production structure, as entrepreneurs undertake more roundabout and time-consuming processes.

In Schumpeterian terms, these new investments can be viewed as *innovations*: manifestations of creative reinterpretation that transform the existing production structure. They embody what Lachmann (1940, p. 271) described as «new forms of progress», or, in Schumpeter's own words, «spontaneous and discontinuous changes in the channels of the circular flow and disturbances of the centre of equilibrium» (Schumpeter, 1911, p. 65). These shifts represent the living core of economic development—the constant reconfiguration of plans and expectations that keeps the capitalist process in motion.

It is at this point that the limitations of the traditional Austrian perspective become visible. While the Austrian Business Cycle Theory correctly explains how *artificial* booms arise from monetary distortions, it does not fully account for the cyclical tensions that emerge even when no such distortions are present. To understand why every process of development inevitably carries within it the seeds of crisis, we must introduce explicitly Schumpeterian elements into the analysis. This will allow us to see that fluctuations are not mere accidents or policy-induced deviations, but intrinsic to the very rhythm of innovation, imitation, and expectation that defines capitalist evolution.

We can therefore begin from Schumpeter's analytical starting point: a hypothetical state of perfect static equilibrium—the "theoretical standard" (Schumpeter, 1939, pp. 132–133)—and explore how the introduction of entrepreneurial innovation disrupts that stillness, transforming it into a dynamic process of change. From this moment, equilibrium ceases to be a resting point and becomes a moving target, constantly reshaped by the interpretative activity of entrepreneurs and the responses of the market. It is within this framework that the concept of the natural cycle can be meaningfully developed.

Schumpeter's reconstruction begins with an abstract condition he called the *theoretical standard*: a state of perfect static equilibrium in which all magnitudes are constant, population remains unchanged, no savings occur, and every agent simply repeats yesterday's actions today (Schumpeter, 1939, pp. 132–133). Within such a circular flow, production and consumption perpetuate themselves indefinitely, and no genuine development takes place. Yet this image of stillness is deliberately artificial: it serves only as a foil against which the essence of capitalism — change — can be revealed. For Schumpeter, the capitalist economy is not an organism seeking rest, but a living process propelled by the initiative of individuals who *see* differently, who imagine new combinations and dare to act upon them.

In every society, there are always some individuals who conceive and elaborate, each with varying promptness and audacity, plans for new ventures inspired by distinct anticipations of profit. These are the entrepreneurs — those who break with routine and set out to do "a new and unfamiliar thing". They establish new firms, build new plants, and demand from existing producers the machines, equipment, and materials needed to realize their vision. To finance their projects, they borrow from banks, and through their spending they withdraw productive resources from their previous employments and redirect them toward novel uses. In this way, innovation is born not as an abstract idea but as a *reallocation of meaning and resources* within the economic structure. The flow of credit channels command over existing goods toward new purposes, transforming expectations into action.

The entrepreneur's bids for producers' goods initiate a process of creative reorganization. At first, only a few innovators move, but their example soon attracts others — imitators, financiers, and suppliers — who are drawn by the promise of new opportunities. Gradually, experience accumulates, obstacles diminish, and the path of innovation becomes smoother for those who follow (Schumpeter, 1939, pp. 133–134). What begins as an isolated act of interpretation — the entrepreneur's perception of a new possibility — unfolds into a collective transformation of the economic landscape. Here, Schumpeter's analysis resonates deeply with the interpretative view of the market: progress arises from acts of understanding, from the continual reinterpretation of existing possibilities in light of new expectations.

Then the scene begins to change. The new commodities—let us say, new consumers' goods—start to flow into the market. If expectations are broadly fulfilled, they are rapidly absorbed at the very prices entrepreneurs had anticipated. A stream of receipts begins to flow back to these pioneers, sufficient to repay the debts incurred, cover the interest due, and yield a genuine entrepreneurial profit. As Schumpeter notes, «*t*he new firms, getting successively into working order and throwing their products into the market of consumers' goods, increase the total output of consumers' goods» (Schumpeter, 1939, p. 136). What was once a bold projection of imagination now materializes as a new reality — production expands, income circulates, and prosperity becomes visible.

Yet, precisely because new goods are introduced faster than the market can fully absorb them, the process of adjustment becomes uneven. Established firms and late imitators encounter frictions: some adapt successfully to the new order, others are forced to exit, and still others attempt to survive through rationalization or cost-cutting strategies (Schumpeter, 1939, pp. 137–138). Over time, the pioneering advantage erodes. As new products proliferate and competitive imitation spreads, profit margins contract while debt repayment obligations persist. The initial burst of entrepreneurial activity gradually loses momentum, and the economy begins its slow movement toward a new equilibrium.

In this transition, the outlines of cyclical motion begin to appear. The sequence of events—rising investment, expanding incomes, resource scarcity, profit compression, and eventual readjustment—reproduces the familiar pattern of prosperity followed by recession. «Our model», writes Schumpeter, «reproduces, by its mere working, that very sequence of events which we observe in the course of those fluctuations in economic life which have come to be called business cycles» (Schumpeter, 1939, p. 142). In other words, the cycle is not an external disturbance imposed on the economy but a natural expression of its inner vitality. The same forces that generate growth—innovation, imitation, and expectation—also generate the necessity of correction and renewal.

Schumpeter's second approximation of the cycle elaborates this insight further. As innovations are embodied in new plant and equipment, expenditures on both capital and consumer goods rise in tandem. Prosperity spreads through two channels: established firms respond to the new environment, while others engage in speculative behaviour, betting that current rates of growth will persist indefinitely (Schumpeter, 1939, pp. 150–151). This second phenomenon transforms sound expansion into exuberance. Transactions begin to rest on anticipated price increases rather than on real productivity gains, and a *secondary wave* of prosperity is set in motion — more visible, more intense, and ultimately more fragile.

Even this secondary prosperity, however, contains within it the seeds of its own disruption. Every phase of expansion, even when driven by genuine innovation, necessarily involves a period of failures and liquidation. The market eliminates outdated combinations, adjusts relative prices, and reallocates resources toward more viable uses. In Schumpeter's own words, the cycle unfolds across four characteristic phases — *prosperity, recession, depression,* and *recovery* — forming the complete rhythm of capitalist evolution (Schumpeter, 1939, p. 142).

From this point of view, crisis is not an anomaly but an intrinsic moment of the creative process — the necessary counterpart of progress. The downturn does not negate the preceding boom; it fulfils it by restoring coherence and paving the way for new combinations to emerge. Development, therefore, is cyclical because understanding itself is cyclical: entrepreneurs interpret, act, err, and reinterpret. Through this constant oscillation between expectation and revision, the market learns, adapts, and evolves.

For our purposes, it is essential to emphasize the distinctive feature of what Schumpeter called *secondary prosperity*: the role of imitation in amplifying and extending the initial growth process. As Lachmann (1986, p. 15) later observed, every competitive process unfolds in two stages. The first is driven by innovation — the creative act of seeing opportunities that others overlook. The second is driven by imitation — the adaptive response of those who follow the pioneers once the path has been opened. Innovation and imitation thus form the twin rhythms of capitalist evolution, mutually reinforcing and inseparable.

The expansionary phase of the cycle is therefore marked by a temporal extension of the production structure, concentrated in sectors where profit expectations have risen most sharply. The success of pioneering investments reshapes the informational landscape: it changes how other agents perceive reality. As optimism spreads, new entrepreneurs and investors reinterpret the boom as a signal of enduring opportunity. Their additional investments, often financed through credit, multiply the effects of the initial expansion and deepen the momentum of growth. In this way, imitation acts as an accelerator — a psychological and financial multiplier of the boom.

Building upon Schumpeter's and Lachmann's insights, we may thus regard crises not as an external disruption but as an *immanent* outcome of the very process of development. Every phase of prosperity inevitably gives rise to speculative and imitative behaviour, which in turn requires a corrective adjustment. Sustainable and artificial booms are not distinguished by whether they end in crisis — for all expansions must eventually be followed by readjustment — but by the *character and intensity* of that crisis. In a "healthy" expansion, the downturn serves a restorative purpose, liquidating only the least viable ventures. In an artificial boom, driven by monetary distortions, the subsequent collapse is deeper and more destructive.

Expectations and imitation are thus the crucial variables of this entire sequence. As early as 1929, Hayek (1929, p. 147) had already underscored the central role of profit expectations in determining the direction of entrepreneurial action. When expectations turn optimistic, entrepreneurs naturally adopt a more future-oriented outlook, and the equilibrium rate of interest rises accordingly. Profit expectations, in this sense, act as both a signal and a catalyst: they transmit information about perceived opportunities and initiate the process of reallocation that defines economic change.

In what follows, these elements — expectations and imitation — will become the building blocks of a broader synthesis. They explain why expansions, even in the absence of monetary manipulation, contain an inner tendency toward crisis. This recognition leads us to a necessary revision of the Austrian framework: to move from a theory of *artificial* cycles, induced by monetary distortion, to a theory of *natural* cycles, born from the interpretative dynamics of the market process itself.

In the idealized setting where no central bank imposes a monetary rate of interest, time-intensive investment processes arise whenever the structure of expectations shifts forward. When consumers lead the change, higher savings lower the natural rate and encourage entrepreneurs to invest in longer production processes. When entrepreneurs initiate the change, rising profit expectations push the natural rate upward, attracting additional savings to finance new projects. In both scenarios, the mechanism is the same: changes in time preferences and expectations jointly generate a sustainable expansion.

Here, the *Natural Cycle* begins to take shape. Business expectations give rise to the first wave of genuine, innovation-led investment — a *primary expansion* supported by real savings and a consistent intertemporal structure. Yet, as optimism spreads and imitators enter the scene, a *secondary expansion* emerges, increasingly detached from underlying preferences and real resources. This second wave magnifies the boom but also plants the seeds of its own liquidation. The eventual downturn — the *corrective crisis* — does not erase the progress achieved; it merely restores the coherence between plans and means, clearing the ground for new acts of innovation.

Thus, the *natural cycle* represents a deeper and more general understanding of capitalist dynamics. It encompasses both the creative and the corrective phases of development, showing that growth and crisis are not opposites but complementary moments of the same process. In every cycle, expectations expand, interpretations multiply, and coordination must be rediscovered. Economic life, seen through this lens, is not a succession of equilibria but a continuous dialogue between human imagination and the constraints of reality.

To summarise, the emergence of *primary expansion* within the natural cycle occurs whenever expectations and time preferences shift toward the future, generating a genuine lengthening of the production structure. When profit expectations rise, entrepreneurs become more forward-looking, and the natural rate of interest tends to increase. This upward movement attracts additional savings, allowing investment projects to be financed through real resources rather than artificial credit. Conversely, when consumers lead the change by increasing their savings, the natural rate declines, encouraging entrepreneurs to undertake more roundabout and time-intensive production processes. In both cases, the engine of development is the same: a collective reinterpretation of the future that reorients action, reorganizes capital, and gives rise to a sustainable path of growth.

In this framework, as long as the expansion originates in authentic changes in expectations and preferences—and as long as the interest rate remains a faithful signal of those changes—resources will be available to complete investment projects. The market process, when left undistorted, enables agents to reveal their plans to one another through prices and to adjust them dynamically in real time. The system thus evolves in a coherent and self-correcting way, not toward a final equilibrium but through successive moments of coordination and learning.

Yet even this virtuous mechanism harbours a source of tension. Every phase of expansion contains within it a rhythm of acceleration and delay. Once the first wave of entrepreneurial investments—the *primary expansion*—sets the process in motion, the economic landscape itself begins to change. The success of the pioneers reshapes expectations across the market: profits appear attainable, risk seems reduced, and the atmosphere becomes charged with optimism. It is this change in perception that triggers a second, broader wave of investment—the *secondary expansion*—driven no longer by discovery but by imitation.

Imitation is not an accident but an inherent feature of capitalist evolution. As Schumpeter observed, true innovations are never mass phenomena; they originate from a few individuals capable of imagining new combinations. But as the initial successes become visible, others reinterpret these achievements as reproducible opportunities. Drawn by the momentum of the boom, imitators enter with the hope of sharing in the prosperity already underway. Their participation, however, introduces a temporal misalignment: investments are initiated not from genuine insight but from the expectation that present trends will persist. As more projects are launched, the demand for loanable funds expands, putting upward pressure on the natural rate of interest.

At first, this acceleration appears self-reinforcing: new ventures stimulate demand, incomes rise, and optimism strengthens. But as the expansion proceeds, the underlying structure of preferences may fail to keep pace. Consumers may not increase their savings sufficiently to finance the additional investment, and banks—buoyed by the euphoria of prosperity—begin to extend credit beyond the limits set by real resources (Minsky's Financial Instability Hypothesis). The very mechanism that once ensured coordination now starts to generate divergence. Optimism transforms into overextension, and the natural rate's guiding role weakens as credit is created in anticipation of a future alignment that may never occur.

Thus, the transition from the primary to the secondary wave marks a critical turning point. The economy moves from a phase of genuine innovation and sustainable growth to one of imitation and speculative expansion. What was initially an interpretative advance—the discovery of new meanings and opportunities—gradually degenerates into the repetition of existing patterns under changing expectations. The seeds of crisis are sown not by external shocks but by the inner logic of temporal coordination itself: when too many plans lean on the same vision of the future, that vision can no longer sustain them all.

The *natural cycle*, therefore, unfolds as a self-contained process comprising three interlinked stages. The first is *primary expansion*, driven by authentic shifts in expectations and preferences that extend the structure of production coherently. The second is *secondary expansion*, propelled by imitation and speculative optimism, which magnifies the boom but weakens its foundations. The third is the *corrective crisis*, a phase of liquidation and realignment through which the economy restores the consistency between plans, preferences, and resources.

In this light, crisis is not the negation of progress but its necessary complement. The downturn represents the moment in which false expectations are purged and the interpretative process of the market is renewed. The capitalist economy advances through these alternating movements of interpretation and re-interpretation—of creation, imitation, and correction. Development, therefore, is not a straight path toward equilibrium but a rhythmic sequence of understanding, misunderstanding, and renewed understanding.

At the peak of expansion, when optimism is widespread and investment projects multiply, a decisive shift begins to unfold beneath the surface. Rising demand for loanable funds pushes the natural interest rate upward, signalling the need for additional real savings to sustain the growing structure of production. Yet, as we have seen, the capacity of consumers to save is not limitless. Consumption remains a necessity, imposing a natural ceiling on the expansion of savings. More importantly, the psychological atmosphere of prosperity often reverses the direction of preferences: as incomes rise and optimism prevails, individuals tend to consume more, not less.

The result is an increasing strain between the structure of production and the underlying intertemporal preferences of society. While entrepreneurs continue to lengthen the production process, consumers reassert their preference for present goods. Wages rise to attract labour into expanding industries, and the price of consumer goods begins to climb. The balance of profitability shifts. Sectors closer to final consumption, benefiting from higher demand and faster turnover, become relatively more attractive. This mechanism—first elaborated by Hayek—constitutes what he called the Ricardo Effect: as real wages rise and profit margins on capital-intensive projects shrink, resources naturally flow back toward shorter, labour-intensive methods of production (Moss, 2005, pp. 8–9).

In this way, the Ricardo Effect acts as the endogenous corrective force of the market process. It is the manifestation, in real time, of the system's effort to re-establish coherence between plans and preferences. When the relative profitability of long-term projects declines, many of them become unsustainable; they are liquidated, releasing resources to more urgent and profitable uses. A wave of bankruptcies may follow, particularly among firms that extended their production structures the furthest or relied most heavily on optimistic credit. Yet, from a broader perspective, this liquidation is not a pathological event. It is the market's hermeneutical moment of *re-interpretation* — the stage at which the economy corrects the misread signals and realigns its productive structure with the genuine pattern of time preferences.

The distinction between sustainable growth and an artificial boom, therefore, lies not in the presence or absence of crisis but in its *nature and severity*. In the defective, monetary cycle—where central-bank intervention has driven a wedge between the natural and the monetary rate—the ensuing collapse is deep and destructive. Capital combinations conceived under false price signals must be dismantled wholesale, and the process of reconstruction is long and painful. In the *natural cycle*, by contrast, the crisis performs a limited and restorative function. It liquidates speculative and imitative ventures without erasing the real progress achieved during the primary expansion. What emerges is not depression but rebalancing: a shorter downturn that purges excesses and prepares the ground for renewed innovation.

We may thus describe the full rhythm of the natural cycle as a triadic sequence:

- Primary Expansion, initiated by genuine shifts in expectations and preferences that lengthen the structure of production in harmony with time preferences;
- Secondary Expansion, fuelled by imitation and speculative optimism that overextend the process beyond the limits of real savings; and
- Corrective Crisis, the necessary phase of liquidation and re-interpretation through which equilibrium between expectations and resources is restored.

Seen in this light, crisis is not an external shock or a moral failure but an integral part of capitalist vitality — the counterpart of creativity itself. The same interpretative openness that allows entrepreneurs to envision new possibilities also exposes them to error; the same freedom that generates innovation inevitably generates misjudgment. But it is through this very process of continual revision that the market learns, evolves, and sustains its dynamism.

In sum, the *natural cycle* embodies the living logic of the market as a process of understanding in motion. Growth and crisis are not opposites but two moments of the same interpretative journey — one of anticipation, disappointment, and renewed discovery. Each phase represents a different configuration of human expectations, bound together by the unending dialogue between the future imagined and the future realized. In that dialogue lies the essence of economic life: a ceaseless effort to make sense of an ever-changing world.

4. A summary

This chapter so far has developed an integrated interpretation of business cycles that combines the insights of the Austrian tradition—particularly Mises, Hayek, and Lachmann—with the Schumpeterian and Spiethoffian vision of development as a dynamic and evolutionary process. The central thesis is that cyclical fluctuations do not represent a pathological deviation from equilibrium but rather the *very form* through which capitalist growth manifests itself. The cycle is not an anomaly to be cured but the physiological rhythm of an economy driven by innovation, expectation, and time-based coordination.

At the methodological level, the chapter rejects the mechanistic conception of equilibrium and embraces a subjectivist and process-oriented approach. Human action, guided by purposes and expectations, lies at the heart of economic dynamics. Consequently, the business cycle cannot be explained by static models or equilibrium conditions, but only by understanding the interaction of entrepreneurial plans and shifting expectations in real time.

The discussion begins by revisiting the traditional Austrian Business Cycle Theory (ABCT), in which monetary expansion and artificially low interest rates distort intertemporal coordination and generate malinvestment. Yet while this interpretation remains analytically powerful, the chapter advances beyond it by incorporating a *real-time, expectation-based framework* in which even "sustainable" booms—those not driven by credit manipulation—contain within themselves the seeds of cyclical readjustment.

In this re-elaboration, two types of cycles are distinguished:

- The *Monetary Cycle*, corresponding to the classical Austrian description of unsustainable expansions generated by credit inflation and leading to deep depressions.
- The *Natural Cycle*, which originates from genuine shifts in time preferences and profit expectations in a context free from monetary distortion. This cycle also culminates in a crisis, though one of adjustment rather than destruction—a process that liquidates speculative and imitative ventures while preserving the genuine achievements of the first wave of innovation.

Figure 3.1: Natural and monetary cycles, stylized representation.

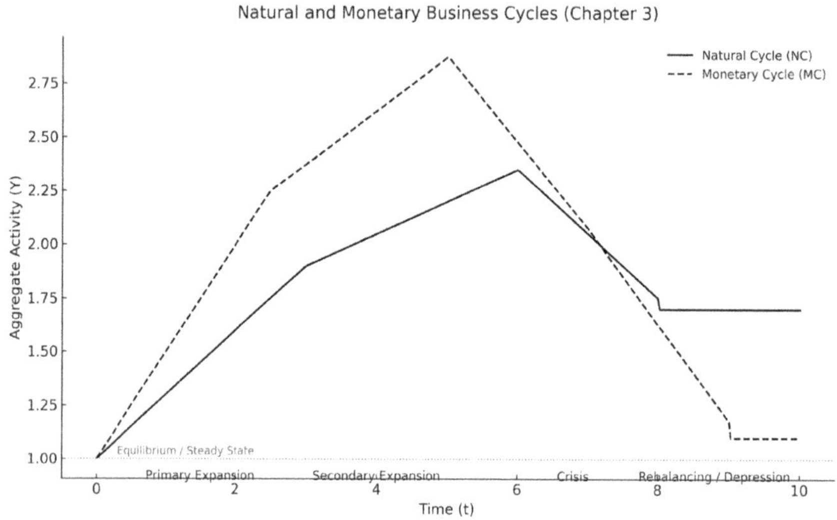

The natural cycle thus reflects the dual nature of capitalist evolution: expansion through entrepreneurial innovation and subsequent correction through the reabsorption of excessive optimism. It captures the dialectical rhythm of development, where every stage of progress generates its own internal limits and, through crisis, prepares the ground for renewal.

The analysis further highlights the sequential logic of primary and secondary waves of investment. The first wave is driven by genuine innovators who extend the production structure in response to altered expectations; the second, by imitators and speculators who amplify the expansion but, by their very excess, make correction inevitable. The crisis that follows—shorter and milder in scope than in the artificial, credit-driven case—is not the failure of the market process but its essential mechanism of learning and re-coordination.

5. The *Natural Cycle* and Hyman Minsky's *Financial Instability Hypothesis*

Although this framework arises from Austrian and Schumpeterian roots, it bears a striking structural resemblance to Hyman Minsky's *Financial Instability Hypothesis (FIH)* (Minsky, 1982 and 2008). Both perspectives, in different languages, portray capitalism as an inherently cyclical and self-transforming system in which stability breeds instability and periods of prosperity generate the very conditions for their own reversal.

Minsky's model describes how financial systems evolve through stages of *hedge, speculative,* and *Ponzi* finance. During the hedge phase, investment is financed on the basis of expected cash flows that are sufficient to meet both interest and principal obligations. As optimism rises and economic agents revise their expectations upward, financial positions become more fragile: speculative finance emerges, where cash flows cover only interest payments, and eventually Ponzi finance, where agents depend on rising asset prices or continual refinancing to sustain their obligations. The process culminates in crisis once expectations are disappointed, liquidity evaporates, and debt structures collapse.

This sequence parallels the transition from the primary to the secondary phase in the natural cycle. In both theories, the system's own success generates behavioural shifts—rising optimism, imitation, and risk-taking—that gradually undermine the foundations of stability. The Austrian–Schumpeterian *secondary wave* of imitative investment corresponds closely to Minsky's *speculative* and *Ponzi* stages: in each, expansion continues beyond the bounds of real resources or fundamental profitability, sustained by financial innovation and optimism rather than by genuine saving or productivity.

Furthermore, both frameworks emphasise the role of expectations, leverage, and feedback mechanisms. For Minsky, the transformation of financial practices under prolonged stability is endogenous: agents reinterpret risk and adapt their balance sheets accordingly. Similarly, in the natural cycle, changing expectations and imitative behaviour generate an endogenous tendency toward overextension, even without monetary manipulation. The difference lies primarily in the analytical focus—*finance* in Minsky's case and *capital and time preferences* in the Austrian–Schumpeterian tradition—but the underlying logic is analogous.

Another point of convergence lies in the *endogeneity of instability*. Minsky rejects the notion of exogenous shocks, arguing that instability is inherent in capitalist dynamics. The present theory of the natural cycle reaches the same conclusion from a different ontological route: even when monetary authorities abstain from interference, endogenous forces—expectations, innovation, imitation—drive the system through alternating phases of expansion and liquidation. The market, far from being a static equilibrium mechanism, is a living process of experimentation, correction, and renewal.

Yet the two perspectives diverge in their normative implications. Minsky's analysis often leads to policy recommendations aimed at stabilising finance through regulation and counter-cyclical intervention. The natural cycle, by contrast, interprets crises as functional episodes of re-coordination—painful but necessary corrections that preserve the vitality of the capitalist process. Rather than suppressing instability, it suggests that policy should avoid amplifying it through artificial credit expansion or excessive fiscal manipulation.

In short, the *Natural Cycle* framework complements Minsky's *Financial Instability Hypothesis* by offering a deeper micro-foundational and entrepreneurial interpretation of the same systemic rhythm. Where Minsky sees financial fragility as the outcome of cumulative leverage, the natural cycle interprets it as the manifestation of intertemporal discoordination between plans, expectations, and real resources. Both agree, however, that capitalism's strength—its capacity for innovation and growth—is inseparable from its vulnerability to cycles of euphoria and correction. Stability, in this sense, is not the absence of fluctuation but the ability of the system to renew itself through them.

6. Measuring business cycles: From quantification to understanding

6.1. The historical evolution of measurement

Since the emergence of modern macroeconomics, the business cycle has been primarily measured through variations in aggregate output—initially through industrial indices and later through the concept of Gross Domestic Product (GDP). From Kuznets's early national income estimates to Burns and Mitchell's (1946) *Measuring Business Cycles*, the analytical focus was on quantifying expansions and contractions in "economic activity". This legacy shaped the practice of cycle dating by institutions such as the National Bureau of Economic Research (NBER), which still defines cycles as fluctuations in real GDP and related indicators.

While this tradition brought statistical discipline to empirical analysis, it also redefined the phenomenon itself. The business cycle became a numerical pattern rather than a complex process of human interpretation. The richness of the cyclical experience—the changing expectations, learning processes, and capital reconfigurations that occur through time—was reduced to the oscillation of a single aggregate variable.

6.2. The limits of GDP as a measure of cyclical reality

From the perspective developed throughout this book, GDP is an inadequate lens through which to observe cyclical dynamics. It embodies a conception of the economy as a machine producing measurable output, rather than as a kaleidic process of interpretation unfolding in historical time. Several problems arise from this reductionism.

First, GDP is an *ex-post* accounting construct, recording the value of final goods and services already exchanged. It captures results, not processes. Consequently, it is silent on the intertemporal structure of production—the changing combinations of capital goods, entrepreneurial expectations, and plans that define the true rhythm of the cycle.

Second, GDP conflates monetary and real phenomena. Because it is denominated in money terms and adjusted only imperfectly for price changes, its movements often reflect monetary disturbances rather than shifts in the real allocation of resources. In the Austrian sense, monetary expansions that distort the structure of production may increase GDP, even as they sow the seeds of future contraction.

Third, GDP assumes that economic value is additive and homogeneous. Yet as Lachmann emphasized, value arises from subjective interpretation, not objective aggregation. Each act of valuation is context-bound, historically situated, and hermeneutical. The attempt to compress such qualitative phenomena into a single quantitative index therefore leads to a loss of meaning.

Finally, the GDP-based measurement of cycles reinforces the illusion of control. If fluctuations can be described as deviations from a stable growth trend, policymakers can imagine that stability can be restored by adjusting fiscal or monetary levers. This belief underpins the very "counter-cyclical" policies that, as shown later in this book, often become the source of new monetary and financial cycles.

6.3. Toward a hermeneutical measure of cyclical dynamics

A hermeneutical approach calls for rethinking what it means to *measure* a cycle. To measure hermeneutically is not to assign a single numerical value, but to interpret the evolving meanings that actors attach to their circumstances—meanings that manifest in expectations, investment plans, and intertemporal coordination.

From this standpoint, a cycle can be understood as a sequence of interpretative phases rather than mechanical stages of output variation. These phases correspond to the changing *meanings* that economic agents attribute to their environment: optimism and discovery in the boom; imitation and overextension in the secondary expansion; recognition, adjustment, and learning in the downturn. The rhythm of the cycle thus reflects a rhythm of understanding.

An interpretative indicator of cyclical activity would not seek to compress these processes into a single aggregate. Instead, it would observe qualitative and structural dimensions of change—for example:

- *Patterns of capital reconfiguration*, capturing shifts in the composition and roundaboutness of production.
- *Expectational divergence and convergence*, traced through surveys, market signals and entrepreneurial narratives.
- *The alignment between monetary signals and real time preferences*, reflected in the relation between market and natural rates of interest.
- *Hermeneutical coherence*, or the degree to which individual plans remain mutually compatible within a changing environment.

Such a framework would not replace quantitative data but reinterpret it within a context of meaning. Prices, profits, and investment flows become *signals* to be read hermeneutically, not mechanical indicators to be aggregated. The economist's task, therefore, is to reconstruct the evolving logic of coordination and miscoordination—the living process by which expectations are formed, tested, and revised.

6.4. From measurement to interpretation

In this sense, the measurement of business cycles should be understood as a form of *verstehen*: a disciplined interpretation of how societies experience change through time. The cycle is not a pathology to be suppressed but an expression of human creativity and fallibility within real time. It reflects the interplay between vision and revision, between entrepreneurial imagination and the learning imposed by market feedback.

A hermeneutical measurement of cycles would thus abandon the pursuit of mechanical precision in favour of interpretative adequacy. It would accept, with Hayek, that «true but imperfect knowledge» is preferable to «a pretense of exact knowledge». Its ultimate goal would not be to predict turning points, but to understand the meanings, expectations, and structural transformations that constitute the cyclical process itself.

6.5. Measuring without losing meaning: A Hermeneutical Cycle Index (HCI)

First principles and differences with GDP

- Cycles are processes of interpretation-expectations, plans, imitations, and liquidations – not mere oscillations in a single output aggregate.
- Two engines coexist: a *Natural Cycle* (NC)-innovation, imitation, liquidation-and a *Monetary Cycle* (MC) driven by misalignment between the market/credit rate and the natural rate (policy or credit pushing the market rate below the natural rate).
- Financial booms can diverge from "real" activity; stability in prices can still fuel financial upswings and later Minsky moments.
- Therefore, GDP may move "up" while coordination worsens-we need indicators that read meaning, not just volume.

The HCI architecture

We build a composite, comparable index with two layers:

Layer A — Five Pillars (standardized, 0–100)

Each pillar is a *readable sign* of expectations, plans, and coordination—not a mechanical "output" count.

1. Capital Reconfiguration & Roundaboutness (CRI)
    - Share of long-gestation investment (structures, machinery, R&D) in total GFCF; average asset life; WIP/inventories days; capex/opex mix.

- Reads the lengthening of the production period typical of the boom's first wave.

2. Expectation Dispersion & Narrative Pulse (EDI)
   - Dispersion (cross-sectional variance) in business/consumer expectations (PMIs, surveys); analyst forecast dispersion; IPO and earnings-call text metrics (uncertainty/opportunity lexicons).
   - Captures the kaleidic, interpretive swing of optimism, imitation, and reassessment.
3. Monetary–Real Alignment Gap (AG)
   - Proxy the natural rate (NR) from slow-moving preference signals (household saving, demographic age structure, consumption growth trend) and compare with observed market/credit rate (MR).
   - AG = MR – NR (z-scored); persistent negative AG flags MC-type booms (policy/credit below NR).
4. Financial Imbalance Index (FII)
   - Credit-to-income gap, leverage of non-financials, duration mismatch (short-term funding of long assets), asset price-to-income ratios; share of credit to non-tradables.
   - Detects the fuel of financial booms even under price stability.
5. Coordination Stress & Plan Coherence (CSI)
   - Inventory-to-sales deviations, order-backlog vs capacity-utilization mismatch, cash conversion cycle stretch, ROIC spread (P75–P25) across firms/industries.
   - Tracks how well heterogeneous plans continue to fit together as novelty arrives.

Computation: For each country-month/quarter, standardize each input (z-score within country), aggregate to its pillar (equal weights or expert weights), then min-max to 0–100.

Layer B — Cycle Typology Signals

Rules interpret the five pillars to classify phase and type:

- NC signature: Rising CRI + EDI, modest FII, AG near zero, then rising CSI as imitation swells and liquidation follows.

- MC signature: Sustained negative AG (MR < NR) with rising FII; CRI may lengthen "for the wrong reasons", CSI eventually jumps when miscoordination is revealed.

The index

Here is how we can build our HCI (0–100), as an *interpretative* coincident index (Function 3.1):

$$\mathrm{HCI}_t = \sum_{k=1}^{5} w_k \cdot \mathrm{Pillar}_{k,t}, \quad \sum w_k = 1$$

It is possible to begin by assigning equal weights to all variables, while maintaining the flexibility to introduce scenario-specific adjustments. For instance, in credit-intensive economies, it may be appropriate to give greater importance to Alignment Gap (AG) and Financial Imbalance Index (FII), reflecting their more dominant role in driving cyclical dynamics.

Next, we can decompose the overall Hermeneutical Cycle Index (HCI) into the portions attributable to Natural Cycle (NC) drivers—such as the Capital Reallocation Index (CRI), Expectation Dispersion Index (EDI), and Coordination Stress Index (CSI)—and those linked to Monetary Cycle (MC) drivers—namely Alignment Gap (AG) and Financial Imbalance Index (FII). Both contributions should be reported distinctly, to capture the interaction and relative strength of real versus monetary impulses.

Finally, we can assign each observation to a specific phase of the cycle—Primary Expansion, Imitative Expansion, or Liquidation/Adjustment—using rule-based thresholds and turning-point indicators. For example, simultaneous increases in CRI and EDI signal a primary expansion; a rise in both EDI and CSI indicates an imitative expansion; and the combination of a CSI peak with a CRI decline identifies a liquidation or adjustment phase.

To ensure cross-country comparability while remaining faithful to local contexts, each raw series should first be standardized within its own country using z-scores. This approach respects domestic institutions, data practices, and measurement conventions while allowing meaningful international comparisons.

When structural differences are substantial—such as economies with a heavier concentration in construction or manufacturing—sectoral adjustments are required. The Capital Reallocation Index (CRI), for example, should be corrected using fixed industry weights based on an international classification, thereby preventing a bias in favour of construction-heavy countries.

Further, temporal alignment is crucial. Data series must be synchronized according to common calendars and vintages: release lags should be harmonized, and each dataset should carry an "as-of" vintage label to allow for full real-time replicability.

Lastly, transparency is a central principle. For every country, the complete list of series must be publicly disclosed. Whenever proxies are used in place of preferred indicators, the semantic meaning of each pillar should be preserved. For instance, if the Purchasing Managers' Index (PMI) is unavailable, a comparable domestic business-survey dispersion measure should be substituted while maintaining the same interpretative role within the framework.

Reading the index and how it preserves meaning

The Hermeneutical Cycle Index (HCI) is not intended to replace understanding with a mere number. Rather, it serves as a structured summary of interpretative signals that, as argued in the book, underlie real economic processes—changes in entrepreneurial plans, patterns of imitation, and emerging coordination tensions observable in real time.

Narratives remain central. The Expectation Dispersion Index (EDI), in particular, explicitly captures expectations and language, while the other pillars act as signs to be interpreted—inputs for understanding, not statistical endpoints.

The distinction between Natural Cycle (NC) and Monetary Cycle (MC) remains explicit throughout. The pair AG (Alignment Gap) and FII (Financial Imbalance Index) continues to represent the monetary transmission channel, conceptually distinct from the structural and Schumpeterian dynamics embodied in CRI, EDI, and CSI.

Minimal data kit

To maintain replicability, the framework relies on data series that are commonly accessible across economies:

- CRI (Capital Reallocation Index): derived from national accounts on gross fixed capital formation by asset type; manufacturing work-in-progress and inventories; listed-firm capex/opex data; or, alternatively, customs records on machinery imports.

- EDI (Expectation Dispersion Index): based on PMIs or national business and consumer surveys; forecast dispersion among analysts; and, where possible, basic natural-language processing on earnings calls or press releases.
- AG (Alignment Gap): captures policy and lending rates, term-structure spreads, saving rates, and consumption trends—serving also as a proxy for the natural rate, with transparent documentation of any applied filters.
- FII (Financial Imbalance Index): includes credit to households and firms, leverage ratios, price-to-income indicators for housing, equity valuation metrics, and average funding tenor.
- CSI (Coordination Stress Index): reflects inventory-to-sales ratios, capacity utilization, order backlogs, dispersion in firm-level return on invested capital (ROIC), and cash-conversion cycles.

Table 3.2: The Hermeneutical Cycle Index (HCI).

Purpose	To operationalize the hermeneutical understanding of business cycles by creating an interpretative yet comparable measure of cyclical dynamics across countries.
Core Principle	The HCI measures *processes of interpretation*—changes in expectations, coordination, and capital structures—rather than mere variations in output.
Structure	Five standardized pillars, each 0–100, combined into a composite index:
	1. Capital Reconfiguration Index (CRI): share of long-gestation investment, asset life, inventories, capex/opex mix.
	2. Expectation Dispersion Index (EDI): variance in business/consumer expectations, forecast dispersion, text-based optimism/pessimism measures.

	3. Alignment Gap (AG): gap between market rate (mr) and estimated natural rate (nr). AG < 0 signals monetary expansion below real-time preference.
	4. Financial Imbalance Index (FII): credit-to-income gap, leverage, duration mismatch, asset-price indicators.
	5. Coordination Stress Index (CSI): inventory-to-sales deviation, capacity-utilization mismatch, ROIC dispersion, cash-conversion stretch.
Formula (3.2)	$HCI_t = \sum_{k=1}^{5} w_k \, Pillar_{k,t}$ with $\sum w_k = 1$. Default $w_k = 0.2$.
Cycle Typology Rules	NC (Natural Cycle): CRI↑ + EDI↑ + moderate FII + AG≈0 → healthy innovation/adjustment. MC (Monetary Cycle): sustained AG < 0 + rising FII → credit-driven boom; liquidation when CSI spikes.
Phase Classification	• Primary Expansion → CRI↑ & EDI↑ • Imitative Expansion → EDI↑ & CSI↑ • Liquidation → CSI peaks & CRI declines
Output	• Headline HCI (0–100) • NC/MC driver shares • Phase flag • Commentary on interpretative context
Computation Frequency	Quarterly (preferred) or monthly if high-frequency data exist.
Cross-Country Standardization	z-score each raw series by country; align sectoral weights; maintain transparent metadata for local proxies.
Interpretation	Higher HCI → increased interpretative dynamism (creative re-coordination or overextension). Falling HCI → consolidation or adjustment. Use qualitatively, not mechanistically.

Table 3.3: Sources for HCI.

Pillar	Typical global sources
CRI	National Accounts (GFCF by asset type); World Bank WDI; OECD Investment by Assets; UNIDO INDSTAT for manufacturing WIP.
EDI	S&P Global PMI; Conference Board Confidence Indices; Consensus Forecasts dispersion; text metrics from earnings calls or press (using lexicon-based sentiment).
AG	Central-bank policy rate; market yield curve; saving rate and consumption trend for nr proxy. Filter nr with five-year Hodrick–Prescott or Kalman trend.
FII	BIS credit gaps; IMF FSI; national balance-sheet data; real estate and equity price indices.
CSI	OECD inventory/sales ratios; capacity utilization; firm-level financial reports (ROIC, CCC); national survey of order backlogs.

Table 3.4: Interpretation dashboard.

Metric	Meaning
HCI	Overall cyclical intensity—aggregate interpretative activity.
ΔHCI	Change → acceleration/deceleration in cycle.
NC Share	Portion of HCI explained by CRI, EDI, CSI. High → structural/innovative cycle.
MC Share	Portion of HCI explained by AG, FII. High → monetary/credit cycle.
Phase	Qualitative stage: primary / imitative / liquidation.
Commentary	Hermeneutical reading: alignment of expectations and reality, coordination stress, policy signals.

Conclusion

The analysis presented in this chapter has redefined the business cycle as a process of interpretation rather than a mechanical oscillation of measurable aggregates. Drawing on the combined insights of Mises, Hayek, Lachmann, and Schumpeter, we have argued that cycles embody the temporal rhythm of capitalism itself—a rhythm made of expectations, discoveries, imitations, and revisions. The economy does not move along a predetermined trajectory of equilibrium; it learns, experiments, and adjusts through the continuous dialogue between the future imagined and the future realized.

Two interwoven dimensions shape this rhythm. The *Natural Cycle* originates in authentic shifts in time preferences and entrepreneurial expectations, where innovation and imitation drive real capital reconfiguration. The *Monetary Cycle*, by contrast, arises when artificial signals—monetary or financial distortions—amplify and misdirect these processes. Yet both forms reveal the same underlying logic: market economies evolve through alternating phases of coherence and discoordination, of overextension and correction. The crisis is not an anomaly but a phase of re-interpretation—an indispensable moment in the learning process through which the economy renews itself.

The chapter has also challenged the empirical foundations on which most modern macroeconomic analyses rest. GDP, though indispensable for national accounting, fails to capture the hermeneutical dimension of economic life. It measures the result, not the process; it quantifies output, not understanding. The pursuit of policy control through such aggregates has too often produced the very instabilities it sought to suppress. A meaningful science of cycles must therefore move beyond quantification toward interpretation.

The proposed *Hermeneutical Cycle Index (HCI)* represents a first attempt to reconcile measurement with meaning. By combining indicators of capital structure, expectations, monetary alignment, financial imbalances, and coordination stress, the HCI provides a framework for observing cyclical dynamics without reducing them to a single aggregate magnitude. It enables cross-country comparison while remaining faithful to the subjectivist foundation of the Austrian–Schumpeterian tradition: that economic activity is an interpretative process unfolding in real historical time.

In this perspective, the role of the economist changes profoundly. The task is no longer to predict or to smooth fluctuations, but to *understand* how economic actors interpret signals, form expectations, and realign their plans. Policy, too, must abandon the illusion of engineering stability and instead aim at preserving the institutional conditions for entrepreneurial discovery, flexibility, and adaptation.

Ultimately, the business cycle is not the failure of capitalism—it is its language. Through expansions and contractions, optimism and correction, the market communicates, learns, and re-creates itself. To interpret those rhythms is to rediscover economics as a human science: a science not of objects, but of meanings in motion.

References

Burns, A.F. and Mitchell, W.C. (1946), *Measuring Business Cycles*, Cambridge, National Bureau of Economic Research.

Fanno, M. (1931), *Production Cycles, Credit Cycles and Industrial Fluctuations*, in H. Hagemann (Ed.), *Business Cycle Theory. Selected Texts 1860-1939*, Volume II: *Structural Theories of the Business Cycle*, London: Pickering and Chatto, 2002, pp. 225-261.

Ferlito, C. (2011), *Sylos Labini's Unpublished Notes on Schumpeter's Business Cycles*, «The Quarterly Journal of Austrian Economics», 14, 1, pp. 88-129.

Ferlito, C. (2013), *Phoenix Economics. From Crisis to Renascence*, New York, Nova Publishers.

Ferlito, C. (2014), *The Natural Cycle: Why Economic Fluctuations are Inevitable. A Schumpeterian Extension of the Austrian Business Cycle Theory*, «Journal of Reviews on Global Economics», 3, pp. 200-219. DOI: http://dx.doi.org/10.6000/1929-7092.2014.03.16.

Garrison, R.W. (2006), *The Natural Rate of Interest in Theory and Policy Formulation*, «The Quarterly Journal of Austrian Economics», 9, 4, pp. 57-68.

Hayek, F.A. von (1929), *Monetary Theory and the Trade Cycle*, New York, Kelley, 1966.

Hayek, F.A. von (1931), *Prices and Production*, New York, Kelley, 1967.

Hayek, F.A. von (1932), *A Note on the Development of the Doctrine of "Forced Saving"*, «Quarterly Journal of Economics», XLVII, pp. 123-133.

Hayek, F.A. von (1933), *Price Expectations, Monetary Disturbances and Malinvestments*, in F.A. von Hayek, *Profits, Interest and Investment and Other Essays on the Theory of Industrial Fluctuations*, Clifton, Augustus M. Kelley, 1975, pp. 135-156.

Hayek, F.A. von (1939), *Profits, interest and Investment*, in F.A. von Hayek, *Profits, Interest and Investment and Other Essays on the Theory of Industrial Fluctuations*, Clifton, Augustus M. Kelley, 1975, pp. 3-71.

Huerta de Soto, J. (1998), *Money, Bank Credit, and Economic Cycles*, Auburn, Ludwig von Mises Institute, 2006.

Hülsmann, J.G. (2013), *Krise der Inflationskultur. Geld, Finanzen und Staat in Zeiten der Kollektiven Korruption*, Munich, Finanzbuch Verlag.

Koppl, R. (2014), *From Crisis to Confidence. Macroeconomics after the Crash*, London. The Institute of Economic Affairs.

Kurz, H.D. (2003), *Friedrich August Hayek: la teoria monetaria del sovrainvestimento*, in J. Ternowetz (Ed.), *Friedrich A. von Hayek e la Scuola Austriaca di Economia*, Rubbettino, Soveria Mannelli, pp. 175-207.

Lachmann, L.M. (1940), *A Reconsideration of the Austrian Theory of Industrial Fluctuations*, in W.E. Grinder (Ed.), *Capital, Expectations, and the Market Process*, Kansas City, Sheed Andrews and McMeel Inc., 1977, pp. 267-286.

Lachmann, L.M. (1956), *Capital and Its Structure*, Kansas City, Sheed Andrews and McMeel, 1978.

Lachmann, L.M. (1986), *The Market as Economic Process*, Oxford, Basil Blackwell.

Minsky, H.P. (1982), *Can "It" Happen Again? Essays on Instability and Finance*, London and New York, Routledge, 2016.

Minsky, H.P. (2008), *Stabilizing an Unstable Economy*, New York, McGraw-Hill.

Mises, L. von (1912), *The Theory of Money and Credit*, Indianapolis, Liberty Fund, 1980.

Mises, L. von (1936), *The "Austrian" Theory of the Trade Cycle*, in R.M. Ebeling (Ed.), *The Austrian Theory of the Trade Cycle and Other Essays*, Auburn, Ludwig von Mises Institute, 1980, pp. 25-35.

Mises, L. von (1949), *Human Action. A Treatise on Economics*, Auburn, Ludwig von Mises Institute, 1998.

Moss, L.S. (2005), *The applied economics of the modern Austrian School*, in J.G. Bakhaus (Ed.), *Modern Applications of Austrian Thought*, London and New York, Routledge, pp. 3-19.

Prychitko, D.L. (2010), *Competing Explanations of the Minsky Moment: The Financial Instability Hypothesis in the light of Austrian Theory*,« The Review of Austrian Economics», 23, pp. 199-221.

Rothbard, M.N. (1969), *Economic Depressions: Their Cause and Cure*, Auburn, Ludwig von Mises Institute, 2009.

Salerno, J.T. (2012), *A Reformulation of Austrian Business Cycle Theory in Light of the Financial Crisis*, «The Quarterly Journal of Austrian Economics», 15, 1, pp. 3-44.

Schumpeter, J.A. (1911). *The Theory of Economic Development. An Inquiry into Profits, Capital, Credit, Interest and Business Cycle*, New Brunswick and London, Transaction Publishers, 1983.

Schumpeter, J.A. (1939), *Business Cycles. A Theoretical, Historical, and Statistical Analysis of the Capitalist Process*, Chevy Chase and Mansfield Centre, Bartleby's Books and Martino Publishing, 2005. Abridged version used here: 2008 edition digitalized by Didier Lagrange.

Spiethoff, A. (1925), *Business Cycles*, in H. Hagemann (Ed.), *Business Cycle Theory. Selected Texts 1860-1939*, Volume II: *Structural Theories of the Business Cycle*, London, Pickering and Chatto, 2002, pp. 109-205.

Steele, G.R. (2001), *Keynes and Hayek. The money economy*, London and New York, Routledge.

Sylos Labini, P. (1954), *Il problema dello sviluppo economico in Marx e Schumpeter*, in P. Sylos Labini, *Problemi dello sviluppo economico*, Bari, Laterza, 1977, pp. 19-73.

Sylos Labini, P. (1984), *The Forces of Economic Growth and Decline*, Cambridge and London, MIT Press.

PART III

INFLATION AND MONETARY POLICY

CHAPTER 4:
Inflation and Its Link to Unemployment[32]

Co-author: John Hearn

1. Defining inflation

When we hear the word *inflation*, we instinctively think of rising prices—and soon after, we realize that our purchasing power is deteriorating, that we are, in effect, becoming poorer. A quick look at popular definitions of inflation, such as those found on Wikipedia and Investopedia, reveals how this common understanding has shaped even formal economic definitions.

According to Wikipedia, in economics, «inflation refers to a general progressive increase in prices of goods and services in an economy. When the general price level rises, each unit of currency buys fewer goods and services; consequently, inflation corresponds to a reduction in the purchasing power of money»[33]. Similarly, Investopedia defines inflation as «the decline of purchasing power of a given currency over time. A quantitative estimate of the rate at which the decline in purchasing power occurs can be reflected in the increase of an average price level of a basket of selected goods and services in an economy over some period of time. The rise in the general level of prices, often expressed as a percentage, means that a unit of currency effectively buys less than it did in prior periods»[34].

Delving deeper, traditional economics textbooks distinguish between *demand-pull inflation* and *cost-push inflation*.

The first refers to a situation in which aggregate demand exceeds the economy's productive capacity. In other words, total demand for goods and services rises beyond what can be produced, leading to upward pressure on prices. According to standard explanations, such a scenario may result from increased consumption, credit expansion, or deficit spending (Baranzini and Marangoni, 1995, pp. 272–273).

32 This is a slightly revised version of J. Hearn and C. Ferlito (2021), *The cause of inflation, its link to unemployment and the need for sound monetary control*, «CME Edupaper», 8, Subang Jaya, Center for Market Education. The section on Malaysia is new.

33 https://en.wikipedia.org/wiki/Inflation.

34 https://www.investopedia.com/terms/i/inflation.asp.

Cost-push inflation, on the other hand, occurs when prices rise because production costs increase faster than productivity. This may stem from higher costs of production factors (Baranzini and Marangoni, p. 274), as well as from increases in the prices of raw materials, energy, or transportation.

However, such definitions represent a misuse of the term *inflation*. While it may be politically convenient for policymakers to blame businesspeople, trade unions, or even consumers for causing inflation, this attribution is misleading. As Friedman and Friedman (1980, pp. 253–254) explain,

> these can produce high prices for individual items; they cannot produce rising prices for goods in general. They can cause temporary ups or downs in the rate of inflation. But they cannot produce continuing inflation for one very simple reason: none of the alleged culprits possesses a printing press on which it can turn out those pieces of paper we carry in our pockets; none can legally authorize a bookkeeper to make entries on ledgers that are the equivalent of those pieces of paper.

In other words, while specific actors or market conditions can influence particular prices or temporarily affect the inflation rate, sustained inflation can only arise from an expansion in the money supply.

Instead, inflation's «original and proper meaning is an excessive increase in the quantity of money, leading in turn to an increase in prices» (Hayek, 1979, p. 44). This clarification was particularly important to stress during the COVID-19 pandemic, as monetary and political authorities continued to attribute rising prices primarily to supply-side shocks—many of which were themselves triggered by policy responses to COVID-19, such as stay-at-home orders—while neglecting the role of monetary expansion beyond the rate of output growth. Little attention was given to how such monetary growth stemmed from fiscal and monetary measures introduced to counter the very disruptions those restrictions caused. Government deficit spending and expansionary monetary policies were largely omitted from the discussion.

We can therefore conclude that inflation arises from «a more rapid increase in the quantity of money than in the quantity of goods and services available for purchase, and such an increase raises prices in terms of that money» (Friedman and Friedman, 1980, p. 252).

Milton Friedman explained this most clearly in his *First Wincott Memorial Lecture*, titled *The Counter-Revolution in Monetary Theory* (Friedman, 1970):

> Briefly stated, there is a consistent, though not precise, relationship between the rate of growth of money and the rate of growth of nominal national income. Today's income growth depends on what has been happening to money in the past.

This lagged relationship between changes in monetary demand and changes in nominal national income typically spans about 6 to 9 months, though it may take up to 18 months before it manifests as inflation. In Friedman's own words,

> Inflation is always and everywhere a monetary phenomenon in the sense that it is, and can be, produced only by a more rapid increase in the quantity of money than in output.

We will return to this point in Section 3.

2. Is there a cost-push inflation?

What we have seen in the first section appears to contradict the dominant narrative, which tends to attribute inflation to rising costs. How, then, did the "myth" of cost-push inflation emerge? The story that follows applies to virtually every country with a government and a central bank and is well illustrated by the experience of the UK economy. To the best of our knowledge—though this can certainly be verified—no economics textbook published before Keynes's death in 1946, or even before the 1960s, contained any reference to cost-push inflation as a cause of rising prices.

During the 1960s, Keynesians were eager to test their theories of countercyclical policy. However, every time the government attempted fiscal stimulus, it was constrained by the fixed exchange rate. An expansion of domestic aggregate demand increased imports, pushing the current account into deficit and placing downward pressure on the exchange rate, as the currency became overvalued. When this happened, fiscal stimulus was halted—only to be restarted once economic conditions improved, or more often, just before the next election.

Thus, what the 1960s truly witnessed was a *Stop–Go Cycle*—or, more accurately, a *Go–Stop Cycle*—driven by alternating phases of expansion and restraint dictated by political and external pressures rather than sound economic reasoning.

In 1971, the Gold Exchange Standard—which had underpinned the fixed exchange rate system—was permanently suspended, and major currencies began to float freely on foreign exchange markets. This development gave Keynesians the opportunity they had long awaited: freed from the constraints of a fixed exchange rate, they could now pursue expansionary fiscal policies without fear of external imbalances. A plan was soon introduced to stimulate the economy, not only to achieve full employment but also to target a 5% annual growth rate.

After an initial boom in 1971–72, however, the Keynesian framework began to unravel. Successive budget deficits led to a sharp rise in inflation. To understand this outcome, a brief clarification is necessary. There are two primary ways to finance a budget deficit. The first—non-inflationary—occurs when the government sells its debt to private investors on financial markets. The second—potentially inflationary—arises when unsold debt is held by the central bank and new money is created to match its value. By 1977, inflation in the United Kingdom had soared to 26% per year, unemployment was high, and economic growth had nearly stalled. The government's 5% annual growth target had instead turned into a meagre 0.6%. These conditions marked the onset of *stagflation*—a phenomenon that Keynesian theory had failed to predict or explain.

According to Keynesian theory, fiscal stimulus should create jobs and stimulate growth with little risk of inflation, so long as there remains an *output gap* between actual output and potential full-employment output. When confronted with accelerating inflation and a persistently wide output gap, Keynesian economists argued that inflation could not be demand-pull in nature—since output was below potential and unemployment remained high. Instead, they claimed that the economy was experiencing *cost-push inflation*, driven by sharp increases in crude oil prices, wage growth, and a depreciating exchange rate that raised import costs.

In 1975, the UK government even distributed a public pamphlet titled *Attack on Inflation: A Policy for Survival* (Government of the United Kingdom, 1975). The leaflet stated:

> No reasonable person can put all the blame for runaway inflation on wage rises or the Trade Unions. There are many other causes. There was a steep increase in 1972/3 in world costs of food and raw materials and the colossal rise in oil prices in 1973/4.

Notably, the pamphlet referred exclusively to cost-push factors. Nowhere did it acknowledge the true cause of inflation as understood in monetary terms. Throughout the 1970s, Keynesians continued to assert that the economy suffered from deficient aggregate demand, high cost-push inflation, and damaging supply-side shocks. In retrospect, this interpretation was deeply flawed—and it brings us to the conclusion that *cost-push inflation* is largely a myth.

By definition, inflation reflects an increase in the amount of money used to conduct the same number of transactions. Inflation would be impossible in a barter economy, where any price increase would be offset by an equivalent decrease elsewhere. Oil companies, farmers, miners, and importers cannot expand the supply of money in an economy—only the central bank in a fiat money system can do so. Central banks exercise full control over the issuance of currency (counterfeiting aside) and over the extent of money creation permitted through the banking system. Consequently, *central banks are the sole and ultimate cause of inflation*. It simply cannot be otherwise.

3. The monetary nature of inflation

The relationship between an increase in the quantity of money—exceeding the growth of output—and the consequent rise in prices is therefore central to a proper understanding of inflation. As Hayek (1979, pp. 44–45) explained:

> A general rise in prices, for instance one brought about by a shortage of food caused by bad harvests, is not inflation. Nor could we properly call 'inflation' a general rise in prices caused by a shortage of oil and other sources of energy that led to an absolute reduction of consumption, unless this shortage had been the pretext for a further increase in the quantity of money. There may also be inflation that considerably harms the working of the market without any rise in prices – if the rise is prevented by controls. Indeed, such a 'repressed' inflation tends to disorganize economic activity even more than open inflation.

It is thus unsurprising that, following the Russian Revolution of 1917, no inflation was recorded—since all prices were fixed and the allocative mechanism shifted instead to shortages and queues.

Inflation, in essence, «occurs when the quantity of money rises appreciably more rapidly than output, and the more rapid the rise in the quantity of money per unit of output, the greater the rate of inflation» (Friedman and Friedman, 1980, p. 254). The same line of reasoning can be found not only among Monetarists such as Friedman and Austrians like Hayek, but also in a prominent figure of the New Institutional Economics, Armen A. Alchian. As Alchian (1979, p. 249) observes:

> Inflation usually means a continuing general rise in most prices, not a one-time jump in most prices without a continuing rise. The difference is important; they are caused by different events.
>
> The second can be caused by any disaster which reduces production, such as a crop failure, a drought, invasion, war, plague of insects, or earthquake. In these cases, with a smaller stock of goods and the same amount of money in the society, prices will rise. [...] These events usually are transient [...].
>
> The necessary and sufficient condition for a persisting, increasing price level is that the quantity of money be increasing relative to the stock of real goods and services. That and only that is the source of a persisting inflation.
>
> History records no instances of a persisting (several years) inflation without the amount of money increasing relative to real goods [...].
>
> In every case, the increase in money relative to goods occurred because the supply of money persistently increased [...].

Even Keynes (1936, chapter 21) acknowledged that «prices are governed by the quantity of money, by its income-velocity, [and] by the velocity of circulation relative to the volume of transactions». Yet, ironically, it was from *The General Theory* that later Keynesians began to advance another supposed cause of inflation—*cost-push inflation*—which Keynes himself never identified (Hearn, 1979).

In summary, according to the view shared by Monetarists and, to a considerable extent, by the Austrian School of Economics, the single cause of inflation is *too much money chasing too few goods*. In contrast, Keynesians—and, incidentally, most modern textbooks—point to two causes: *demand-pull* and *cost-push* inflation.

It is also essential to recall that in today's world, «when the commonly accepted media of exchange have no relation to any commodity, the quantity of money is determined in every major country by government. Government, and government alone, is responsible for any rapid increase in the quantity of money»" (Friedman and Friedman, 1980, p. 253).

Failing to recognize this fact prevents a clear understanding of the true cause of inflation. Unsurprisingly, policymakers are often reluctant to accept responsibility for creating inflation and prefer instead to deflect blame. As mentioned earlier, today's politicians attribute rising inflation to supply-side disruptions; in other contexts, they have accused businesspeople, trade unions, or even consumers. Yet, as Friedman and Friedman (1980, pp. 253–254) emphasized:

> All these can produce high prices for individual items; they cannot produce rising prices for goods in general. They can cause temporary ups or downs in the rate of inflation. But they cannot produce continuing inflation for one very simple reason: none of the alleged culprits possesses a printing press on which it can turn out those pieces of paper we carry in our pockets; none can legally authorize a bookkeeper to make entries on ledgers that are the equivalent of those pieces of paper.

4. Inflation and unemployment

To emphasize the monetary nature of inflation and the government's central role in creating it, it is crucial to note that changes in the quantity of money do not merely affect the *general price level*—they also distort the *structure of relative prices*. As Hayek (1979, pp. 42–43) warned, this distortion is the source of «the most harmful effects of inflation: the misdirection of resources it causes and the unemployment that ultimately results from it».

Friedman (2007, p. 17) likewise observed that «a second related effect of increased volatility of inflation is to render market prices a less efficient system for coordinating economic activity». The reason lies in the price system itself. As Hayek (1945) explained, prices convey the information necessary for economic agents to decide what to produce and how to produce it. This coordination depends on *relative prices*. When inflation becomes volatile, however, «the more volatile the rate of general inflation, the harder it becomes to extract the signal about relative prices from the absolute prices: the information about relative prices is, as it were, being jammed by the noise coming from the inflation broadcast» (Friedman, 2007, p. 17). This "jam" in the information-transmission mechanism leads to resource misallocation, which in turn generates unemployment and stagnation.

The Phillips Curve and the myth of the inflation/unemployment trade-off

The relationship between money creation, inflation, and unemployment is fundamental. For many years, the so-called Phillips Curve dominated macroeconomic thinking, promoting the belief in «a stable negative relation between the level of unemployment and the rate of change of wages» (Friedman, 2007, p. 4). In short, the Phillips Curve suggested a trade-off: lower unemployment could be achieved at the cost of higher inflation. Yet the emergence of *stagflation* in the 1970s—a combination of inflation, unemployment, and stagnant growth—directly contradicted this assumption and challenged the theoretical foundations of post-war Keynesian full-employment policies.

How, then, did these policies gain such popularity? As Hutchison (1977) noted, there is no evidence of cost-push inflation in Keynes's own writings—only a faint suggestion that cost pressures might affect *relative* prices. It is therefore worth examining how the idea that cost-push factors could raise *average* prices and cause inflation became entrenched.

The logic and limits of countercyclical fiscal policy

Before World War II, economists widely believed that capitalist economies were inherently unstable, fluctuating between booms and depressions. Moreover, government budgets tended to reinforce these cycles: during booms, rising revenues encouraged higher spending, while in recessions, declining revenues forced spending cuts, deepening the downturn.

Keynes and his followers proposed reversing this pattern by using fiscal policy in a *countercyclical* manner to smooth fluctuations. When the economy contracted and revenues fell, government should increase spending and run a deficit; when the economy expanded rapidly and risked overheating, spending should be restrained, creating a surplus. Keynesians likened this to a thermostat: switching off fiscal stimulus when the economy overheated (surplus) and turning it on again when it cooled (deficit). In theory, this "fine-tuning" could stabilize aggregate demand around a high level of employment—the so-called full-employment equilibrium.

The inflationary consequences of fiscal stimuli

In practice, however, such policies proved harmful, generating a vicious cycle of inflation and unemployment. It is true, as Friedman and

Friedman (1980, p. 264) acknowledged, that higher government spending *need not* cause inflation if it is financed through taxation or borrowing from real investors. In that case, increased government spending merely substitutes for reduced private spending. Inflation arises only when government deficits are financed by *creating new money*.

Because taxation is politically unpopular and borrowing raises interest rates—making debt repayment harder for households and firms—governments often resort to the more expedient route of monetary financing. This allows them to pursue expansionary policies without immediately imposing new taxes, at the cost of future inflation.

When deficits are financed by selling bonds to private investors, the increased demand for funds pushes up interest rates. This crowds out private investment:

> While a subsequent rise in interest rates may elicit some increase in the amount of total saving in the economy, the residual amount of saving available to meet private-sector demands for loanable funds will fall. Utilization of savings by government to finance its deficit will crowd out utilization of savings for private investment. (Buchanan and Wagner, 1977, p. 69).

Higher interest rates make long-term projects less profitable, causing resources to shift from investment in capital goods toward the production of consumer goods. As Garrison (2001, p. 87) noted, this slows economic growth and shifts the debt burden onto future generations. Moreover, as White and Garrison (1999, p. 8) pointed out, governments find deficit spending politically attractive because it postpones the costs of current expenditure onto future taxpayers who are not represented in today's borrowing decisions.

The vicious circle of inflation and unemployment

This cycle can easily spiral when central banks begin monetizing government debt—creating new money to purchase bonds. Such monetization distorts the money supply, undermines confidence, and increases uncertainty about how and when the debt will be repaid. Governments thus become ever more tempted to expand the money supply further to sustain full-employment policies without raising taxes.

As Hayek (1950) and Friedman and Friedman (1980, p. 266) both observed, these policies not only produce inflation but also fail to sustain employment. Inflation distorts the structure of relative prices, misdirecting resources and ultimately leading to higher unemployment once the temporary stimulus fades.

While rising nominal incomes may temporarily boost employment, Hayek (1950, p. 176) warned that the fundamental error lies in believing that unemployment stems from insufficient aggregate demand. If spending is misallocated across sectors, increased demand cannot solve the problem. As he wrote (1950, p. 177):

> Unemployment can be the consequence of the fact that the distribution of labour is different from the distribution of demand... Where the cause of unemployment and of low aggregate incomes is such a discrepancy, only a reallocation of labour can lastingly solve the problem in a free economy.

Monetary expansion, by redirecting demand toward sectors that would not otherwise be favoured, creates artificial patterns of employment that collapse once inflationary growth stops. When this occurs, unemployment may rise above pre-stimulus levels, as previously induced investments and jobs become unsustainable.

<u>The inevitable outcome</u>

Inflation-induced unemployment can only be managed through growing government intervention—more control, more spending, and more money creation. This leads to diminishing economic freedom and an ever-tightening cycle of dependency on expansionary fiscal and monetary policy. Eventually, this dynamic risks two extreme outcomes: social upheaval (as living standards collapse) or authoritarian control (as governments attempt to stabilize discontent through intervention).

In conclusion, there is only one true cause of inflation: the expansion of monetary demand by the central bank at a pace faster than the growth of output. Keynesian attributions of inflation to cost-push factors are mistaken—an attempt to rationalize why unemployment remains high even as prices rise. All inflations, without exception, result from excessive monetary expansion, regardless of the prevailing level of employment or unemployment.

5. Addressing inflation

Once inflation has been fuelled by full-employment policies financed through money creation or the monetization of debt, only a few possible courses of action remain. As Hayek (1979, p. 4) summarized:

> 1. To allow a rapidly accelerating inflation to continue until it has brought about a complete disorganization of all economic activity.
>
> 2. To impose controls on wages and prices that would for a time conceal the effects of continued inflation but would inevitably lead to a centrally directed, totalitarian economic system.
>
> 3. To terminate resolutely the increase in the quantity of money—a step that would soon, through the appearance of substantial unemployment, make manifest all the misdirection of labour that the inflation of past years has caused and that the other two procedures would further increase.

Clearly, options (1) and (2) are undesirable—yet this does not make them unlikely. When inflation spirals out of control, «we will come to see our salvation as residing in the use of power. Power is always sought to promote the good, of course, never the bad. We are being bombarded with increasing intensity with calls for incomes policies, price and wage controls, national planning, and the like. Each of these aims to achieve its objectives by the imposition of new restrictions on the freedom of individuals»" (Buchanan and Wagner, 1977, p. 76).

The difficult path of stabilization

The third option—ending monetary expansion—cannot avoid triggering a "stabilization crisis" accompanied by significant unemployment. However, while halting monetary growth, policymakers should also prevent a deflationary spiral. To do so, they must clearly communicate this objective to avoid turning a recession into a depression. The priority must be the *stability of the value of money* (Hayek, 1979, pp. 16–17). Achieving this requires a steady reduction in the rate of monetary growth—a goal that ultimately depends on political will (Friedman and Friedman, 1980, p. 270).

A slower monetary expansion following an inflationary period will inevitably produce slower growth and rising unemployment. Friedman and Friedman (1980, pp. 270–271) compared this process to giving up alcohol: painful at first, but beneficial in the long run—the reverse of intoxication, which is pleasant initially but harmful later.

It is important to clarify, however, that slower growth and higher unemployment are not *remedies* for inflation; rather, they are *side effects* of the cure (Friedman and Friedman, 1980, p. 273). For this reason, inflation should be reduced gradually but persistently (Friedman and

Friedman, 1980, p. 277). Hayek, however, disagreed with Friedman's "gradualist" approach, arguing that a slow process would erode political resolve; in his view, a short, sharp shock would be more effective in restoring stability.

The limits of centralized monetary control

Scepticism about whether a centrally controlled currency can deliver lasting monetary stability is well justified. As Hayek (1976, p. 15) warned:

> Without the conviction of the public at large and the painful measures necessary to preserve reasonable stability, we cannot hope that any authority which has the power to determine the quantity of money will long resist the pressure for, or the seduction of, cheap money.

If government monopoly over money creation is a fundamental source of instability, Hayek proposed a radical solution: allow people to choose freely what money they wish to use. He suggested that the countries of the Atlantic Community should

> bind themselves mutually not to place any restrictions on the free use within their territories of one another's—or any other—currencies, including their purchase and sale at any price the parties decide upon, or on their use as accounting units in which to keep books. (Hayek, 1976, p. 17).

In a system of *currency competition*, people would abandon a depreciating national currency, and competition would drive the emergence of stable, value-preserving alternatives. As Hayek (1976, p. 20) predicted:

> The upshot would probably be that the currencies of those countries trusted to pursue a responsible monetary policy would tend to displace gradually those of a less reliable character. The reputation of financial righteousness would become a jealously guarded asset of all issuers of money, since they would know that even the slightest deviation from the path of honesty would reduce the demand for their product.

The need to limit government spending

The next step must be the control of government budgets. As Buchanan and Wagner (1977, p. 182) argued,

> Budgets cannot be left adrift in the sea of democratic politics. They must be constructed within constraints that impose external form and coherence on the particular decisions about size and distribution which an annual budget reflects.

Elected politicians, accountable to their constituents, and bureaucracies responsive to political pressure require an external rule—a "superior" constraint—to resist continuous demands for more public spending and lower taxation. Such a rule should be simple, transparent, and consistent with widely shared civic values (Buchanan and Wagner, 1977, p. 183).

One of Buchanan's long-standing proposals was to restore the primacy of *balanced budgets*—over a three-year cycle—until national debt falls below 30% of GDP. As he and Wagner (1977, pp. 184–185) wrote,

> The simplest rule is to re-establish the primacy and superiority of balanced budgets, which will finally destroy the unhealthy belief in the existence of free lunches.

They further recommended that the rule include an automatic adjustment mechanism: if projected outlays exceed tax revenues, spending must automatically be reduced. For instance,

> If the projected balanced budget proves in error and a budget deficit beyond specified limits occurs, federal outlays shall be automatically adjusted downward to restore projected balance within a period of three months. (Buchanan and Wagner, 1977, pp. 187–188).

Any resulting surpluses, they concluded, should be used exclusively to retire existing debt.

In sum, a credible anti-inflation strategy must combine monetary restraint, fiscal discipline, and institutional rules that prevent both politicians and central bankers from succumbing to the short-term temptations of cheap money and deficit spending.

Conclusion

Inflation—or even hyperinflation—can only result from one cause: the rate of growth of *monetary demand* exceeding the rate of growth of aggregate output. To clarify, *monetary demand* consists of two components: the stock of money (*M*) and the speed at which it circulates through the economy (*V*). Hence, aggregate monetary demand is expressed as M × V.

This implies that both money creation and an accelerating velocity of money influence the rate of inflation. The effect is most visible during episodes of hyperinflation. As inflation accelerates and the value of money erodes more rapidly, individuals rush to spend their cash before it loses further value—thereby increasing velocity and fuelling even faster price increases. The opposite occurs during deflation: as the value of money rises, people prefer to hold onto it, slowing its circulation.

From the analysis conducted so far, we can conclude that the principal agents responsible for generating inflation are governments and monetary authorities, which control the money supply through fiscal and monetary policies. Although inflation is often portrayed as a remedy for unemployment, it is, at best, a temporary palliative that ultimately leads to even greater joblessness once the expansion peaks. Moreover, inflation poses a profound threat to liberal democracies by fostering demands for stronger government intervention and control.

While Hayek proposed a system of *competing currencies* as one possible safeguard against inflationary tendencies, the return to *balanced budgets*—achieved through gradual reductions in public spending—remains the most reliable path to placing national economies on a sound and sustainable trajectory.

Appendix: Seeing the Quantity Theory of Money through the lens of post-Covid Malaysia

Malaysia's fiscal response to Covid-19

The Malaysian government incurred exceptionally high levels of spending in 2020 and 2021 in an attempt to mitigate the economic fallout of lockdowns, which had been introduced in the mistaken belief that they would curb the spread of COVID-19. This massive fiscal effort illustrates a common pattern in policymaking: a later intervention (stimulus packages) is deployed to counteract the unintended negative consequences created by an earlier intervention (lockdowns). As explained by Coyne and Boettke (2020, p. 51):

> In response to these unintended consequences, policymakers have two options. They can remove the initial intervention, which will free the market process to operate without distortions. Alternatively, they can introduce additional policies meant to address these undesirable outcomes. But notice that this second course of action requires expanding the discretionary power of policymakers as they extend their control over additional aspects of economic activity.

In fact, during the pandemic Malaysia recurred to emergency powers and the suspension of Parliament; in order to continue pursuing such a course of action, the government needed to further curb liberties and increase its discretionary powers. However, this is not the place to discuss the worsening political scenario in Malaysia. Instead, we will look at the different fiscal measures implemented by the Malaysian government in an attempt to counter-act the negative consequences produced by lockdowns.

It is estimated that the total value of these so-called relief packages reached RM 305 billion in 2020 (equivalent to 23% of GDP) and RM 225 billion in 2021 (15% of GDP).

Figure 4.1: The total value of all relief packages enacted in 2021 stood at 15 percent of GDP.

		Total Spending		Direct Fiscal Injection	
Year	Program	Value (RM billion)	% of GDP	Value (RM billion)	% of GDP
1H 2020	PRIHATIN	250	18	25	2.0
1H 2020	PRIHATIN SMEs	10	1	10	1.0
1H 2020	PENJANA	35	3	10	1.0
2H 2020	KITA PRIHATIN	10	1	10	1.0
TOTAL		**305**	**23**	**55**	**5.0**
1H 2021	PERMAI	15	1	2	0.0
1H 2021	PEMERKASA	20	1	11	1.0
1H 2021	PEMERKASA+	40	3	5	0.0
1H 2021	PEMULIH	150	10	10	1.0
TOTAL		**225**	**15**	**28**	**2.0**

Source: World Bank (2021, p. 30).

As a result of the extraordinary level of spending and the decline in fiscal revenues, federal government debt rose to 60.7% of GDP in 2020 (a sharp increase from 52.5% in 2019) and further to 63.3% by the end of June 2021 (World Bank, 2021, p. 31). According to BNM (2022, p. 44), total external debt climbed to 67.6% of GDP in 2020 (RM 958.1 billion) and 69.3% of GDP by the end of 2021 (RM 1,070.3 billion).

Meanwhile, the fiscal deficit widened significantly, rising from 3.4% of GDP in 2019 to 6.2% in 2020 and 6.5% in 2021 (World Bank, 2021, p. 33). It subsequently narrowed to 5.6% in 2022 and continued to improve, reaching 5% in 2023 and 4.1% in 2024.

Figure 4.2: Malaysia's fiscal deficit as percentage of GDP, 2013-2024.

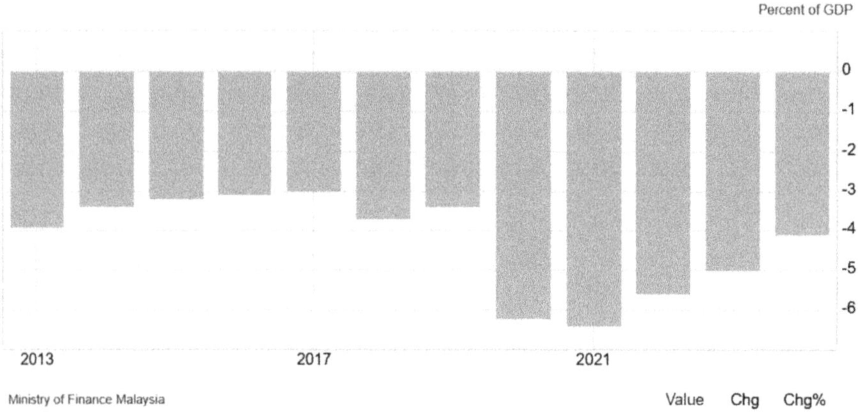

Source: https://tradingeconomics.com/malaysia/government-budget.

The increased government expenditures mixed with an expansionary monetary policy, in the form of historically low interest rates, as shown in Figure 4.3.

Figure 4.3: Malaysia's interest rates – 2015-2025.

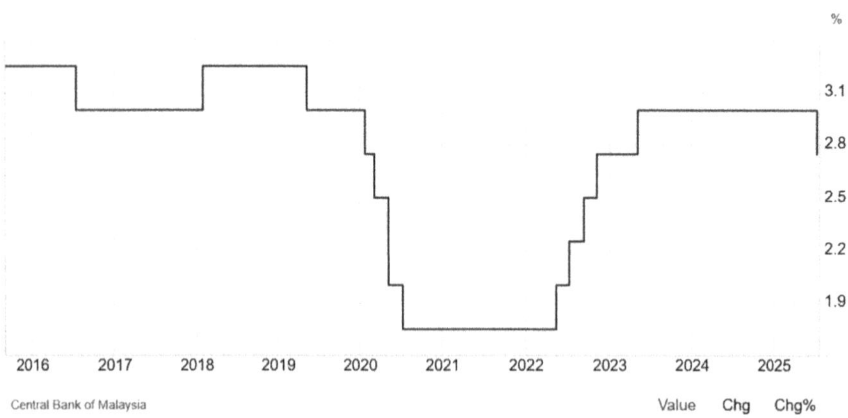

Source: https://tradingeconomics.com/malaysia/interest-rate.

Here is instead the total of the different Covid-19 packages that were introduced between 2020 and 2022 (some of them out-of-budget)[35]. Between February 2020 and October 2021, successive Malaysian governments rolled out stimulus measures amounting to RM 526.3 billion. Approximately 35% of this amount came directly from the government, while the remaining 64% was mobilized from the broader ecosystem and private sector. However, of the government's reported contribution, only half—RM 96.6 billion—qualified as direct fiscal expenditures (Murniati Yusuf, Rode, and Low, 2022). Of this total, RM 55 billion was allocated in 2020 and RM 41.6 billion in 2021.

Other Covid-19 measures with fiscal implications, as noted in the *Pantau Laksana* report, included RM 7.4 billion in foregone revenues between 2020 and 2021.

In 2022, much of the federal budget was still shaped by anti-Covid measures not covered in the *Pantau Laksana* report. Notably, these included RM 8.2 billion in direct cash transfers under Strategy 1, alongside additional recovery initiatives such as:

- RM 8 billion for the Covid Fund;
- RM 2.9 billion in job creation incentives;
- RM 5.645 billion in targeted assistance for various economic sectors.

<u>The inflationary effects of Covid-19 stimuli</u>

The outcomes of these policies—implemented not in response to COVID-19 itself, but to the economic harm caused by stay-at-home orders—can be summarized as follows:

- An excessive money supply, which fuelled inflation;
- GDP struggling to return to its 2019 level, despite expansionary measures;
- A fragile recovery sustained largely by government spending and aid-driven private consumption;

35 In order to assess the actual budget impact of Covid-19 measures, we used the Pantau Laksana dataset produced by IDEAS: https://www.pantauwangkita.com/pantau-laksana/download-the-ideas-pantau-laksana-dataset/. However, the database does not include the Budget 2022 anti-Covid measures, for which we referred to the official budget speech.

- An investment-unfriendly environment, as emergency measures—such as the freeze on foreign worker recruitment—were prolonged well beyond the health crisis.

But let us limit ourselves to the inflationary impact of Covid-19 stimulus packages.

Money supply, inflation and GDP in Malaysia

In line with the definition of inflation presented in the previous sections, the Covid-19 emergency demonstrated how expansionary fiscal measures accelerated the growth of the money supply—proxied by M2—at a rate exceeding that of real output, as measured by GDP. This monetary disequilibrium translated into upward pressures on the general price level, with consumer price inflation (CPI) reaching levels unusually elevated by Malaysian standards. The empirical evidence is reported in Table 4.1.

Table 4.1: Annual variation for M2, GDP, Consumer Price Index (CPI) and Producer Price Index (PPI), 2015-2024.

Year	Annual rate of growth			
	M2	GDP	CPI	PPI
Y-2015	3.35%	5.10%	2.68%	-3.44%
Y-2016	3.22%	4.40%	1.74%	6.54%
Y-2017	5.05%	5.80%	3.51%	0.28%
Y-2018	8.94%	4.80%	0.17%	-3.71%
Y-2019	3.47%	4.40%	0.99%	3.47%
Y-2020	4.46%	-5.50%	-1.39%	-2.14%
Y-2021	6.30%	3.30%	3.23%	9.99%
Y-2022	4.27%	8.90%	3.78%	3.46%
Y-2023	5.88%	3.60%	1.55%	-1.34%
Y-2024	3.68%	5.10%	1.68%	0.51%

Source:
- M2: Bank Negara Malaysia database;
- GDP: World Bank database;
- CPI and PPI: Malaysia's department of statistics database.

Let us now disaggregate these data into the periods before, during, and after Covid-19. What emerges from this comparison? Using 2014 as the base year (2014 = 100), by the end of 2019 M2 had reached 126.32, GDP 127.01, CPI 109.39, and PPI 102.78. This indicates that the growth of the money supply and output proceeded at a comparable pace—5.26% and 5.40% per annum, respectively—while inflation remained below the 2% target, averaging 1.88% per annum.

Table 4.2: M2, GDP, CPI and PPI assuming 2014 values equal 100.

Year	IF 2014=100			
	M2	GDP	CPI	PPI
Y-2015	103.35	105.10	102.68	96.56
Y-2016	106.68	109.72	104.47	102.87
Y-2017	112.07	116.09	108.14	103.16
Y-2018	122.08	121.66	108.32	99.33
Y-2019	126.32	127.01	109.39	102.78

During the two pandemic years, taking 2019 as the base year (2019 = 100), the money supply (M2) expanded to 111.04, while real output (GDP) contracted to 97.62. This pronounced divergence between monetary expansion and real economic activity reflects a condition of monetary disequilibrium, wherein excess liquidity outpaced productive capacity. Consequently, the CPI rose to 105.64 by the end of 2022, consistent with the lagged transmission mechanism through which increases in the money supply exert upward pressure on the general price level. In effect, the economy experienced a contraction in output alongside rising prices—an instance of inflationary pressure driven by excess money relative to goods and services available for exchange.

Table 4.3: M2, GDP, CPI and PPI assuming 2019 values equal 100.

Year	IF 2019=100			
	M2	GDP	CPI	PPI
Y-2020	104.46	94.50	98.61	97.86
Y-2021	111.04	97.62	101.80	107.64
Y-2022	115.78	106.31	105.64	111.36
Y-2023	122.59	110.13	107.28	109.87
Y-2024	127.10	115.75	109.08	110.43

After Covid-19, we can see that in 2022 the quantity of money grew at a slower pace than the output, so that in 2023 inflation slowed down to 1.55%. Instead, with a further acceleration of the quantity of money beyond the GDP rate of growth in 2023, at the end of 2024 inflation rose to 1.68% after having touched 2% in July 2024. During the past year, instead, output growth outpaced money supply and this is now reflected in an yearly rate of inflation – measured by CPI – at 1.2% as per July 2025.

Figure 4.4: Malaysia inflation rate – July 2024-July 2025.

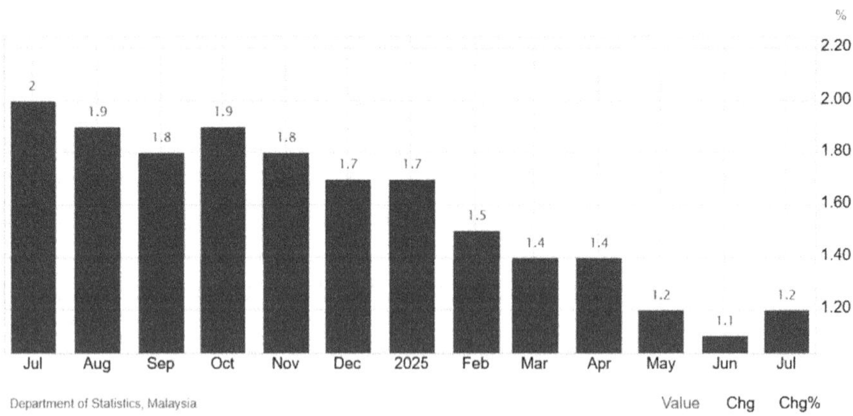

Source: https://tradingeconomics.com/malaysia/inflation-cpi.

In the post-Covid period, monetary dynamics shifted. In 2022, the money supply expanded at a slower pace than output, leading to a deceleration of inflation, which fell to 1.55% in 2023. However, as monetary growth once again outstripped GDP growth in 2023, inflation accelerated, reaching 2% in July 2024 before settling at 1.68% by year-end. Over the past year, by contrast, output growth has exceeded the expansion of the money supply, and this is now reflected in a lower annual inflation rate—measured by the CPI—of 1.2% as of July 2025.

The parallelism between the rate of growth of consumer prices and money supply is shown in the figure below.

Figure 4.5: Rate of growth of CPI and M2 in Malaysia, 2015-2025.

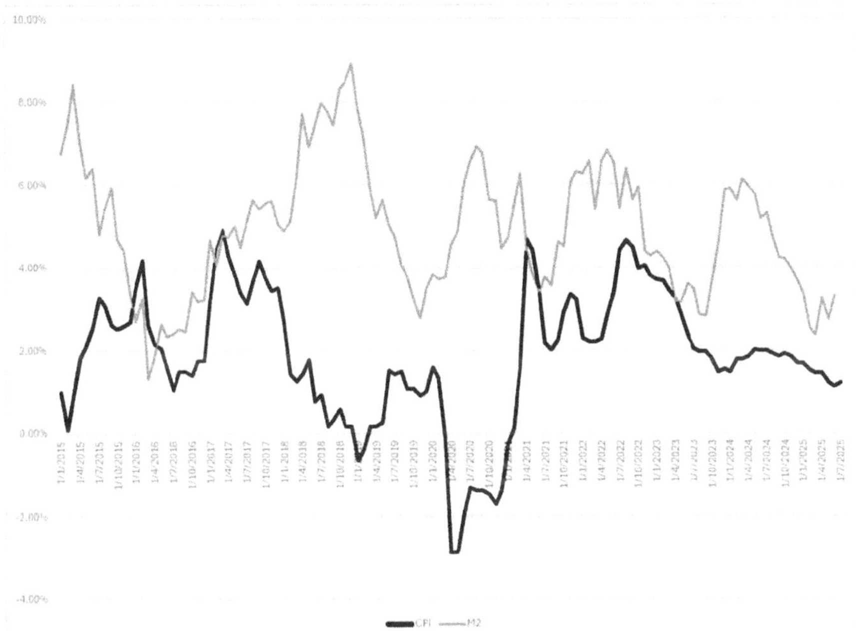

Source: our re-elaborations on data from Bank Negara Malaysia (BNM) and Department of Statistics of Malaysia (DoSM).

The long-term linkage between CPI and M2 in Malaysia can be formally examined using a log–log linear regression. Estimating the relationship between the natural logarithm of CPI and the natural logarithm of M2 over the period 2013–2025 reveals a strong positive co-movement, with a correlation coefficient of 0.9706. This result suggests a high degree of elasticity of consumer prices with respect to monetary aggregates, consistent with the theoretical expectation that sustained monetary expansion exerts upward pressure on the general price level.

Figure 4.6: Correlation between CPI and M2 in Malaysia, 2013-2025.

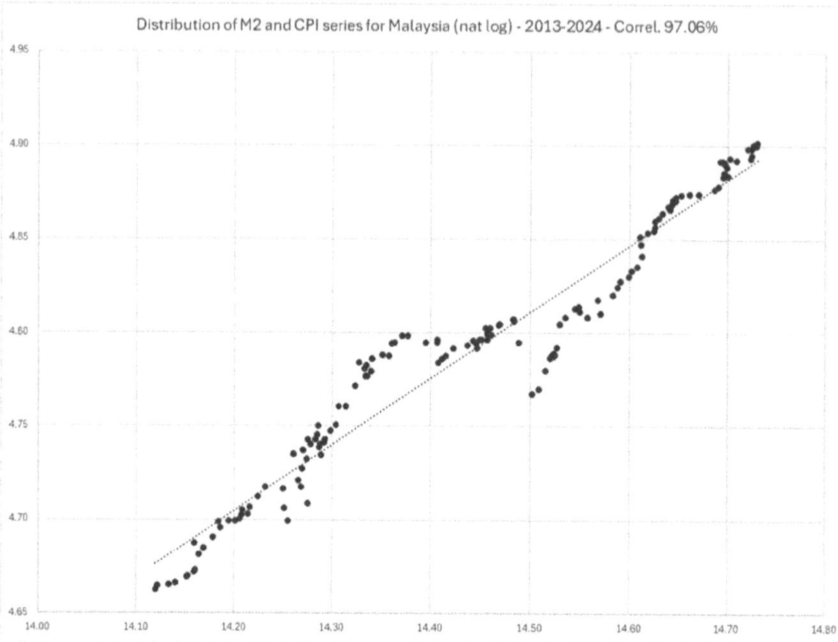

Source: our re-elaborations on data from Bank Negara Malaysia (BNM) and Department of Statistics of Malaysia (DoSM).

The horizontal axis reports the ln values for M2, while on the vertical axis the ln values for CPI are reported.

Conclusion and expectations

The Malaysian experience during and after the Covid-19 crisis offers a compelling illustration of the quantity theory of money in practice. The massive fiscal interventions introduced to mitigate the effects of lockdowns, coupled with an expansionary monetary stance, created a situation of monetary disequilibrium in which liquidity expanded far more rapidly than real output. As both Monetarist and Austrian traditions would predict, this imbalance eventually translated into higher consumer prices, confirming that inflation is fundamentally a monetary phenomenon rather than a mere by-product of cost pressures or external shocks.

The post-pandemic phase has shown a partial return to stability as fiscal consolidation and more cautious monetary management have allowed output growth to outpace money supply expansion, leading to a moderation of inflation. Yet the persistence of populist fiscal initiatives, such as the Madani cost-of-living package, signals the risk of repeating past mistakes—where short-term political gains override the pursuit of long-term price stability and sustainable growth.

Ultimately, Malaysia's recent trajectory reaffirms a classical principle: stable money and disciplined fiscal policy are the indispensable foundations of lasting prosperity. When governments succumb to the temptation of monetary expansion to finance interventionist ambitions, inflation becomes not an accident but an inevitable consequence. The post-Covid recovery thus provides a timely reminder that enduring economic health cannot be engineered through spending, but must instead be built upon sound monetary governance and respect for the self-correcting forces of the market.

References

Alchian A.A. (1979), *There's only 1 cause for inflation*, in D.K. Benjamin (Ed.), *The Collected Works of Armen A. Alchian*, Vol. 1: *Choice and Cost Under Uncertainty*, Indianapolis, Liberty Fund, 2006, pp. 249-252.

Baranzini, M. and Marangoni, G. (1995), *Macro e Microeconomia. Teoria e Applicazioni*, Padua, CEDAM.

BNM (2022), *BNM Quarterly Bulletin*, 36, 4, Kuala Lumpur, Bank Negara Malaysia.

Buchanan, J.M. and Wagner, R.E. (1977), *Democracy in Deficit. The Political Legacy of Lord Keynes*, Carmel, Liberty Fund, 2000.

Coyne, C.J. and Boettke, P.J. (2020), *The Essential Austrian Economics*, Vancouver, The Fraser Institute.

Friedman, M. (1970), *The Counter-Revolution in Monetary Theory*, in K. Matthews and P. Booth (Eds.), *Issues in Monetary Policy: The Relationship between Money and the Financial Markets*, Hoboken, 2006, pp. 171-183.

Friedman, M. (2007), *Milton Friedman on Economics. Selected Papers*, Chicago and London, The University of Chicago Press.

Friedman, M. and Friedman, R.D. (1980), *Free to Choose. A Personal Statement*, New York and London, Harcourt Brace Jovanovich.

Garrison, R.W. (2001), *Time and Money. The macroeconomics of capital structure*, London and New York, Routledge.

Garrison, R.W. (2003), *The Trouble with Deficit Finance*, «The Free Market», 21, 4, pp. 3-4.

Government of the United Kingdom (1975), *Attack on inflation. A policy for survival. A guide to the Government's programme*, London.

Hayek F.A. von (1945), *The Use of Knowledge in Society*, «American Economic Review», 35, pp. 519-530.

Hayek F.A. von (1950), *Full Employment, Planning and Inflation*, «Institute of Public Affairs Review», IV, 6, pp. 174-184.

Hayek, F.A. von (1976), *Choice in Currency. A Way to Stop Inflation*, London, Institute of Economic Affairs.

Hayek, F.A. von (1979), *Unemployment and Monetary Policy. Government as Generator of "Business Cycle"*, San Francisco, Cato Institute.

Hearn, J. (1979), *Keynes was a Monetarist*, https://jbhearn.wordpress.com/.

Hutchison, T.W. (1977), *Keynes versus the 'Keynesians'...?*, London, The Institute of Economic Affairs.

Keynes, J.M. (1936), *The General Theory of Employment, Interest and Money*, A Project Gutenberg of Australia eBook, 2003.

Murniati Yusuf, S., Rode, A. and Low, Z.T. (2022), *Pantau Laksana: Assessing Malaysia's Transparency and Accountability Initiatives in Implementing Emergency Fiscal Responses*, «Policy IDEAS», 76, Kuala Lumpur, Institute for Democracy and Economic Affairs (IDEAS).

White, L.H. and Garrison, R.W. (1999), *Do Deficits Matter?*, «The Free Market», 17, 2, pp. 5-8.

World Bank (2021), *Staying Afloat*, Malaysia Economic Monitor (December), Washington, DC, World Bank.

CHAPTER 5

Beyond Price Stability: The Role of Monetary Policy for Sustainable Growth and Social Welfare[36]

1. A methodological introduction

Methodologically, this paper sets itself apart from much of contemporary academic literature in three key areas: the treatment of the literature, the vision and role assigned to economic theory, and, as a consequence, the scope and limits of policy prescriptions.

First, the reader will not find here a "literature review" in the conventional sense. The main shortcoming of the traditional literature review is that, while it may demonstrate the author's awareness of the relevant debates and body of work, it often risks creating a separation: on one side, a list of references, and on the other, a paper that develops its argument in relative isolation from them.

To avoid this pitfall, my paper seeks to engage with the literature in an open and dynamic manner, allowing the development of the argument itself to emerge as both a dialectical and hermeneutical outcome of this intellectual dialogue. I share the view of the history of economic thought (HET) as a «living laboratory of economic theorizing» (McCaffrey, Salerno, and Dorobat, forthcoming). In this sense, the perspective offered here is constructed in continuous dialogue with theories from different times and contexts. Similar approaches can be found, for instance, in the extensive work of the late Axel Leijonhufvud (see Ferlito, 2022b), or more recently in Yeager and Hanke (2024), and—through a more contemporary lens—in Benigno (2024).

This paper also distinguishes itself by resisting the dominant trend in economics to imitate the "hard" sciences. While many contemporary economists increasingly «view the economy as a machine that can be 'repaired' by experts when it malfunctions, and that they are those experts who can fix it» (Daou and Marciano, forthcoming), I align myself more closely with the «classical political economists

36 Originally published as C. Ferlito (2025), *Beyond Price Stability: The Role of Monetary Policy for Sustainable Growth and Social Welfare*, «CME Policy Paper», 7, Subang Jaya, Center for Market Education.

[who] were scholars, using different approaches to understand the complexities of the society of which economics was a part» (Daou and Marciano, forthcoming).

Such a perspective carries two main implications, both rooted in the recognition of complexity:

1. In economics, there are no strict, "hard" cause–effect relationships. Genuine uncertainty, inseparable from the passage of real time (Meacci and Ferlito, 2018), is the only true constant.
2. Human nature is not mechanical: «human behaviour is not solely determined by external constraints that individuals may not comprehend or acknowledge». On the contrary, it requires «acknowledging that individuals possess agency and strive to shape their own destinies rather than passively accepting their circumstances» (Daou and Marciano, forthcoming).

This view implies that the future is, by its very nature, open-ended. It also means that historical facts—or data—are insufficient on their own to explain reality, which must instead be interpreted through the lens of theory (Ferlito, 2023).

Consistent with this perspective on complexity, the paper will "fluctuate" between micro- and macroeconomic analyses, without drawing a rigid boundary between the two fields. It was only with Keynes (1936) that macroeconomics came to be understood as the realm of aggregation. Here, however, I adopt Erik Lindahl's (1919) approach, according to which microeconomics concerns individual choices, while macroeconomics examines the outcomes of the social interactions generated by those choices. As Wagner (2020, p. vii) notes: «[m]icro denotes the individual entities whose actions and interactions generate the phenomena we designate as macro».

Finally, it is important to clarify that this paper embraces a flexible approach to policy prescriptions. The economic system has no automatic mechanisms, and thus one cannot expect policy *a* to deliver result *b* within a defined time frame *x*. In short, reality cannot be controlled or "fixed"; it is an emergent and evolving process.

> The central narrative of complexity science involves viewing the social system as a complex evolving system—beyond control of government or anyone. It is more a living entity than a mechanical entity. Its fundamental nature does not allow for the type of governmental control that unsophisticated

> liberals are seen to be advocating. Likewise, seeing the social system as a complex evolutionary system is quite different from seeing it as a self-steering system requiring the government to play no role, as seems to be suggested by unsophisticated market advocates. Instead, it sees the social system as complex and adaptive, developing multiple endogenous control mechanisms that make it work, and which are continually evolving over time. Government is just one component of those endogenously evolved control mechanisms (Colander and Kupers, 2014, p. 5).

Echoing Keynes, Leijonhufvud (2009, p. 755) recognized that «a modern economy is "a delicate machine, the workings of which we do not understand" and that "blundering" in the control of it can bring misery to millions and endanger the social order». Humility is a lesson that, according to Leijonhufvud, we should learn from Keynes: «the economics profession might be humbled by recent events [the Great Recession]». This is the same call advanced by Friedrich Hayek (1974): the necessity to humble ourselves before the complex network of human relationships that constitutes the economy.

In the current political economy environment, the struggle for humility probably is the most significant battle between those who believe in measurable and achievable-in-size policy targets (pretence of knowledge) and those who believe that *There are more things in heaven and Earth, Horatio, / Than are dreamt of in your philosophy* (W. Shakespeare, *Hamlet*) (limits of knowledge). Presently, this distinction is more important than any traditional boundary among schools in economics (Ferlito, 2022, p. 308).

This implies that the policy recommendations put forward in this paper are intended to support the spontaneous evolution of the economic system, enabling it to realize what it can best achieve through its own inner dynamics, rather than attempting to steer it exogenously. Such an approach abandons «the presumption that political agents are a special breed of humanity that is wise in ways that ordinary people are not» (Wagner, 2020, p. vi).

Indeed, most practical decisions—including policy choices—are made under conditions of radical uncertainty. This refers to situations in which historical data cannot provide reliable guidance, rendering statistical models, grounded in probabilistic reasoning, inadequate for capturing the essence of the decision and the broader context in which it is made (Kay and King, 2020).

2. What is interest rate?

Any discussion on monetary policy cannot avoid dealing with the interest rate. However, it is not possible to deal with it, in particular, in terms of policy prescriptions, if it is not clearly defined. In fact, despite its common usage in commercial language and theoretical jargon, a clear-cut definition of the interest rate is yet settled.

2.1. Interest rate and interest rate*s*

In everyday conversation, it is common to refer to the interest rate as the *cost of money*[37]. It is a rather narrow perspective on the interest rate that drives contemporary monetary policy: raising the cost of money should cool down overheated price dynamics, while lowering the cost of money – or loan pricing – should stimulate a stagnant economy (French, 2011, p. 7).

Such a view cannot be considered completely wrong, from a commonsense point of view, but it is a limited perspective which fails to grasp the essence of the interest rate. Therefore, here, I will distinguish between interest rates and *the* interest rate. Let us proceed with order: to explain the phenomenon of interest rate, I will follow a particular theory of interest which, for more than a century now, «has been again and again discussed, refuted, defended, ignored, forgotten and rediscovered; somehow it has managed to survive. This theory is the pure time-preference theory (often to be referred to [...] as PTPT)» (Kirzner, 1993, p. 99).

Such a theory originated with Carl Menger's causal-realist tradition in economics (Herbener, 2011, p. 11), an approach which seeks to explain the essence of things, reflecting a philosophical approach that can be traced back to Aristotle (Kirzner, 1993, p. 121). The PTPT was fully developed by American economist Frank Fetter (1904)[38] in a time when economic theory was painfully trying to grasp the essence of both capital and interest through the contributions of giant theorists such as Eugen von Böhm-Bawerk (1884, 1889), Knut Wicksell (1893, 1898) and Irving Fisher (1906, 1907, 1911).

37 Even Schumpeter (1911), while recognizing the importance of time preference as described below, remained trapped in the idea that interest is a sort of remuneration for capital; he linked his perspective with the idea that bankers create purchasing power to finance entrepreneurial innovations, and interest is the remuneration due to them for such anticipation of purchasing power.

38 Summarized and further refined in Fetter (1914).

Fetter's development is based on the simple fact that people prefer present goods to future goods and *the* interest rate measures the intensity of such a preference[39].

> Time Preference is the insight that people prefer "present goods" (goods available for use at present) to "future goods" (present expectations of goods becoming available at some date in the future), and that the social rate of time preference, the result of the interactions of individual time-preference schedules, will determine and be equal to the pure rate of interest in a society. The economy is pervaded by a time market for present as against future goods, not only in the market for loans [...], but also as "natural rate" in all processes of production (Rothbard, 1987, p. 59).

As Murray Rothbard (1987) highlighted, time preference could have been both a theoretical and moral justification for interest rate as was hinted by the late Scholastics such as Conrad Summenhart (1465-1511) and MartÍn de Azpilcueta Navarrus (1493-1586). Yet, it was the famous Neapolitan abbé Ferdinando Galiani (1728-1787) who expressed a rudimental version of the theory in his *Della Moneta* (1751)[40]. A higher degree of development was brought in by Anne Robert Jacques Turgot (1727-1781).

Although Menger (1871) clearly recognized the principle of time preference, he never extended it from value theory to the theory of interest. That step was taken by Eugen von Böhm-Bawerk (1884), who, however, seemed to have stepped back to a productivity approach in Böhm-Bawerk (1889) (Rothbard, 1987, pp. 64-65). That confusion was also not solved by Fisher and Wicksell[41].

In a nutshell, according to the productivity view, some present goods contain the capacity to generate ("produce") income for the future; such a capacity is measured by the interest rate, intended thus as a capital productivity.

---

39 We may say that it is the formal recognition that time has a value and that therefore interest can be considered the price of time rather than the price of money, as asserted by Thomas Wilson in 1752 (Chancellor, 2022, pp. 25-27).

40 In his monumental *History of Economic Analysis*, Schumpeter (1954, p. 279) referred to Galiani as «one of the ablest minds that ever became active in our field».

41 Even Hayek later remained trapped in the confusion: while he seemed to prefer the productivity approach in Hayek (1941), he opened to the time preference theory few years later (Hayek, 1945b), trying to find a compromise. Furthermore, while in Hayek (1947) productivity is associated to peculiar features of capital goods, in Hayek (1927) it is associated with the passage of time.

The PTPT, instead, is fully consistent with a subjectivist approach to value (marginal theory): interest is «the discount of future goods as against present goods» (Mises, 1949b, p. 67). Such a discount, rather than productivity, explains the difference in value between current inputs and future output of the production process. The value of inputs lies in the expected value of the future output they contribute to produce: the theory of value cannot admit to the creation of a higher value, *ex nihilo*, because of some sort of productivity; rather, the value of inputs should coincide with the expected value of future output; the difference lies in the temporal dimension of the production process, and therefore the value of present inputs is the discounted value of the expected future output, and the discount depends on time preference.

> Currently existing means are valued in the marketplace in accordance with the *discounted* value of the corresponding (future) ends. Because of this discounting, the total value of the currently existing factors of production falls short of the value of the future output that these factors make possible. It would be misleading to claim that there is "growth" in value between the employment of inputs and the emergence of output. And the value difference (between output and inputs) does not constitute a "surplus" in any meaningful sense.
>
> The existence of (positive) time preferences – the general preference for achieving ends sooner over achieving them later – is both necessary and sufficient for the emergence of the market phenomenon called interest. [...]
>
> If market participants do discount the future, then the value of present inputs will be systematically less than the value of future output. The value difference is the interest (Garrison, 1988, p. 164).

What we have seen so far can be called, following Ludwig von Mises, as *originary interest*, and it is not a price «determined on the market by the interplay of the demand for and the supply of capital or capital goods. Its height does not depend on the extent of this demand and supply. It is rather the rate of originary interest that determines both the demand for and the supply of capital and capital goods» (Mises, 1949b, p. 71). Such a distinction is very important because it means that the «loan market does not determine the rate of interest. It adjusts the rate of interest on loans to the rate of originary interest as manifested in the discount of future goods» (Mises, 1949b, p. 71). This also means that it is not the originary interest which influences decisions about investing or saving. Changes in the originary rate of interest and changes in the amount of savings are two sides of the same coin; a lower time preference means a higher amount of savings which is reflected in a lower originary rate of interest.

So, if interest «is always and everywhere a time-preference phenomenon» (Garrison, 1988, p. 161), it cannot be negative, as time preference can rise or decline, but cannot become negative[42].

Recognizing the existence of *the* originary rate of interest as the measure of the intensity of the preference for present goods over future goods does not mean denying the existence, at the same time, of different interest rates intended as market prices arising in the financial markets because of the interaction between the supply and demand of financial means, or loanable funds (Fetter, 1914, p. 137). Those rates of interests, which are different across different markets, are market prices of money loans and they are the reflection of the time preference (Fetter, 1914, p. 139).

2.2. Interest rate as a price

It is only under this more limited perspective that we can look at interest rate *as a price*. Although it is interest arising in the capital markets and not *the* interest rate but a reflection of it, and while the supply and demand for loanable funds depend on the originary interest rate, focusing on this special case is of primary importance. In fact, it is this rate that central banks try to influence with the determination of official discount rates (overnight policy rate, or OPR, in the case of Malaysia).

Affirming that loanable fund market interest rates are prices is a crucial fact to be stated with clarity. Why? Worldwide, no matter how high or low the degree of economic freedom of a country, one of the most fundamental prices of the economic system, affecting crucial saving and investment decisions – the interest rate – is, yes, determined at different levels in different markets. Indeed, we cannot just speak of *one* interest rate, as many interest rates are present at the same moment in different markets within the same economy. However, interest rates movements are affected or guided by central banks' decisions about the so-called reference level.

42 Others, like Yeager and Hanke (2024), following Cassel and Fisher, have tried to explain interest rate as the price or productivity of an additional production factor called *waiting* (Kirzner, 1993), and they included the possibility of negative interest rates. For a critique, see Rothbard (1988).

Re-stating such an obvious fact has profound implications. In fact, we can say that, where the interest rate is concerned, most of the world's economies experience a high degree of price control, despite the fact that «[p]rice controls create a mess, and the mess expands» is very well known. «*Microeconomics* textbooks explain why, but none of this inexorable logic makes its way into the typical *macroeconomic* textbook» (Rangley, Koppl and Richer, 2024, p. 27). It seems that economists fail to recognize that messing with interest rates create a mess just as interfering with other prices (Rangley, Koppl and Richer, 2024, p. 26).

To understand why playing with prices creates a mess[43], it is important to fully grasp what prices are. In fact, *price theory* should regain a central role in teaching economics (Cutsinger and Salter, 2024). Tyler Cowen and Alex Tabarrok (2010, p. 115) emphatically argue that a «price is a signal wrapped up in an incentive. [...] Prices convey important information and they create an incentive to respond to that information in socially useful ways». Their approach echoes the one of Hayek (1945a), stating that the

> most significant fact about this system is the economy of knowledge with which it operates [...] by a kind of symbol [the price], only the most essential information is passed on and passed on only to those concerned. [...] The marvel is that in a case like that of a scarcity of one raw material, without an order being issued, without more than perhaps a handful of people knowing the cause, tens of thousands of people whose identity could not be ascertained by months of investigation, are made to use the material or its products more sparingly; i.e., they move in the right direction.

While we are all equipped with our own subjective preferences and expectations, which determine our subjective values, we bring those subjective elements to the marketplace, where, in the never-ending interaction with other individuals, they generate the objective – but evolving and ever-changing – synthesis called *prices* (McCaffrey, 2020).

Therefore, talking about *prices* and *market prices* is the same thing, as prices which are not the emergent synthesis of market interactions simply are not prices at all. While the market process generates prices, market-generated prices, in turn, exercise an information transmission function which allows the market process to be a coordination process,

43 On the damages of price controls see, among other, Coyne and Coyne (2015) and Bourne (2024).

where rational decisions about resource allocation can be taken (Bregu, 2021).

> Prices are not just the point on a graph where supply meets demand. Prices allow people to allocate resources and use information in a decentralized way and solve the coordination problem of who gets what. Starting with the price role of information, we immediately focus on problems associated with dispersed knowledge and imperfect information. It is not a God's eye view of the supply and demand curve where everyone knows everything (Albrecht and Hendrickson, 2023).

This process unfolds over time: prices emerge and evolve through time, and the price structure itself is inherently intertemporal (Hayek, 1928). If prices did not result from market interactions, such coordination could never arise. Economic decisions would instead be guided by distorted signals; prices would cease to represent the synthesis of subjective evaluations of objective reality, and would instead mirror what policymakers deem to be "just". As economic theory has long demonstrated, the negative consequences of substituting policymakers' will for bottom-up market processes are well known.

One obvious implication is that without market prices, rational economic calculation becomes impossible—one of the key reasons why central planning cannot succeed (Phaneuf, 2020). Markets and their outcomes—prices—may indeed be imperfect, but they still constitute an order, more precisely, a spontaneous order (Andersson, 2021). Attempts to correct these imperfections by imposing politically determined prices would not result in a better order, but rather in the absence of any order at all.

With specific reference to monetary policy, moreover, understanding interest rate as a price would naturally drive to the conclusion that, even in a narrow sense of cost of money, interest rates cannot be negative: prices can rise or decline, but they cannot go below zero, despite reputed and influential economists such as N. Gregory Mankiw (2009), following the Great Recession, declared that «[i]t may be time for the fed to go negative»[44].

Therefore, seeing interest rates as prices and even looking at them simply from the money market perspective, simply adds to the PTPT perspective according to which *the* interest rate cannot be negative.

44 Like Keynes before him, Mankiw suffered from a certain fascination with the extremely "unorthodox", if not anti-economical, views of Silvio Gesell (French, 2011, p. 8).

2.3. Three rates: A summary

In conclusion, we can distinguish three distinct types of interest rates, and it is important to specify which one we are referring to when using the term.

1. The originary interest rate – reflecting the intensity of time preference (originary rate or OR)[45].
2. Market interest rates – those emerging in the various markets for loanable funds or financial instruments which, in the absence of reference rates set by monetary authorities, would mirror the originary rate (market rate or MR)[46].
3. The central bank rate – the reference discount rate determined by the central bank (central bank rate, or CBR).

This threefold classification moves beyond the traditional dichotomy between the natural rate (NR) and the monetary rate (MOR) and represents, perhaps, the most original contribution of the present paper.

The distinction between natural (or normal) and monetary (or bank) interest rate was introduced by Knut Wicksell (1898) to explain price fluctuations. It is necessary here to summarize the main aspects of Wicksell's explanation, in order to show where and how my explanation differs and open the doors to what shall be seen in the next sections. Furthermore, Wicksell's approach was so important that it generated a series of explanations of business cycles all based on the interaction between saving and investment decisions mediated by the interest rate: «Cassel, Lindahl, Ohlin, and Myrdal; Mises and Hayek; Hawtrey, Robertson, and Keynes were among those who put the theme squarely in the center of major works of theirs. After the *General Theory*, however, the theme is no longer prominent. It was abandoned by monetary economists and left to antiquarians» (Leijonhufvud, 1979, p. 133).

According to Wicksell (1898, p. 102), there «is a certain rate of interest on loans which is neutral in respect to commodity prices, and tends neither to raise nor lower them. This is necessarily the same as the rate

45 To put it from the perspective of price theory, we may say that the interest rate is the market price of present goods in terms of future goods (Huerta de Soto, 2000, p. 51).

46 It is important to stress that, from the general perspective of the interest rate theory, the market for loanable funds represent a limited portion of the total relationship between future and present goods (Huerta de Soto, 2000, p. 51).

of interest which would be determined by supply and demand if no use were made of money and all lending were effected in the form of real capital goods. It comes to much the same thing to describe it as the current value of the *natural rate of interest on capital*».

The Swedish economists thus explained that the normal or natural rate of interest depends on supply and demand for real capital that is not yet invested:

- The supply of capital is generated from individuals who postpone consuming part of their income and so accumulate wealth.
- The demand for capital depends on profit expectations (defined by Wicksell as the marginal productivity of capital).
- The natural interest rate is generated by supply and demand interactions.

The natural rate, however, applies only to the exchanges between individuals, while the presence of banks complicate things, as financial institutions are not limited in their lending activity by their own funds.

If the bank lending rate is below the natural rate, saving will be discouraged. As a consequence, demand for consumption goods and services rises. At the same time, profit expectations are pushed to later, and with them the demand for loanable funds for investment in time-consuming investment projects, making the demand for workers and other production factors to rise too. All these elements push upwards the prices of consumption goods while their supply is not increased. This brings prices to grow even more. A cumulative upward price movements begins which will not stop as long as the bank rate of interest is below the natural level.

The opposite happens when the bank rate is above the natural rate. While the obvious policy recommendation would be to set the bank rate at the level of the natural one, Wicksell was aware that the latter would not be observable. Therefore, Wicksell advised to start raising interest rates only when prices are on an upward trend and stop doing so after stabilization. The opposite should be done when prices fall. Here we see the theoretical root of contemporary monetary policy.

In the later development of what Leijonhufvud (1979) termed the *Wicksell Connection*, the natural rate came to be understood as the equilibrium rate in capital markets—«one which assured correspondence between the intentions of the consumers and the intentions of the entrepreneurs. And with a constant rate of saving this would be the rate of interest arrived at on a market where the supply of money, capital was of exactly the same amount as current savings» (Hayek, 1933, p. 145). This is also the sense in which Garrison (2001) employs the concept of the natural rate, as will be discussed later.

How can we integrate OR, MR and CBR with Wicksell's distinction between NR and MOR?

1. OR is an originary phenomenon, reflecting, at any given time, a society's structure of time preferences. Whether one conceives it as the market price of present goods in terms of future goods (following Huerta de Soto) or, as Mises argued, not a price at all, it remains a non-observable and continuously evolving magnitude.
2. MR emerges in the market for loanable funds from the interaction between savings and investment (*S* and *I*). n unhampered markets, it tends to gravitate toward its natural, or market-clearing, level, NR. Deviations from this equilibrium level, when generated by monetary factors, can be identified as MORS.
3. In the absence of external monetary disturbances, NR will tend to mirror the underlying OR.
4. The CBR, by contrast, is institutionally determined and, in principle, detached from both time preference and the spontaneous dynamics of the loanable-funds market. Established for policy purposes — originally inspired by Wicksell's idea that it could influence price movements — it is intended to guide MR toward NR. In practice, however, it often becomes a source of monetary distortions and cyclical fluctuations.

To fully grasp the relationships among these "entities", one must approach them outside the confines of comparative statics or dynamic stochastic general equilibrium (DSGE) models. In the perspective adopted here, the economic system is conceived as an *emergent and evolutionary process*, not as a fixed state of affairs. It is therefore perpetually in motion. While equilibrating forces are continuously at work — alongside countervailing forces that resist them (Lachmann, 1973) — the process itself is never at rest (Wagner, 2020, p. 21). This captures the essence of an *open-ended evolutionary* (OEE) framework (Wagner, 2020, p. 11).

3. Defining sustainable growth and social welfare

Having outlined the theoretical foundations of the main instrument of monetary policy — the interest rate — and building on what was discussed in Section 1, I will now define both *sustainable growth* and *social welfare* in a deliberately narrow and flexible sense. Within the domain of monetary policy, these objectives must be approached with realism. We should not assign to central banks goals that lie beyond the boundaries of economics itself, nor expect from economic policy in general — and from monetary policy in particular — what properly belongs to other spheres of social life.

3.1. Sustainable growth

I therefore define *sustainable growth* as a pattern of economic expansion that proceeds with minimal — or, ideally, no — cyclical fluctuations. I acknowledge that business cycles cannot be completely eliminated (Ferlito, 2014[47]); to some extent, they are an inherent feature of market dynamics. However, as will be shown, their amplitude can be mitigated by isolating the "natural" component of cyclical movements — driven mainly by profit expectations and imitative entrepreneurial behaviour — from the *monetary disturbances* that tend to amplify them.

While the difference between natural and monetary cycles will be explained in Section 4, here, it is worth to dig deeper into the concept of sustainable growth, for which I will refer to the analysis developed by Roger Garrison (2001) with his capital-based macroeconomics (CBM). In order to develop its concept of sustainable growth as a growth without booms and busts, the American economist used three diagrams, representing respectively (1) the market for loanable funds, (2) the production possibilities frontier and (3) the intertemporal structure of production (Garrison, 2001, pp. 34-35).

In the first diagram, we see the supply of loanable funds, representing the willingness to lend at different interest rates, and the demand for loanable funds, which represents the eagerness to borrow in correspondence of those interest rates. The intersection between

47 In Ferlito (2014) a list of economists who believed that economic cycles are the form of development in a capitalist economy can be found. The list includes representatives from different schools of thought: Karl Marx, Paolo Sylos Labini, Joseph A. Schumpeter, Marco Fanno, Arthur Spiethoff and, to a certain extent, Hayek.

the two curves, represent the market-clearing level for interest rate, corresponding to a situation in which MR = NR (i_{eq} in the graph).

Figure 5.1: The market for loanable funds.

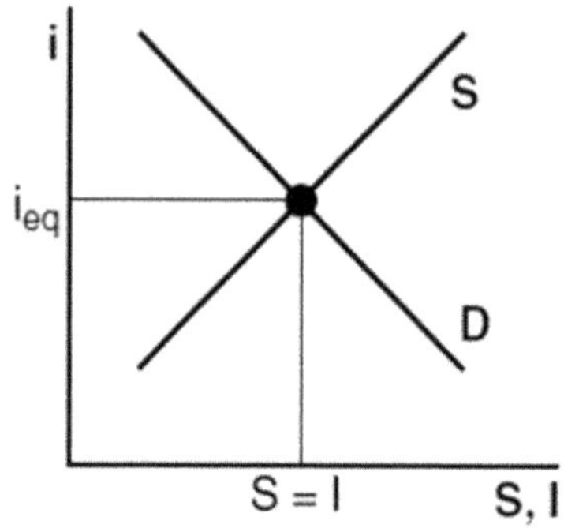

Source: Garrison (2001, p. 37).

In the context of Garrison's CBM, the well-known production possibilities frontier (PPF) is used to show the trade-off between consumption (C) and investment (I) (as shown below). These two tools are then integrated with a representation of the intertemporal structure of production, which

> gives play to both the value dimension and the time dimension of the structure of production. The relationship between the final, or consumable, output of the production process and the production time that the sequence of stages entails is represented graphically as the legs of a right triangle. In its strictest interpretation, the structure of production is conceptualized as a continuous-input/point-output process. The horizontal leg of the triangle represents production time. The vertical leg measures the value of the consumable output of the production process. Vertical distances from the time axis to the hypotenuse represent the values of goods-in-process. The value of a half-finished good, for instance, is systematically discounted relative to the finished good – and for two reasons: (1) further inputs are yet to be added; and (2) the availability of the finished good lies some distance in the future. Alternatively stated, the slope of the hypotenuse represents value added (by time and factor input) on a continuous basis (Garrison, 2001, p. 46).

This latter graph is Garrison's readaptation of the famous Hayek's Triangle (Hayek, 1931, p. 39).

Figure 5.2: The structure of production (continuous-input/point-output).

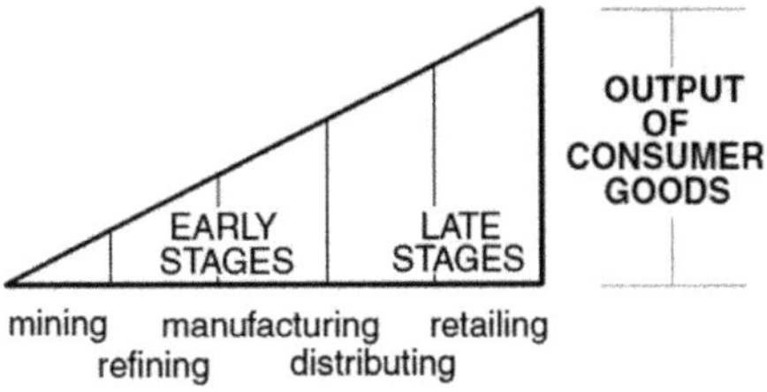

Source: Garrison (2001, p. 47).

The integration of the three components show, for any given intertemporal structure of production, the division of production between consumption and investment goods and the corresponding market-clearing interest rate.

Figure 5.3: The macroeconomics of capital structure.

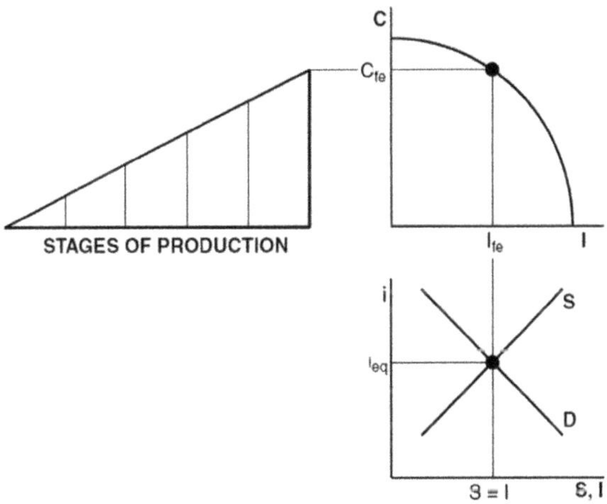

Source: Garrison (2001, p. 50).

In Garrison's model, sustainable growth happens when the market-clearing interest rate changes as a response to an endogenous change in the intertemporal structure of preferences or production: this means that *i* responds to some change in the economic system, exercising – as price – its coordination function. This in turn means that a change in OR generates market interactions that move MR away from NR but at the same time a path is set in motion to restore the equality at a difference level, corresponding with the new OR. On the contrary, a boom-and-bust cycle happens when elements of the intertemporal structure of production or preferences change in response to an exogenous increase in the supply of loanable funds, which can happen through commercial banks *ex nihilo* money creation (as shall be described later) or by moving CBR below NR in the attempt to stimulate the economy[48].

The two cases in which sustainable growth happens, thus, are linked to changes in technology and changes in intertemporal preferences. In the first case, «the frontier shifts outward (and possibly experiences a change in shape depending on the specific nature of the change in technology); the demand for loanable funds shifts to the right, as business firms take advantage of the new technological possibilities. The resulting higher incomes cause the supply of loanable funds to shift to the right as well» (Garrison, 2001, p. 57). To take advantage of the new technologies available – following what Schumpeter would have defined the second wave of imitative innovators – entrepreneurs increase the demand for loanable funds, making *i* to grow; but the increase in interest rates brings about an increase in savings too, making *i* to fall again. Therefore, at the end of the process we will have both more savings and more investments, but also more consumption due to the technological jump.

Figure 5.4: Technology-induced growth.

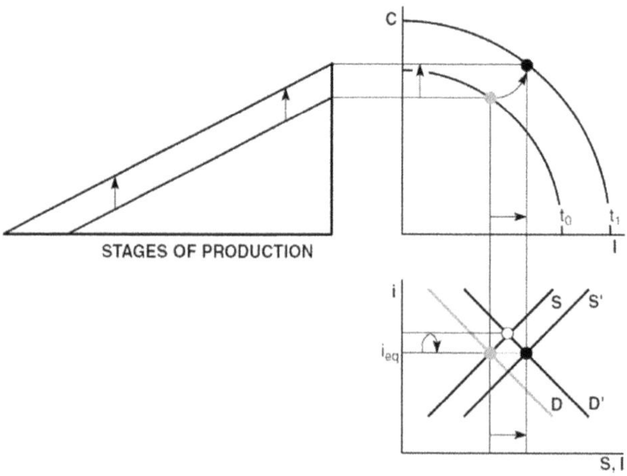

Source: Garrison (2001, p. 59).

48 For a more detailed explanation of Garrison's model and its fiscal and monetary policy implications, see Ferlito (2012, 2013).

As an example of endogenous change in the intertemporal structure of preferences we may consider an increased degree of thriftiness, which, by increasing the supply of loanable funds, brings down the market-clearing level of the interest rate, then reshuffling the production frontiers in favour of more roundabout methods of production, therefore generating a higher level of investment (higher demand for loanable funds).

Figure 5.5: Saving-induced capital restructuring.

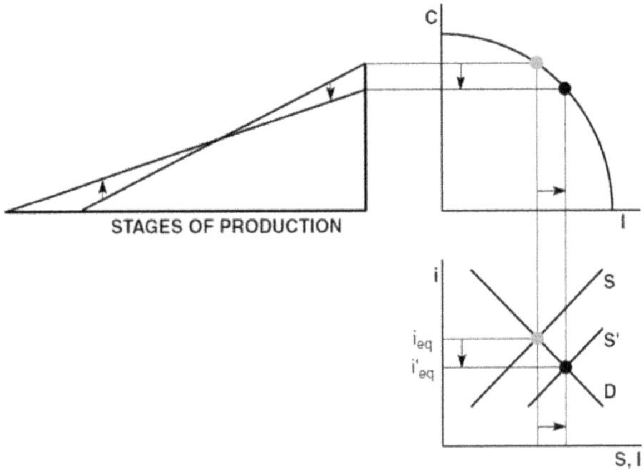

Source: Garrison (2001, p. 62).

In a nutshell, the economy can be on a sustainable growth path if the interest rate can fluctuate in a way to exercise an equilibrating function between supply and demand for loanable funds (savings and investment) after an endogenous change in the intertemporal system of preferences; or, and it is the same, if the interest rate can fluctuate in a way to constantly seek its *natural* or *market-clearing* level (Leijonhufvud, 1979, p. 154), as explained below.

The opposite case, when the intertemporal change of preferences is not endogenous, but induced by monetary or fiscal policy, will be discussed in Section 4.

3.2. Social welfare

While the current paper aims at going *beyond price stability*, it does not claim that a stable level of prices is not an important target; rather, it emphasizes that it is not a strong enough target *per se*. As we shall see, pursuing price stability does not impede the emergence of asset bubbles and business fluctuations.

However, price stability remains a socially crucial target. Social welfare will be here defined in a very narrow way, consistently with what we can realistically expect from monetary policy and without establishing targets that may induce the emergence of distortionary policies which can be worse than the disease they aim to address.

Therefore, social welfare is here defined as a situation where the value of the currency is stable and the best possible employment is achieved which is consistent with the structure of production dictated by the intertemporal system of preferences (without exogenous stimuli).

3.2.1. *Price stability*

There is no doubt that price stability, intended as a stable purchasing power of the currency, is a socially desirable objective. It nurtures certainty for economic exchanges and protects individuals and households. Furthermore, it promotes savings and therefore is an intergenerational alliance for stable economic growth.

In fact, inflationary regimes – which are often accompanied by other anti-growth policies (Heymann and Leijonhufvud, 1995, p. 38) – make critical the coordination of expectations and create a very difficult environment for decision-making (Heymann and Leijonhufvud, 1995, p. 44). Relative prices then begin to lose their coordination ability (Leijonhufvud, 1975, p. 34).

Historically, the ethical desirability of monetary stability was recognized by Saint Thomas Aquinas in the 13th century (Hülsmann, 2008, p. 74) and it remained a constant element in intellectual reflection, although a clear definition for it struggled to emerge.

Moreover, monetary or price stability is not only difficult to define but arguments may arise as to which monetary system is better suited to achieve it. I will not deal with this second issue here; it will be discussed in the next sessions. Furthermore, I shall not follow the predominant definition of price stability (price growth below 2%)[49]. As

49 «Monetary stability is a synonym for price stability. Price stability refers to a stable price level or a low level of inflation and not to stable individual prices. There is no doubt that changing relative prices play a crucial and beneficial part in economic adjustment and decision making by individual actors be it companies or households. Part of the costs of inflation can be related to the fact that these relative price signals will be blurred more and more the higher the rates of inflation. Although there are some issues concerning the most relevant composition and measurement of the price index and the optimal horizon over which to define price stability, in general the concept is widely accepted and relatively straightforward to handle,

price fluctuations are a normal component of the market process, price stability here is intended as the possibility for relative prices to adjust according to the normal conditions of supply and demand, without external monetary shocks induced by fiscal and monetary policies. In the past, «the general adoption of a positive (+2%) inflation target has prevented the downward adjustment of prices that would be the natural product of increases in productivity and positive supply shocks. As a result, prices have been drifting upwards (and significantly) for decades» (White, 2024, p. 86).

Therefore, in this paper, that target is extended to the fact that price deflation should not be feared or impeded; instead, in particular, after a boom induced by virtual money creation, deflation is a positive and necessary phenomenon. Therefore, productivity growth deflation should be allowed to nurture an environment conducive to innovation. Furthermore, cash-building deflation should be allowed too, as savings are the necessary means for enhancing a process of sound growth (Bagus and Ferlito, 2022, p. 35).

Coming back to Wicksell (1898), thus, price stability is granted when MOR = NR.

3.2.2. *Best possible employment*

The second characteristic of social welfare is *the best possible employment* given the structure of the economy. This means renouncing active full employment policies. Hayek (1950, pp. 174-175) argued that inflationary dynamics is the price to be paid for implementing persistent full-employment policies (stimulating aggregate demand). In fact, Hayek precisely disputed that a higher level of employment (full employment) can be achieved and *maintained* by means of monetary pressures (Hayek, 1950, pp. 175-176). The Austrian economist's central thesis is that short-term injections of money (via fiscal or monetary policy) may well help maintain jobs at a higher level than would be possible otherwise; nonetheless, in the long term, the employment level resulting from these policies is destined to fall (Hayek, 1950, pp. 175-176).

both conceptually and in central banking practice. An example of an explicit definition of price stability is the one chosen by the ECB, which refers to a year-on-year increase in the Harmonised Index of Consumer Prices for the euro area of below 2 percent, which is to be maintained over the medium term» (Issing, 2003).

While it is true that an increase in monetary incomes may increase employment, the basic mistake is to believe that unemployment is due to insufficient aggregate demand and that pressure on it may therefore automatically generate *stable* employment (Hayek, 1950, p. 176): if spending is spread across the various sectors in a manner other than that in which employment is spread in the relevant sectors, then it cannot be assumed that an increase in spending has a positive effect on employment.

> Unemployment can evidently be the consequence of the fact that the distribution of labour is different from the distribution of demand. In this case the low aggregate money income would have to be considered as a consequence rather than as a cause of unemployment. Even though, during the process of increasing incomes, enough expenditure may "spill over" into the depressed sectors temporarily there, to cure unemployment, as soon as the expansion comes to an end, the discrepancy between the distribution of demand and the distribution of supply will again show itself. Where the cause of unemployment *and* of low aggregate incomes is such a discrepancy, only a re-allocation of labour can lastingly solve the problem in a free economy (Hayek, 1950, p. 177).

Active full employment polices create a distortion in the system of resource allocation. Monetary and fiscal expansions direct demand towards sectors that, without exogenous stimulation, would not be favoured. When such expansion comes to an end, probably because inflation has reached an unsustainable level, demand will be forced to return in the direction expressed by the temporal preferences in existence prior to monetary injections. Therefore, employment created artificially in all probability will not be permanent. The new unemployment level may even be higher than the pre-stimulus situation, if monetary injections encouraging demand have not only increased employment but have also stimulated the creation of new economic initiatives in the sectors so stimulated. This is why the result of inflation is worse than the problem intended to be resolved.

The core message here is that the relationship between an increase in aggregate spending and full employment does not hold true. In fact, the inflation generated by increased spending, while producing desirable effects in the short term (increase in employment and monetary wages), ends up being more damaging. Indeed, distorting the structure of employment in order to maintain an artificial level of employment requires continual injections of money. Yet this situation is not indefinitely sustainable and situations such as the Great Inflation in Austria and German in the 1920s are clear proofs. When further artificial inflation is no longer possible, the system will begin to move towards realignment, that entails the loss of such artificially created employment as well as the closure of economic activities launched in sectors where aggregate demand had been artificially stimulated. The outcome is consequently a situation worse than the one preceding the stimulus.

Is there perhaps a remedy for all this? A radical new approach to policy should be conceived (as we will see later in this paper), and it entails depriving political authority of control over money. Agreeing with Hayek, Leijonhufvud observed that inflation is political in nature[50] and therefore it cannot avoid dealing with the adequacy of the political regime, in particular, its readiness to fall to the song of the inflation tax and seigniorage (Ferlito, 2022). As argued by Michael Bordo and Lars Jonung (1994, p. 11), as

> long as money is produced by a government controlled monopolist, that is by a central bank, the money supply process will be the subject of political pressure. Sooner or later the monetary system will be exposed to a disturbance that induces political manipulation of the money supply, creating inflation. Once inflation begins, it tends to become entrenched in the monetary regime.
>
> One method to create strong credibility for the purchasing power of the currency is to take the money supply out of the control of the political system. Creating a truly independent central bank whose only responsibility is to maintain price stability is one way to do this.

What Hayek (1979, p. 17) said is that «our aim must be, not the maximum of employment that can be achieved in the short run, but a "high and stable [i.e., *continuing*] level of employment" [...]. We can achieve this, however, only through the re-establishment of a properly functioning market which, by the free play of prices and wages, establishes the correspondence of supply and demand for each sector».

Therefore, while monetary policy, by controlling fluctuations in the quantity of money, can affect employment, the effects on employment should not be of primary importance, as the «*primary aim must again become the stability of the value of money*» (Hayek, 1979, p. 17).

50 On the relationship between inflation and politics see also Phelps (1985, pp. 573-598).

Then, again, monetary policy can achieve social objectives related to employment only indirectly: by maintaining a stable value of money, misallocation of resources is minimized and therefore the best possible employment arises which is consistent with the structure of production resulting – at any given moment – by the system of intertemporal preferences.

I will define here that that level of unemployment – the one consistent with the intertemporal structure of production – as *the natural level of unemployment*[51], further specifying that it can be achieved only when the interest rate moves towards its natural level (Leijonhufvud, 1979, p. 185).

3.3. Wrapping up

Wrapping up what has been said so far, we can conclude that the basic condition for achieving both sustainable growth and social welfare is

MR = NR = OR

Indeed, what has been said so far can be summarized by saying that:

- Business fluctuations can be moderated if MR is allowed to seek its path toward NR and if NR is a reflection of OR (Garrison).
- The equivalence – dynamically intended – between MR and NR is the condition for achieving price stability (Wicksell).
- The natural or structural level of unemployment can be achieved only when MR moves toward NR (Leijonhufvud).

How this can be obtained shall be analyzed in the next sections.

4. Price stability, asset bubbles and monetary policy

4.1. Price stability as a policy target: Necessary, but not enough

In July 1927, a meeting took place in Long Island, United States, to discuss cooperation among leading central banks. The host was Benjamin Strong, president of the New York Federal Reserve, and the participants included Montagu Norman (Governor of the Bank of England), Charles

51 This is not to be confused with the NAIRU (Non-Accelerating Inflation Rate of Unemployment), the unemployment rate consistent with price stability according to the current mainstream economic thought; in fact, accepting NAIRU implies a certain degree of acceptance of the universal validity of the short and long-run Phillips curve, while I believe that the theory of unemployment must be considered historically conditioned (Sylos Labini, 1987).

Rist (Deputy Governor of the Bank of France), and Hjalmar Schacht (President of the Reichsbank). In the aftermath of World War I, the major central banks agreed at this meeting to pursue a new course of monetary policy: restoring a measure of currency stability through the Gold Exchange Standard and targeting price stability via interest rates—specifically to prevent deflation, which was deemed politically unacceptable. This objective was supported by prominent economists such as Keynes, Ralph Hawtrey, and Irving Fisher (Chancellor, 2022, pp. 82–87).

The new course brought low interest rates in the United States. However, while prices remained stable and the Roaring Twenties were ... roaring, stock prices accelerated and an asset bubble emerged, as was warned by Benjamin Anderson, chief economist at Chase National Bank. Easy money fostered credit growth and credit growth generated speculative excesses (Chancellor, 2022, pp. 87-90). The rest is history[52].

The 1930s in the US were characterized by massive losses in output and employment, but the depression was not preceded by any considerable inflation (White, 2006, p. 7); instead, an asset bubble collapsed in October 1929 (Laidler, 2003, p. 6).

The years of the Great Depression not only fuelled the production of the best available literature on business cycles, with particular attention to the effect of monetary phenomena, but they also initiated reflection within central banking circles. In a Federal Reserve bulletin from 1937 we read that, while «wide fluctuations in the price level are disastrous», «price stability should not be the sole or principal objective of monetary policy». In fact, «unstable economic conditions may develop, as they did in the 1920's, while the price level remains stable». However, while recognizing the limits of monetary policy and the need for integration with fiscal policy, the Fed reiterated the fear of deflation (Federal Reserve, 1937, pp. 827-828).

After World War II, the rise of the *New Economics* placed aggregate demand management at the core of activist policies, with the goal of maintaining full employment. These policies initially appeared capable of delivering both sustained prosperity and price stability. However, their apparent success was soon eclipsed by the emergence

52 The technical and financial details of the process are well described in Phillips, McManus and Nelson (1937); the authors also report the history of the legal framework which permitted the credit expansion to happen in the United States.

of stagflation in the 1970s (Orphanides and Williams, 2004). In fact, ever since the Employment Act of 1946, U.S. policy had been characterized by expansionary measures that fuelled an upward trend in prices well before stagflation fully set in (Orphanides, 2000, p. 1).

As a result, the emphasis on price stability grew even stronger—and rightly so—after the inflationary surge of the 1970s and Volcker's decisive monetary tightening. Yet, by the late 1980s, some economies still experienced real estate bubbles without corresponding inflationary pressures (Laidler, 2003, p. 1).

The same happened during the 1997-1998 financial crisis in Southeast Asia, where for «some countries the costs could be measured as double digits of GDP, with associated increases in unemployment [...]; [however], these difficulties were not preceded by any inflationary excesses but rather by sharp increases in credit, asset prices, and fixed investment. On the financial side, an important influence was exerted by large-scale capital inflows, which subsequently and suddenly reversed as the crisis worsened» (White, 2006, p. 8).

Again, after these new turbulences, a period of price stability followed, accompanied by general macroeconomic stability. It was a time when Fed chairman Ben Bernanke popularized the expression *Great Moderation*[53]. In the 1990s, central banks placed increased emphasis on price stability, and monetary policy increasingly oriented itself towards low and stable inflation (Barro, 1995). That stability, though, did not impede the emergence of the dotcom bubble first and the housing bubble later. The two new cycles, which emerged during the Fed tenures of Alan Greenspan and Bernanke, were possible precisely because of periods of extremely low interest rates; asset bubbles were fuelled within a context of price stability[54].

This demonstrates that price stability, while important, is not a sufficient condition for macroeconomic stability, intended as the avoidance of boom-and-bust cycles.

---

53 Just before the emergence of the Great Recession, Bernanke (2007, p. 145) wrote: «One of the most striking features of the economic landscape over the past twenty years or so has been a substantial decline in macroeconomic volatility».

54 Price stability is mentioned as both the central bank mandate and the primary monetary policy objective for all the central banks of the ASEAN-5 group, which includes Indonesia, Malaysia, Philippines, Singapore and Thailand (Khor, Guajardo and Peiris, 2018).

The objective of price stability, however, appeared to lose its priority—at least temporarily—during the Great Lockdown. In the Western world in particular, fiscal and monetary policies became so accommodative that the potential inflationary consequences of the so-called Covid packages were largely disregarded by policy makers. Expansionary fiscal policies were politically attractive, while central banks were likely operating under significant pressure from political authorities. This resulted in major forecasting errors on inflation, which in turn led to misguided interest rate policies and the return of inflation in the Western world to levels not seen since the 1970s. Notably, the Federal Reserve's models failed to account for the historical relationship between budget deficits and accommodative monetary policy (Levy, 2024, pp. 261, 272). Moreover, the fact that the link between lower short-term interest rates and stronger lending activity tends to vanish in persistently low-rate environments (Borio and Gambacorta, 2017, p. 2) was overlooked[55].

From 2022, the two major Western central banks realized that inflation was again "a thing" and embarked on a journey towards higher interest rates: price stability was at risk. In fact, «US inflation has declined from its forty-year high in 2022. Yet it remains above the Fed's 2% target, and throughout the current disinflation, US financial markets have been ignoring a simple reality. There is no historical precedent for a painless return from moderate to low inflation» (Chari and Blair Henry, 2024, p. 159).

However, although the recent monetary policy efforts have slowed down price dynamics, an excess amount of liquidity was produced with the Covid-19 fiscal policy packages that has fuelled new bubbles, as testified by the Silicon Valley Case (Quarles, 2024; Ferlito and Calzolari, 2023) and by the 5 August 2024 Black Monday (Ferlito and Chong, 2024).

The point can be summarized by saying that counter-cyclical policy aimed at stabilizing the "real circuit" create monetary disorder within the "financial circuit" (Palley, 2023, p. 331). What may have misled several economists is the expectation that such monetary disorder manifests itself in the form of inflation. Instead, price increases can be one of the ways in which monetary disorder induced by money injections take shape; the other two are currency disorder and asset price bubbles (Palley, 2023, pp. 316 and 322).

55 Not to mention that very low interest rates can keep alive zombie firms in scarcely productive activities (Weizsäcker and Krämer, 2021, p. 21).

This happens because a narrow focus on near-term inflation "blinds" policymakers on the connection between the business cycle and the financial cycle: economic booms within a regime of price stability create abundant fuel for financial booms (Borio, 2012, p. 6) and the emergence of Minsky moments.

Figure 5.6: Interactions between real circuit and financial circuit due to monetary injections.

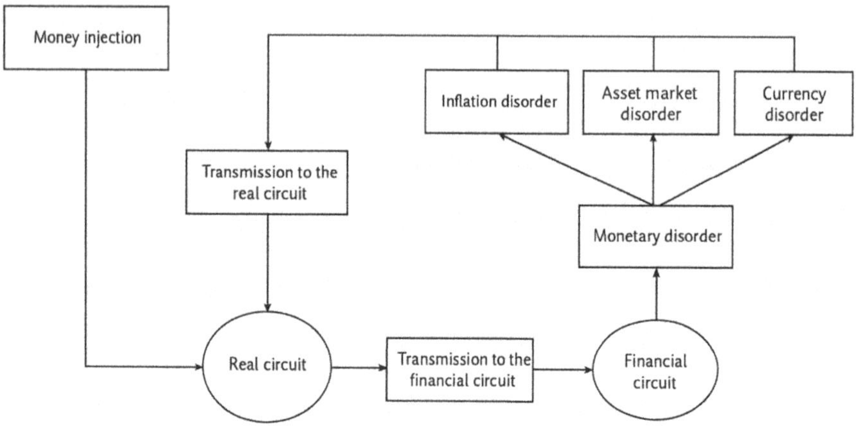

Source: My re-adaptation from Palley (2023).

Ironically, such a scenario was "predicted" by Alan Greenspan, who in 1997 said: «What I want to suggest is that we confront the question of whether we are trying to stabilize prices or trying to stabilize the financial system. That is where the issue of asset prices comes in; [...] I also suspect that by around the year 2006, this very tricky question may involve what [it is] we are endeavoring to stabilize and may be the focus of our policy actions. My own guess is that we are going to be dealing with asset prices, the question of nomina long-term interest rates, and probably the outlook for nominal GDP as well. In any event, our task will surely be tougher than it is today, and the issue will be how we should proceed» (Connolly, 2023, pp. 86-87).

Greenspan saw what was about to come in 2007-2008. How monetary phenomena contribute to creating bubbles that burst is discussed in section 4.2.

4.2. Business cycles: Natural and induced

The biggest regret I have so far with regard to my short life as a modest economist is the inability to fully clarify my position on business cycles and the co-existence of structural – or natural – fluctuations with money-expansion-induced ones[56]. I defined these cycles as the natural cycle (NC) and the monetary cycle (MC) (Ferlito, 2016, Chapter 3). Herewith, I will try to explain the point the best I can.

A boom is generally initiated when entrepreneurs see unexploited profit opportunities. When experiencing positive profit expectations, they become future-oriented and ready to invest in long-term investment projects. Such a situation encourages the onset of major investments in production assets, or capital goods, whereby the economy becomes, in general, more capital-intensive and the production period is extended (Hayek, 1931, pp. 35-36). However, even if entrepreneurs become more future-oriented, such a change does not necessarily bring about a modification of consumer preferences, and we encounter a difference between entrepreneurial decisions and consumer choices (Hayek, 1933, pp. 143-148), which lies at the very root of business cycles (Bresciani-Turroni, 1936).

Here we can observe two possible scenarios. The first one is the one described above as sustainable growth: the banking system does not accommodate the increasing demand for loanable funds with the creation of money, but rather supply is allowed to grow thanks to the interplay of market forces and the subsequent growth in MR, tending towards the new NR generated by rising profit expectations[57].

Although Garrison's CBM – inspired by the Austrian Theory of the Business Cycle – does not consider the possibility of a cycle in this scenario, it instead appears because of the disruptive nature of the outcome of entrepreneurial production processes set in motion by the expansion of the period of production (Schumpeter, 1939). It is the fight between the new that emerges and the old that tends to survive that generates a more or less extended process of liquidations, which however is a structural part of the attempt of the economic system to reach its new equilibrium level. This is made all the more true by the fact that the first wave of investors is usually followed by a swarm of imitators, who enters the game attracted by rising profit expectations.

56 I hope that, through the substantial and thorough revision of my analysis of monetary and natural cycles presented in Chapter 3 of this book, I have succeeded in clarifying and deepening my position.

57 The role of profit expectations is emphasized in Hayek (1933, 1939) and Bresciani-Turroni (1936).

It is likely that these imitative initiatives are unable to survive the re-adjustment process and the market's attempt to absorb the outcome of new investments.

Such a three-phase cycle (boom first wave, imitative second wave and liquidation), which I identify with the NC, corresponds to a large extent with Schumpeter's (1939) first approximation, and partially extends to its second one.

The second scenario, instead, can be generated in three ways, resulting in the same effects:

1. Entrepreneurial new orientation towards the future is generated by a CBR keeping MOR (or MR) below NR (via monetary policy).
2. Financial resources to respond to that change in preferences are supplied by the banking system through the *ex-nihilo* creation of money via loans: new supply does not meet demand naturally, but artificially, without a re-alignment of the system of intertemporal preferences. MOR is pushed below NR, because of artificial new supply.
3. Excess of financial means are supplied to the system via expansive fiscal policies. Again, MOR is pushed below NR, because of artificial new supply.

I would like to clarify that, while the traditional version of the Austrian Business Cycle Theory (ABCT) emphasizes case 1., I tend to believe that monetary disorders are, in the current scenario, mostly comprising a mix of the three. Furthermore, while the ABCT tends to see the monetary expansion at the root of the cycle, as able in itself to stimulate entrepreneurial impulses, I tend to believe that increased profit expectations are the prime mover: they can either be allowed to interact with savings via the interest rate (NC), or provided with additional capital through the three ways mentioned above (MC)[58].

Before further progressing with the explanation, a few words need to be devoted to point 2, as it may seem odd to most readers. In fact, the common belief is that, when they make loans, banks lend out depositors' money (endogenous monetary theory). However, this is not the case

58 My vision is closer to Schumpeter *and* Keynesian *animal spirits*. A similar hybrid perspective in this regard can be found in Weizsäcker and Krämer (2021, p. 21).

(Rangeley and White, 2024, p. 3)[59]. Instead, we can find in explanations given by the Deutsche Bundesbank, the Banco de España and the Bank of England (Rangeley and White, 2024, pp. 3-4), that when a bank grants a loan, it posts the associated credit entry for the customer as a sight deposit by the latter. So, commercial banks can create money, «in the form of bank deposits, by making new loans. When a bank makes a loan [...] it credits [someone] bank account with a bank deposit of the size of the mortgage. At that point money is created» (McLeay, Radia and Thomas, 2014).

New money supply, thus, can be created by commercial banks without an accommodative intervention of the central bank or without expansionary fiscal policies. The compulsory reserve coefficient is ineffective as new money is precisely created by posting new deposits and therefore automatically increasing the reserve amount (Rangeley and White, 2024).

What has just been described in terms of accounting practice is consistent with what Schumpeter (1911, p. 73) argued from a theoretical standpoint, suggesting that entrepreneurial innovations are financed with «the creation of purchasing power by banks», adding that the «banker, therefore, is not so much primarily a middleman in the commodity "purchasing power", as a *producer* of this commodity. [...] He is the ephor of the exchange economy» (Schumpeter, 1911, p. 74)[60].

In these situations, as consumers are not necessarily saving more to finance the new investment decisions, a general expansion of the capital supply becomes crucial in supporting an emerging boom. Most investments are made in the expectation that the supply of capital will for some time continue at a level consistent with the new demand for loanable funds. In other words, entrepreneurs regard the present supply of capital and the present rate of interest as an indication that approximately the same situation will continue to exist for some time (Hayek, 1933, p. 142).

59 To understand the quantitative importance of commercial bank loans in Malaysia, let us consider that they amounted to RM 1.25 trillion in 2023 (https://www.statista.com/statistics/1422122/malaysia-total-loans-of-commercial-banks/), while narrow money (M1) amounted to just RM 655 billion and M2 to RM 2.4 trillion (https://data.gov.my/dashboard/money-supply).

60 A technical description of Schumpeter's concept of money creation can be found in Sylos Labini (1992, pp. 25-27).

While entrepreneurs invest in new processes for the production of capital goods, savers are frustrated in their desire to consume, because what they want is not being produced. The forced saving phenomenon (Hayek 1932) thereby results: we observe a gradual reduction in the production of consumer goods and therefore an involuntary limitation of consumption (Hayek, 1933, pp. 145-146).

The entrepreneurial impetus towards new investments, on the other hand, initially involves an increase in raw material prices and consequently of the capital goods produced with them. And the impetus becomes particularly violent when the wave of the first innovative entrepreneurs is joined by the pressure of imitators, who grasp profit opportunities only in a second stage and attempt to benefit by following the "fashion".

At the same time, demand for labour increases, attracting workers towards the new investments, making relative wages increase: this in turn encourages demand for consumer goods, and prices in this sector also increase. In order to be sustainable, this process requires further credit expansion, which would bring about a cumulative increase in prices that sooner or later would exceed every limit. The conflict seems to be evident when demand for consumer goods exceeds the funds available for investment in terms of absolute value. At this point, the interest rate cannot but rise, frustrating demand for capital goods precisely when their price has also risen. A considerable part of the new plant installed, designed to produce other capital goods, remains unused since the additional investments required to complete production processes cannot be made (Hayek, 1933, p. 148). As a result, in an advanced stage of the boom, growth in demand for consumer goods brings down demand for capital goods (Hayek,1939, p. 31).

At the peak of the boom, the economy discovers that it is unable to sustain a production oriented beyond its possibilities. Demand for capital goods runs out, taking with it the over-production in the particular sector where the boom started, and it is here where problems arise. Many economic initiatives set up through excessive reliance on profit expectations, on speculation fever or on credit cannot be completed, although the debts still have to be paid. Many companies have to be expelled from the system. Capital is scarce[61] (Bresciani-Turroni, 1936, p. 174) and banks raise interest rates. A period of adjustment and return to equilibrium begins, only it has the aspect of a depression.

It is important to emphasize that the *secondary wave of investments* generates additional demand for loanable funds. This represents an attempt to prolong the expansionary process, thereby heightening uncertainty. The more time the process takes, the greater the range of possible outcomes — opening the door to higher productivity, but also to greater instability.

Moreover, during this secondary phase, the optimistic sentiment and profit expectations that become *incandescent* at the end of the primary expansion also influence the behaviour of banks. Precisely because of the prevailing euphoria, it becomes highly probable that banks will extend additional *virtual funds* — credit not backed by genuine savings — under the assumption that consumer preferences will eventually adjust through higher savings, seemingly justified by the confidence inspired by the boom itself.

As Hyman Minsky's *financial instability hypothesis* suggests (Minsky, 1982; 2008), during a boom that follows a period of tranquillity, innovative debt practices and speculative excesses proliferate, leading to the emergence of a fragility that often goes unrecognized until the cycle reverses (Prychitko, 2010, p. 206)[62].

61 As explained by Yeager (1956, pp. 5-6), the «most striking characteristic of depression is not overproduction of some things and underproduction of others but, rather, a general "buyers' market," in which sellers have special trouble finding people willing to pay money for goods and labor».

62 The model described so far, which includes elements from different scholars such as Hayek, Schumpeter and Minsky, presents a dynamics which can be read also with the Keynesian lens, and in particular in light of the multiplier-accelerator model of business cycles. In Keynesian models, the initial impulse comes from autonomous investment (generated by innovation or public decisions). An autonomous investment makes consumption rise and thus, via the multiplier, income rises too. The income increase, in turn, causes further investments via the accelerator. This way a spiral mechanism is created; it reinforces itself, until it breaks down, when full utilization of productive resources is imminent. At this point, the rate of increase in income tends to slow down, then fall. The decrease, first relative to the multiplier, becomes absolute: income falls (Ferlito, 2011, p. 112).

Again, Garrison's model can be used for a diagrammatic representation[63].

Figure 5.7: Boom and bust (policy-induced intertemporal disequilibrium).

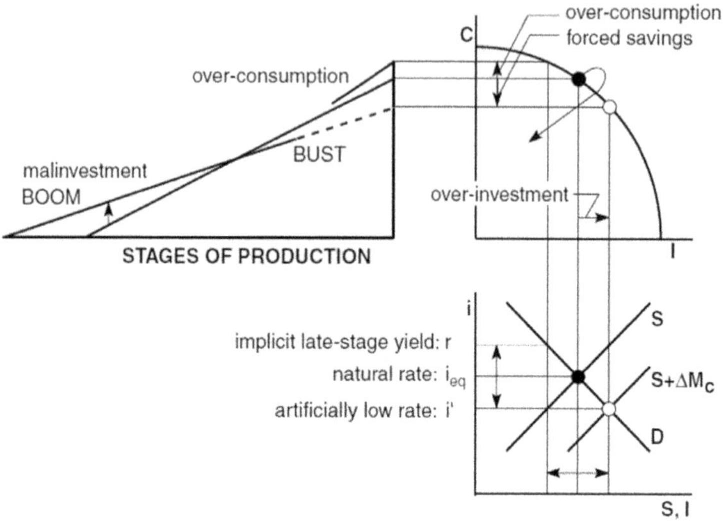

Source: Garrison (2001, p. 69).

The different configurations of *Natural Cycles (NC)* and *Monetary Cycles (MC)* can be summarized as follows:

Case 1: Pure Natural Cycle (NC)

- Phase 1 – Primary Expansion: Triggered by a change in intertemporal preferences, the economy moves from point *a* to point *b*, where *b* > *a*.
- Phase 2 – Secondary Expansion: Imitative entrepreneurial processes follow, pushing the economy further from *b* to *c*, where *c* > *b*.
- Phase 3 – Liquidation: The system seeks a new equilibrium consistent with the revised time preferences. Some of the investments initiated during Phase 2 must be liquidated, as they were the temporary product of euphoric expectations. The economy stabilizes at point *d*, where *b* < *d* < *c*.

63 Further specific cases related to fiscal policies are summarized in Ferlito (2012).

Case 2: Pure Monetary Cycle (MC)

- Phase 1 – Primary Expansion: Initiated by a monetary expansion, the economy moves from a to b_1, where $b_1 > a$ and $b_1 > b$ (the latter referring to the corresponding point in the NC case).
- Phase 2 – Secondary Expansion: Imitative processes amplify the boom, driving the system from b_1 to c_1, where $c_1 > b_1$ and $c_1 > c$.
- Phase 3 – Liquidation: As monetary distortions accumulate and the demand for consumer goods overtakes that for investment goods, the unsustainability of the growth path becomes evident. The system adjusts toward a new equilibrium at d_1, where $b_1 < d_1 < c_1$.
- Phase 4 – Crisis: Liquidation deepens into a full-fledged crisis, accompanied by capital destruction and deflation. The process concludes at point e_1, where $a < e_1 < d_1$, or possibly $a > e_1$, depending on the severity of the downturn.

Case 3: Hybrid Cycle

- Phase 1 – Primary Expansion: Stimulated by a change in intertemporal preferences, the economy moves from a to b_2, where $b_2 > a$.
- Phase 2a – Secondary Expansion: Imitative entrepreneurial behaviour propels the system from b_2 to c_2, where $c_2 > b_2$.
- Phase 2b – Tertiary Expansion: A subsequent monetary expansion adds further momentum to the boom, shifting the system from c_2 to d_2, where $d_2 > c_2$.
- Phase 3 – Liquidation: The economy begins to realign with the new time preferences. Some of the initiatives undertaken during Phases 2a and 2b must be liquidated, as they were driven by temporary exuberance. The system settles at e_2, located between c_2 and d_2.
- Phase 4 – Crisis: Monetary disorder intensifies the liquidation process, leading to capital destruction and deflation. The crisis culminates at point f_2, positioned above a but below the preceding peaks, depending on its severity.

Figure 5.8: Natural, monetary and hybrid cycles, stylized representation.

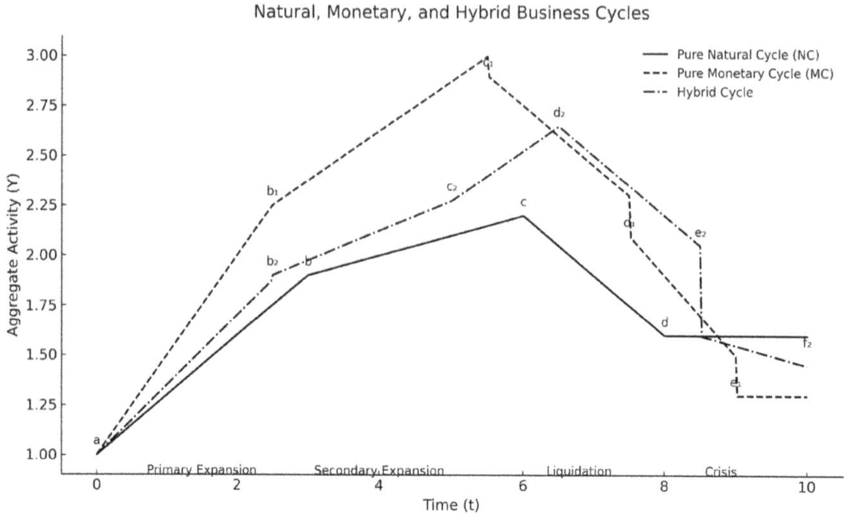

4.3. A growing post-Wicksellian consensus

A crucial point for a "new" realization that discretionary monetary policy can drive interest rates to a level which is not consistent with a sustainable growth path even *within* a context of price stability is stated by Taylor (1993a), where the famous Taylor Rule is presented (Taylor, 1993a, p. 202[64]). The success of the rule is probably due to the fact that it «synthesized (and provided a compromise between) competing schools of thought in a language devoid of rhetorical passion» (Asso and Leeson, 2007, p. 5).

Focusing on short-term interest rates as the main tool for monetary policy, the rule, which aims at being prescriptive (Khan, 2007, pp. 64 and 68), suggests how interest rates should be accommodated in reaction to fluctuations in the levels of prices and output, so as to maintain an inflation target of 2%. Indeed, the rule, in its simplicity includes both the Keynesian focus on output (*y*) and the Wicksell/Fisher tradition on the price level (*p*).

The reason why I consider the Taylor Rule a paradigmatic point of arrival – or departure, depending on one's perspective – in the post-Wicksellian tradition is that it is clear how John Taylor identifies

64 Original formulation: $r = p + .5y + .5(p - 2) + 2$.

disturbances created by an interest rate where it is and not where it should be. In fact, his approach can be seen as a formalization of the natural rate hypothesis (Nelson, 2007, p. 131).

In line with what has been explained in the previous sections, Taylor (2007) recognizes that boom-and-bust cycles are produced by monetary excesses, identified by federal funds rate below what would have been suggested by his rule.

Figure 5.9: Federal funds rate, actual and counterfactual, %.

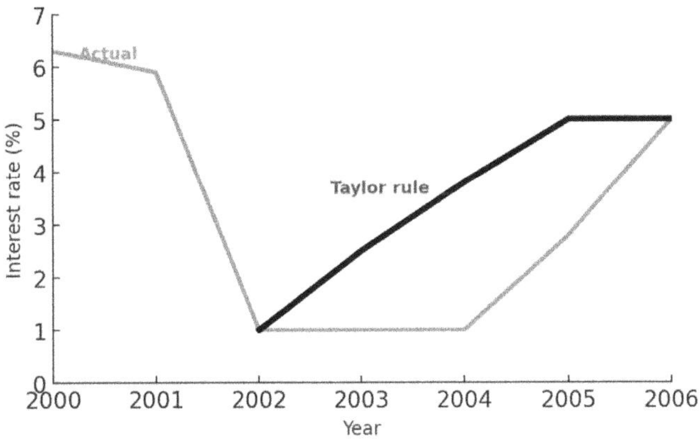

Source: Re-elaborated from Taylor (2009, p. 17).

Furthermore, as per the model previously described, Taylor (2007, p. 165) explains that the bust can be understood only by looking at how the boom was created, and he identifies monetary expansion, via low interest rates, at the root of the Great Recession.

The biggest difference with the approach embraced here, as will be clear in the policy section, is that Taylor suggests that NR can clearly be identified and calculated, therefore the principle of time preference is ignored, making NR unrelated to OR. It follows that the "right" level of interest rate can, according to Taylor, be fixed by the authorities without the need for market forces to be at work. To my natural objection that the natural rate can only emerge and evolve in the market (like any other price), in the struggle to reflect an evolving originary rate, it may be added that a simple rule like the Taylor's one has indeed the advantage of simplicity, but, at the same time, it sacrifices complexity, deals with variables that are not observable (like potential output) and simplifies the concept of inflation (Kohn, 2007).

The major positive points of the Taylor Rule are:

- Relaunching in mainstream economic circles that monetary disturbances can produce real circuit disturbances (via asset market disturbances) even with prices under control
- Indeed, the natural rate of interest should enter into the picture of policy evaluations
- A rule-based policy approach is superior to a discretionary one (Taylor, 1993b, p. 5), as a rule-based policy «is predictable and predictable policy is more effective because it exploits the expectations channel of policy transmission» (Wieland, 2024, p. 36).

An even more explicit reference to Wicksell, and the idea that monetary policy rules should be inspired by the basic Wicksellian system where CBR is adjusted to follow price movements, can be found in several works by MIT professor Athanasios Orphanides. For example, in Orphanides and Williams (2007) we read:

> We find that simple difference rules that do not require any knowledge of the economy's natural rates are particularly well suited to ensure medium-run inflation control when natural rates are highly uncertain. These rules share commonalities with the simple robust strategy first proposed by Wicksell (1936 [1898]), who, after defining the natural interest rate, pointed out that precise knowledge about it, though desirable, was neither feasible nor necessary for policy implementation aimed toward maintaining price stability.

The authors then move into directly quoting Wicksell and his stress that the rate of interest should follow price movements; they concluded that «the main cause of the instability of prices resides in the instability of the banks to follow this rule».

The main strength in such an approach, according to the proponents, is the fact of not having to repeat any estimation for the natural values of interest rate and unemployment, which, they emphasize, are non-observable entities[65] (Orphanides and Williams, 2002). Furthermore, the way indicated by Orphanides is an attempt to design a policy mechanism which does not need to rely on unrealistic informational assumptions (Orphanides, 2000). The main weakness, instead, is moving

65 Like any other equilibrium or market-clearing price, to be true. In fact, market-clearing prices only emerge in the market and cannot be known in advance.

from a mechanical system to another, failing again to recognize the emergent nature of the market process.

A post-Wicksellian reading of 20th Century crises which is more in line with the Austrian school of interpretation but which emerged from mainstream economic circles (the Bank for International Settlements) can be found in White (2006), which emphasized the role of financial liberalization and globalization.

> The dynamics of the process can be described in the following way. Buoyed by justified optimism about some particular development, credit is extended which drives up related asset prices. This both encourages fixed investment (as per Tobin's q), and increases collateral values, which supports still more credit expansion. With time, and underpinned by an associated increase in output growth, this process leads to increasing willingness to take on risks ("irrational exuberance"), which gives further impetus to the credit cycle. Borio et al (2001) provide evidence that credit spreads, asset prices, internal bank risk ratings, ratings from agencies and loan loss provisions all demonstrate this tendency to procyclicality. Subsequently, as exaggerated expectations concerning both risk and return are eventually disappointed, the whole process goes into reverse. As undershoot replaces overshoot, the dampening effect on the real economy of high debt levels and weak investment becomes particularly notable. Frequently, but not necessarily, the financial system is itself weakened and exerts a further dampening effect on the real economy (White, 2006, p. 9).

The description resembles what we have seen with the description of the monetary cycles. The thesis is reinforced by another economist from BIS, Claudio Borio, who showed how «*the financial boom should not just precede the bust but cause it*. The boom sows the seeds of the subsequent bust, as a result of the vulnerabilities that build up during this phase» (Borio, 2012, p. 8). In the same paper, the author calls for a better understanding of business fluctuations to abandon equilibrium models and to rediscover the disequilibrium, as stressed by Wicksell (Borio, 2012, p. 11).

It is now time to conclude with a list of policy recommendations inspired by the view herewith presented.

5. Policy suggestions

It must be clarified from the start of this section that, consistent with the title of this paper, I will not discuss here monetary policy suggestions for price stability. That would require an additional lengthy discussion on the nature of price increases, distinguishing, in particular, between inflation *stricto sensu* and adjustments in relative prices[66]. Therefore, the present section will deal only with policy suggestions aimed at reducing fluctuations and maximizing employment.

It also needs to be added that the present paper is aimed at stimulating discussion within academic circles, and so it dares to present ideas and proposals that may look unrealistic or very difficult to implement. However, I believe it is important to advance provocative ideas that can help us think out of conventional boundaries.

However, while some of the proposals listed below may seem eclectic, they will never be overambitious in the sense of viewing policymakers as mechanics who can fix a machine: the economy is not a machine and it does not evolve in a technical way. Orphanides (2003, pp. 660-661) seems to echo Hayek (1974) when he writes that a «willingness to recognize our ignorance and lower our stabilization objectives accordingly may then be the safest defense against destabilizing fine-tuning. [...] The continuing fallacy is to downplay the degree of our ignorance and at times perhaps mistake the good fortune of the recent past for wisdom. Must we repeat such errors before we learn to respect the limits of stabilization?». My policy suggestions will follow in that tune very much.

My proposals are easy to understand and, while inspired by the Wicksellian connection, will not present any Wicksell-inspired automatic mechanism. Even Taylor (1993b, p. 5), whose rule belongs to the field of centrally-designed mechanical adjustment tools, warned against the risk of a mechanistic approach to policy making: «a policy rule need not be a mechanical formula. It can be implemented and operated more informally by policymakers who recognize the general instrument responses that operating the rule requires judgment and cannot be done by computer».

While not implying a mechanical approach, reforms must also move away from the discretionary approach which have been followed in the past decades. Our proposals will be inspired by:

- The primacy of bottom-up and price-driven discovery processes over centrally-planned price mechanisms, which implies believing

66 For my perspective on the topic see Hearn and Ferlito (2021).

that individuals can fabricate contractual terms able to moderate economic turbulence (Wagner, 2020, p. 47);

- The primacy of the rule of law over the rule of men.

In fact, monetary policy is very much guided by central bankers' discretion, and it is necessary for monetary (and fiscal) authorities to be «constrained by a "higher law" that the monetary authority itself cannot change and is simple enough to admit minimal interpretive latitude» (Boettke, Salter and Smith, 2021, p. 147).

5.1. Suggestion 1: Abolishing CBR

The reader is probably by now ready to understand where our approach is going:

- An originary rate (OR) exists that measures the intertemporal structure of preferences.
- In the market for loanable funds and in the absence of central banks, the supply side (*S*) interacts with the demand side (*I*) generating different monetary rates (MORs); we called market rate (MR) the emerging market-clearing rate able to grant coordination of plans between savers and borrowers.
- Market forces (price mechanism) tend to drive MR towards an equilibrium level – the natural rate (NR) – which would grant equality between *S* and *I*; NR is the reflection on financial markets of the OR.
- The signalling power operated by the price mechanism is jammed by the existence of the central bank rate (CBR).

The natural conclusion of such a reasoning is abolishing the CBR and any artificial alteration of the price mechanism. This is consistent with what we argued in section 3.3., where we concluded that the condition for price stability, sustainable growth and social welfare is MR = NR = OR.

While it is true, as argued in Orphanides and Williams (2002), that the natural rate is in some ways an abstraction, it is also true that any equilibrium price is.

If a certain café serves espresso at MYR 7 and it stays in business, it means that that price level makes enough customers happy for the business to stay open. Is there another price level which will make more customers happy? Maybe yes, maybe not, but this cannot be known ex-ante. It can be discovered only through an entrepreneurial process of price change and acceptance of risk. But MYR 7 is a price which allows a degree of plan coordination allowing the shop to remain in business. Surely MYR 7 is a value tending towards equilibrium – an equilibrium which cannot be known.

In an exchange of emails I had with Professor Orphanides, the MIT scholar used this argument to justify the existence of a centrally-defined level of interest rates. But that argument could be used to justify any price control, while the harm produced by price controls is one of the few topics on which many economists agree.

My reasoning is the opposite of Professor Orphanides's: although unhampered markets do not produce perfect results, the price mechanism allows a better degree of coordination to emerge when compared with the situation in which prices are controlled. The same perspective should therefore be transferred to the market for loanable funds.

Such a reform would allow the first point I mentioned as the source of monetary disorder[67].

5.2. Suggestion 2: On the banking system

Today, money created through banks making loans account for around 80% of the money in modern economies, while central bank reserves account for 15-17% of the total and cash/notes being only 3-5% (Rangeley and White, 2024, p. 10). A first step in recognizing the importance of bank loans and their current effect in creating monetary disorders would be to account for them when measuring the monetary aggregates; in particular, the amount of bank loans that should be considered as part of M2.

Secondly, and to control the second source of monetary disorder previously mentioned and described, the reserve amount to be taken into account in order to know if it is possible for the bank to issue an additional loan should be calculated by deducting from the amount of available deposits those in the name of the loan beneficiary as they were *before* the loan application. In this way, the above-described accounting trick would be avoided.

This suggestion would find a natural complement in the previous one: after having abolished CBR, an increased demand for loanable funds

67 See points 1., 2. and 3. in section 4.2.

would push the market-clearing interest rate upwards, eventually attracting new deposits (therefore increasing the amount of available reserves) and thus increasing the ability of the market process to make new loans possible because of a genuine interaction between supply and demand.

5.3. Suggestion 3: Balanced budgets

The third source of monetary disorder must be addressed recognizing that, without fiscal discipline, the effectiveness of monetary policy efforts will be extremely reduced. It is thus essential limiting government spending and reintroducing the primacy of balanced budgets.

Budgets cannot be left adrift in the sea of democratic politics. They must be constructed within constraints that impose external form and coherence on the particular decisions about size and distribution which an annual budget reflects. The elected politicians, who must be responsive to their constituents, the governmental bureaucracy as well as the electorate, need something by way of an external and "superior" rule that will allow them to forestall the persistent demands for an increased flow of public-spending benefits along with reduced levels of taxation (Buchanan and Wagner, 1977, p. 182).

Such a rule needs to be simple and straightforward; it must offer clear criteria for adherence and for violation and it must reflect and express values held by the citizens (Buchanan and Wagner, 1977, p. 183). In «this regard, the simplest rule is to re-establish the primacy and superiority of balanced budgets, which will finally destroy the unhealthy belief in the existence of free lunches» (Buchanan and Wagner, 1977, pp. 184-185). Such a rule should incorporate an automatic adjustment mechanism in the case of budgeted outlays that are projected to exceed tax receipts (Buchanan and Wagner, 1977, p. 185). For example, if the projected balanced budget shows an error "and a budget deficit beyond specified limits occurs, federal outlays shall be automatically adjusted downward to restore projected balance within a period of three months" (Buchanan and Wagner, 1977, pp. 187-188). Eventual surpluses, instead, should be used to retire existing debt.

Concluding remarks

This chapter has advanced a vision of monetary policy grounded in realism, humility, and the recognition of complexity. It has argued that the economy cannot be engineered through mechanical rules or discretionary interventions but must be understood as an evolving process guided by individual choices, expectations, and intertemporal coordination.

The core message is that monetary policy should not pursue price stability as an end in itself, but as a means toward broader goals—sustainable growth and social welfare. These objectives are attainable only when the market rate of interest is allowed to align dynamically with both the natural and originary rates (MR = NR = OR). Such correspondence ensures that saving and investment decisions remain coordinated, preventing the cumulative distortions that generate financial excesses and boom-and-bust cycles.

Sustainable growth, in this view, is not the elimination of fluctuations but the moderation of those distortions that arise from exogenous monetary interference. Likewise, social welfare does not depend on permanent full employment or artificial stimulation, but on maintaining a stable monetary framework that allows the market process to allocate resources efficiently.

Ultimately, the argument developed here calls for a re-foundation of monetary policy upon the principles of spontaneous order and respect for market-generated prices. Only by freeing the interest rate from administrative control can monetary institutions recover their coordinating role within a complex and adaptive economic system—one that, left to its own discovery process, promotes both prosperity and stability over time.

References

Asso, P.F. and Leeson, R. (2007), *Monetary Policy Rules: From Adam Smith to John Taylor*, in E.F. Koenig, R. Leeson and G.A. Kahn (Eds.), *The Taylor Rule and the Transformation of Monetary Policy*, Stanford, Hoover Institution Press, pp. 3-62.

Albrecht, B. and Hendrickson, J. (2023), *What Is Price Theory?*, «Economic Forces», 5 October, https://www.economicforces.xyz/p/what-is-price-theory.

Andersson, D.E. (2021), *An Introduction to Spontaneous Orders*, «CME EduPaper», 6, Subang Jaya, Center for Market Education.

Bagus, P. and Ferlito, C. (2022), *Why Monetary Policy Should Not Avoid Market Price Deflation*, «CME Policy Paper», 4, Subang Jaya, Center for Market Education.

Barro, R.J. (1995), *Inflation and Economic Growth*, «NBER Working Paper Series», No 5326.

Benigno, P. (2025), *Monetary Economics and Policy. A Foundation for Modern Currency Systems*, Princeton and Oxford, Princeton University Press.

Bernanke, B. (2007), *The Great Moderation*, in E.F. Koenig, R. Leeson and G.A. Kahn (Eds.), *The Taylor Rule and the Transformation of Monetary Policy*, Stanford, Hoover Institution Press, pp. 145-162.

Birner, J. (2002), *The Cambridge Controversies in Capital Theory: A Study in the Logic of Theory Development*, London, Routledge.

Boettke, P.J., Salter, A.W. and Smith, D.J. (2021), *Money and the Rule of Law. Generality and Predictability in Monetary Institutions*, Cambridge, Cambridge University Press.

Böhm-Bawerk, E. von (1884), *Capital and Interest. A Critical History of Economical Theory*, London and New York, MacMillan, 1890.

Böhm-Bawerk, E. von (1889), *The Positive Theory of Capital*, New York, G.E. Stechert, 1930.

Bordo, M.D. and Jonung, L. (1994), *Monetary Regimes, Inflation and Monetary Reform: An Essay in Honor of Axel Leijonhufvud*, Working Paper No 1994-07, New Brunswick, Rutgers University, Department of Economics.

Borio, C. (2012), *The financial cycle and macroeconomics: What have we learnt?*, «BIS Working Papers», No 395.

Borio, C. and Gambacorta, L. (2017), *Monetary policy and bank lending in a low interest rate environment: diminishing effectiveness?*, «BIS Working Papers», No 612.

Bourne, R.A. (Ed.) (2024), *The War on Prices. How Popular Misconceptions about Inflation, Prices, And Value Create Bad Policy*, Washington, Cato Institute.

Bregu, K. (2021), *The Importance of Understanding the Market Process*, «CME EduPaper», 7, Subang Jaya, Center for Market Education.

Bresciani-Turroni, C. (1936), *The Theory of Saving*, «Economica», 3, 10, pp. 161-181.

Buchanan, J.M. and Wagner, R.E. (1977), *Democracy in Deficit. The Political Legacy of Lord Keynes*, Carmel, Liberty Fund, 2000.

Chancellor, E. (2022), *The Price of Time. The Real Story of Interest*, New York, Atlantic Monthly Press.

Chari, A. and Blair Henry, P. (2024), *Disinflation and the Stock Market: Third-World Lessons for First-World Monetary Policy*, in M.D. Bordo, J.H. Cochrane and J.B. Taylor (Eds.), *Getting Monetary Policy Back on Track*, Stanford, Hoover Institution Press, pp. 137-162.

Colander, D. and Kupers, R. (2014), *Complexity and the Art of Public Policy. Solving Society's Problems from the Bottom Up*, Princeton and Oxford, Princeton University Press.

Connolly, B. (2023), *You Always Hurt the One You Love. Central Banks and the Murder of Capitalism*, Lewes, Unicorn.

Cowen, T. and Tabarrok, A. (2010), *Modern Principles: Microeconomics*, New York, Worth, 2015.

Coyne, C. and Coyne, R. (Eds.) (2015), *Flaws and Ceilings: Price Controls and the Damage They Cause*, London, Institute of Economic Affairs.

Cutsinger, B. and Salter, A.W. (2024), *Does Price Theory Have a Future?*, Free Market Institute Research Paper No. 4613078, available at SSRN: https://ssrn.com/abstract=4613078 or http://dx.doi.org/10.2139/ssrn.4613078.

Daou, M. and Marciano, A. (forthcoming), *Teaching Economics as Political Economy*, in G. Ianulardo, J. Davis and R. Crespo (Eds.), *Edward Elgar Handbook for Teaching Philosophy to Economists*, Cheltenham and Northampton, Edward Elgar.

Federal Reserve (1937), *Objectives of Monetary Policy*, «Federal Reserve Bulletin», September, pp. 827-828.

Ferlito, C. (2011), *Sylos Labini's Unpublished Notes on Schumpeter's* Business Cycles, «Quarterly Journal of Austrian Economics», 14, 1, pp. 88-129.

Ferlito, C. (2012), *Garrison's Capital-Based Macroeconomics: The Role of Deficit, Credit Control and Taxation*, in M.-A. Galindo Martin and C. Nardi Spiller (Eds.), *Public Finance: Lessons from the Past and Effects on the Future*, New York, Nova Science Publishers, pp. 105-122.

Ferlito, C. (2013), *Phoenix Economics. From Crisis to Renascence*, New York, Nova Science Publishers.

Ferlito, C. (2014), *The Natural Cycle: Why Economic Fluctuations Are Inevitable. A Schumpeterian Extension of the Austrian Business Cycle Theory*, «Journal of Reviews on Global Economics», 3, pp. 200-219.

Ferlito, C. (2016), *Hermeneutics of Capital. A Post-Austrian Theory for a Kaleidic World*, New York, Novinka.

Ferlito, C. (2022), *Axel Leijonhufvud: A personal recollection from an Austrian perspective*, «PSL Quarterly Review», 75, 302, pp. 299-310.

Ferlito, C. (2023), *History and Economic Theorizing*, in D. Howden and P. Bagus (Eds.), *The Emergence of a Tradition: Essays in Honor of Jesús Huerta de Soto*, Volume I: *Money and the Market Process*, London, Palgrave MacMillan, pp. 113-121, https://doi.org/10.1007/978-3-031-17414-8_11.

Ferlito, C. and Calzolari, S.M. (2023), *The Silicon Valley Bank Collapse And The Business Cycle*, «Business Today», 15 March, https://www.businesstoday.com.my/2023/03/15/the-silicon-valley-bank-collapse-and-the-business-cycle/.

Ferlito, C. and Chong, N. (2024), *Wake-up call from a new 'Black Monday'*, «New Straits Times», 8 August, p. 5.

Fetter, F.A. (1904), *Principles of Economics*, New York, The Century Co.

Fetter, F.A. (1914), *Interest Theories, Old and New*, in J.M. Herbener (Ed.), *The Pure Time-Preference Theory of Interest*, Auburn, Ludwig von Mises Institute, 2011, pp. 127-157.

Fisher, I. (1906), *The Nature of Capital and Income*, New York, MacMillan.

Fisher, I. (1907), *The Rate of Interest: Its Nature, Determination, and Relation to Economic Phenomena*, New York, MacMillan.

Fisher, I. (1911), *Impatience Theory of Interest*, «Scientia», 9.

French, D.E. (2011), *Foreword*, in J.M. Herbener (Ed.), *The Pure Time-Preference Theory of Interest*, Auburn, Ludwig von Mises Institute, 2011, pp. 7-10.

Garrison, R.W. (1988), *Professor Rothbard and the Theory of Interest*, in J.M. Herbener (Ed.), *The Pure Time-Preference Theory of Interest*, Auburn, Ludwig von Mises Institute, 2011, pp. 159-172.

Garrison, R.W. (2001), *Time and Money. The macroeconomics of capital structure*, London and New York, Routledge.

Hayek, F.A. von (1927), *On the Problem of Interest Theory*, in L.H. White (Ed.), *The Collected Works of F.A. Hayek*, Volume XI: *Capital and Interest*, Chicago, The University of Chicago Press, pp. 20-31.

Hayek, F.A. von (1928), *Intertemporal Price Equilibrium and Movements in the Value of Money*, in S. Kresge (Ed.), *The Collected Works of F.A. Hayek*, Volume V: *Good Money, Part I: The New World*, Indianapolis, Liberty Fund, 1990, pp. 186-227.

Hayek, F.A. von (1931), *Prices and Production*, New York, Augustus M. Kelly, 1967.

Hayek, F.A. von (1932), *A Note on the Development of the Doctrine of 'Forced Saving'*, «Quarterly Journal of Economics», XLVII, pp. 123-133.

Hayek, F.A. von (1933), *Price Expectations, Monetary Disturbances and Malinvestments*, in *Profits, Interest and Investment and Other Essays on the Theory of Industrial Fluctuations*, Clifton, Augustus M. Kelley, 1975, pp. 135-156.

Hayek, F.A. von (1939), *Profits, Interest and Investment*, in *Profits, Interest and Investment and Other Essays on the Theory of Industrial Fluctuations*, Clifton, Augustus M. Kelley, 1975, pp. 3-71.

Hayek, F.A. von (1941), *The Pure Theory of Capital*, in L.H. White (Ed.), *The Collected Works of F.A. Hayek*, Volume XII: *The Pure Theory of Capital*, Indianapolis, Liberty Fund, 2007.

Hayek, F.A. von (1945a), *The Use of Knowledge in Society*, «American Economic Review», XXXV, 4, pp. 519-530.

Hayek, F.A. von (1945b), *Time Preference and Productivity: A Reconsideration*, «Economica», 12, pp. 22-25.

Hayek, F.A. von (1950), *Full Employment, Planning and Inflation*, «Institute of Public Affairs Review», IV, 6, pp. 174-184.

Hayek, F.A. von (1974), *The Pretence of Knowledge*, Lecture to the memory of Alfred Nobel, December 11, https://www.nobelprize.org/prizes/economic-sciences/1974/hayek/lecture/.

Hayek, F.A. von (1979), *Unemployment and Monetary Policy. Governments as Generator of the "Business Cycle"*, San Francisco, Cato Institute, 1980.

Hearn, J. and Ferlito, C. (2021), *The cause of inflation, its link to unemployment and the need for sound monetary control*, «CME EduPaper», 8, Subang Jaya, Center for Market Education.

Herbener, J.M. (2011), *Introduction*, in J.M. Herbener (Ed.), *The Pure Time-Preference Theory of Interest*, Auburn, Ludwig von Mises Institute, 2011, pp. 11-58.

Heymann, D. and Leijonhufvud, A. (1995), *High Inflation: The Arne Ryde Memorial Lectures*, Oxford, Clarendon Press.

Huerta de Soto, J. (2000), *The Austrian School. Market Order and Entrepreneurial Creativity*, Cheltenham and Northampton, Edward Elgar, 2010.

Hülsmann, J.G. (2008), *The Ethics of Money Production*, Auburn, Ludwig von Mises Institute.

Issing, O. (2003), *Monetary and Financial Stability: Is There a Trade-off?*, https://www.ecb.europa.eu/press/key/date/2003/html/sp030329.en.html.

Kahn, G.A. (2007), *The Taylor Rule and the Practice of Central Banking*, in E.F. Koenig, R. Leeson and G.A. Kahn (Eds.), *The Taylor Rule and the Transformation of Monetary Policy*, Stanford, Hoover Institution Press, pp. 63-101.

Kay, J. and King, M. (2020), *Radical Uncertainty. Decision-Making beyond the Numbers*, New York, W.W. Norton, 2021.

Keynes, J.M. (1936), *Teoria generale dell'occupazione, dell'interesse e della moneta*, Milan, Milano Finanza, 2006.

Khor, H.E., Guajardo, J. and Peiris, S.J. (2018), *Evolution of Monetary Policy Frameworks*, A. Corbacho and S.J. Peiris (Eds.), *The Asean Way. Sustaining Growth and Stability*, Washington, The International Monetary Fund, Chapter 2.

Kirzner, I.M. (1993), *The Pure Time-Preference Theory of Interest: An Attempt at Clarification*, in J.M. Herbener (Ed.), *The Pure Time-Preference Theory of Interest*, Auburn, Ludwig von Mises Institute, 2011, pp. 99-126.

Kohn, D.L. (2007), *It's Not So Simple*, in E.F. Koenig, R. Leeson and G.A. Kahn (Eds.), *The Taylor Rule and the Transformation of Monetary Policy*, Stanford, Hoover Institution Press, pp. 173-182.

Lachmann, L.M (1973), *Macro-Economic Thinking and the Market Economy: An Essay on the Neglect of the Micro-Foundations and its Consequences*, London, The Institute of Economic Affairs, 1973.

Laidler, D. (2003), *The price level, relative prices and economic stability: aspects of the interwar debate*, «BIS Working Papers», No 136.

Leijonhufvud, A. (1975), *Costs and Consequences of Inflation*, UCLA Economics Working Papers No 58, UCLA Department of Economics.

Leijonhufvud, A. (1979), *The Wicksell Connection: Variations on a Theme*, in *Information and Coordination: Essays in Macroeconomic Theory*, New York and Oxford, Oxford University Press, 1981, pp. 131-202.

Leijonhufvud, A. (2009), *Out of the corridor: Keynes and the crisis*, «Cambridge Journal of Economics», 33, 4, pp. 741-757.

Levy, M.D. (2024), *The Fed: Bad Forecasts and Misguided Monetary Policy*, in M.D. Bordo, J.H. Cochrane and J.B. Taylor (Eds.), *Getting Monetary Policy Back on Track*, Stanford, Hoover Institution Press, pp. 261-290.

Lindahl, E. (1919), *Studies in the Theory of Capital and Income*, London, Allen & Unwin, 1939.

Mankiw, N.G. (2009), *It May Be Time for the Fed to Go Negative*, «New York Times», 18 April.

McCaffrey, M. (2020), *An Introduction to Value, Cost, and Price*, «CME EduPaper», 5, Subang Jaya, Center for Market Education.

McCaffrey, M.C., Salerno, J.T. and Dorobat, C.E. (forthcoming), *The History of Economic Thought as a Living Laboratory*, «Cambridge Journal of Economics».

McLeay, M., Radia, A. and Thomas, R. (2014), *Money Creation in the Modern Economy*, «Bank of England Quarterly Bulletin», 54, 1, pp. 14-27.

Meacci, F. and Ferlito, C. (2018), *The classical roots of the Austrian theory of capital and entrepreneurship*, «The Review of Austrian Economics», 31, pp. 315-339, https://doi.org/10.1007/s11138-017-0407-y.

Menger, C. (1871), *Principles of Economics*, Auburn, Ludwig von Mises Institute.

Minsky, H.P. (1982), *Can "It" Happen Again? Essays on Instability and Finance*, London and New York, Routledge, 2016.

Minsky, H.P. (2008), *Stabilizing an Unstable Economy*, New York, McGraw-Hill.

Mises, L. von (1949), *Human Action: The Rate of Interest*, in J.M. Herbener (Ed.), *The Pure Time-Preference Theory of Interest*, Auburn, Ludwig von Mises Institute, 2011, p 67-84.

Nelson, E. (2007), *A Comparison with Milton Friedman*, in E.F. Koenig, R. Leeson and G.A. Kahn (Eds.), *The Taylor Rule and the Transformation of Monetary Policy*, Stanford, Hoover Institution Press, pp. 103-138.

Orphanides, A. (2000), *The Quest for Prosperity without Inflation*, «European Central Bank Working Paper Series», 15.

Orphanides, A. (2003), *The quest for prosperity without inflation*, «Journal of Monetary Economics», 50, pp. 633-663.

Orphanides, A. and Williams, J.C. (2002), *Robust Monetary Policy Rules with Unknown Natural Rates*, Paper prepared for the September 2002 Brookings Panel on Economic Activity.

Orphanides, A. and Williams, J.C. (2004), *The Decline of Activist Stabilization Policy: Natural Rate Misperceptions, Learning and Expectations*, International Finance Discussion Paper No 804, Board of Governors of the Federal Reserve System.

Orphanides, A. and Williams, J.C. (2007), *Inflation Targeting and Imperfect Knowledge*, in F. Mishkin and K. Schmidt-Hebbel (Eds.), *Series on Central Banking, Analysis, and Economic Policies X: Monetary Policy under Inflation Targeting*, Santiago, Central Bank of Chile.

Palley, T. (2023), *The theory of monetary-disorder: debt finance, existing assets, and the consequences of prolonged ultra-easy policy*, «Paolo Sylos Labini Quarterly Review», 76, 307, pp. 315-335.

Phaneuf, E. (2020), *Can governments intervene in the market in a rational way? The problems of knowledge and economic calculation*, «CME EduPaper», 4, Subang Jaya, Center for Market Education.

Phelps, E.S. (1985), *Political Economy. An Introductory Text*, New York and London, W.W. Norton.

Phillips, C.A., McManus, T.F. and Nelson, R.W. (1937), *Banking and the Business Cycle. A Study of the Great Depression in the United States*, New York, The MacMillan Company.

Prychitko, D.L. (2010), *Competing Explanations of the Minsky Moment: The Financial Instability Hypothesis in Light of Austrian Theory*, «The Review of Austrian Economics», 23, pp. 199-221.

Quarles, R. (2024), *Silicon Valley Bank: What Happened? What Should We Do about It?*, in M.D. Bordo, J.H. Cochrane and J.B. Taylor (Eds.), *Getting Monetary Policy Back on Track*, Stanford, Hoover Institution Press, pp. 79-101.

Rangeley, M. and White, W. (2024), *How Money Is Created in a Modern Economy*, in M. Rangeley (Ed.), *The Age of Debt Bubbles. An Analysis of Debt Crises, Asset Bubbles and Monetary Policy*, Cham, Springer, pp. 3-24.

Rangeley, M., Koppl R. and Richer, H. (2024), *Business Cycles, Debt Bubbles and the Monetary System*, in M. Rangeley (Ed.), *The Age of Debt Bubbles. An Analysis of Debt Crises, Asset Bubbles and Monetary Policy*, Cham, Springer, pp. 25-42.

Rothbard, M.N. (1987), *Time Preference*, in J.M. Herbener (Ed.), *The Pure Time-Preference Theory of Interest*, Auburn, Ludwig von Mises Institute, 2011, pp. 59-66.

Schumpeter, J.A. (1911), *The Theory of Economic Development*, New Brunswick and London, Transaction Publishers, 1983.

Schumpeter, J.A. (1939), *Business Cycles: A Theoretical, Historical and Statistical Analysis of the Capitalist Process*, Chevy Chase and Mansfield Centre, Bartleby's Books and Martino Publishing, 2005.

Schumpeter, J.A. (1954), *History of Economic Analysis*, London and New York, Routledge, 2006.

Sylos Labini, P. (1987), *The Theory of Employment, too, is historically conditioned*, «Banca Nazionale del Lavoro Quarterly Review», 40, 163, pp. 379-435.

Sylos Labini, P. (1992), *Elementi di dinamica economica*, Bari, Laterza.

Taylor, J.B. (1993a), *Discretion versus policy rules in practice*, «Carnegie-Rochester Conference Series on Public Policy», 39, pp. 195-214.

Taylor, J.B. (1993b), *Macroeconomic Policy in a World Economy. From Econometric Design to Practical Operation*, New York and London, W.W. Norton & Company.

Taylor, J.B. (2007), *The Great Deviation*, in E.F. Koenig, R. Leeson and G.A. Kahn (Eds.), *The Taylor Rule and the Transformation of Monetary Policy*, Stanford, Hoover Institution Press, pp. 163-172.

Taylor, J.B. (2009), *Getting Off Track. How Government Actions and Interventions Caused, Prolonged, and Worsened the Financial Crisis*, Stanford, Hoover Institution Press.

Wagner, R.E. (2020), *Macroeconomics as Systems Theory. Transcending the Micro-Macro Dichotomy*, London, Palgrave Macmillan.

Weizsäcker, C.C. von and Krämer, H.M. (2019), *Saving and Investment in the Twenty-First Century. The Great Divergence*, Cham, Springer.

White, L.H. (2007), *Editor's Introduction*, in Hayek (1941), pp. xiii-xxxvi.

White, W.R. (2006), *Is price stability enough?*, «BIS Working Papers», No 205.

White, W. (2024), *Why the Monetary Policy Framework in Advanced Countries Needs Fundamental Reform*, in M. Rangeley (Ed.), *The Age of Debt Bubbles. An Analysis of Debt Crises, Asset Bubbles and Monetary Policy*, Cham, Springer, pp. 85-101.

Wicksell, K. (1893), *Value, Capital and Rent*, London, George Allen & Unwin, 1954.

Wicksell, K. (1898), *Interest and Price*, London, George Allen & Unwin, 1962.

Wieland, V. (2024), *The Taylor Rule at Thirty: Still Useful to Get the Fed Back on Track*, in M.D. Bordo, J.H. Cochrane and J.B. Taylor (Eds.), *Getting Monetary Policy Back on Track*, Stanford, Hoover Institution Press, pp. 31-53.

Yeager, L.B. (1956), *A Cash-Balance Interpretation of Depression*, in G. Selgin (Ed.), *The Fluttering Veil. Essays on Monetary Disequilibrium*, Indianapolis, Liberty Fund, pp. 3-17.

Yeager, L.B. and Hanke, S.H. (2024), *Capital, Interest, and Waiting. Controversies, Puzzles, and New Additions to Capital Theory*, London, Palgrave MacMillan.

PART IV

ENTREPRENEURSHIP, INNOVATION AND MARKET PROCESS

CHAPTER 6

A Fresh Look at Competition: Oligopolies, Innovation, Entrepreneurship and the Market Process[68]

1. Competition: True and false

When I was studying economics at the University of Verona in the early 2000s, our microeconomics textbook (which I still have in my library) described the characteristics of a perfectly competitive market as follows:

- Atomization of the market;
- Homogeneity of the product and anonymity of both producers and consumers;
- Absence of barriers to firms' entry into or exit from the market;
- Perfect mobility of production factors;
- Perfect knowledge of the prevailing technical and economic conditions;
- No firm can earn extra profits in the long run (Baranzini and Marangoni, 1995, pp. 544-545)[69].

In another very popular textbook, we read that, under perfect competition, the only thing that a firm could decide is how much to produce (Varian, 2007, p. 365).

---

68 Originally published as C. Ferlito (2024), *Competition, Innovation and Concentration. A Nietzschean Essay in Honour of Paolo Sylos Labini*, «CME edupaper», 9, Subang Jaya, Center for Market Education.

69 Similarly, Hayek (1946, pp. 106-107) observed that the textbook features of perfect competition are:

«1. A homogeneous commodity offered and demanded by a large number of relatively small sellers or buyers, none of whom expects to exercise by his action a perceptible influence on price.

2. Free entry into the market and absence of other restraints on the movement of prices and resources.

3. Complete knowledge of the relevant factors on the part of all participants in the market».

As we shall see, Hayek too criticized such a view, noting these features simply describe a state of affairs that is eventually brought about by the process of competition, while the «moving force of economic life is left almost altogether undiscussed».

Like most students, I was mainly concerned with passing the exam, and then I digested the definition and its theoretical implications[70]. It was only after reading O'Driscoll and Rizzo (1985) that I realized how blind I was and how far from the *true* nature of competition the definition learned in university was. «It is well known that in economic theory "competition" means the opposite of its meaning either in ordinary language or in commonsense economic discussions of competition»; indeed the «theory of perfect competition analyses the state of affairs or equilibrium conditions that would exist if all competitive activity ceased. *It is not an approximation but the negation of that activity*» (O'Driscoll and Rizzo, 1985, pp. 136-137).

It is evident – even to the eye of the layman – that the features described by my textbook (and criticized by Hayek (1946)) are the opposite of a process of competition: why compete if there is no profit? Where does competition stand if products are homogeneous and the market share is marginal? Is not the very same idea of competition based on differences? Can we compete if knowledge is already perfect and perfectly possessed by everybody? Such an idea of competition looks more like the description of a static ideal state of affairs. Or it serves even better to describe a centrally planned economy, which is the very opposite of an economic system ruled by market competition.

Among other economists, Schumpeter (1911) recognized – in line with Adam Smith and the classics – that competition is a process and not a state of affairs, and this process is based on the conflict between non-homogeneous elements rather than on elements of equality: a competition is won by virtue of a difference, even if it was simply luck or corruption. And for the Austrian economist, the real competitive process is consumed in the struggle between innovations trying to emerge – driven by the entrepreneur with the means provided by the banker – and traditional products and methods trying to survive – supported by common and predominant sense.

Echoing his teacher Schumpeter, the Italian economist Paolo Sylos Labini (1957, p. 52) observed that the «neoclassical economists' perfect competition has never existed anywhere. The static hypothesis and the application of marginal analysis within it led the neoclassical school to ascribe to competition certain characteristics (in particular, perfect

70 For sake of simplicity, we will refer to the textbook vision as neoclassical perfect competition.

homogeneity of goods, horizontal demand curve for the individual firm) which severely limit the realism of the concept».

If the market is a dynamic process unfolding in time, then such a process cannot have a pre-determined outcome, as is instead assumed in equilibrium models (Lachmann, 1986, p. 4).

But Schumpeter was not the only economist to develop an alternative vision of competition and the market process[71]. What is competition beyond the fictional textbook representation? We will focus here on some economists who tried to explain competitions in a way that is closer to the actual meaning that people associate with the word itself; it is in fact immediately clear that the word competition cannot refer, like it happens in conventional textbooks, to something static and to a state of affairs; competition is indeed *dynamic* and *a process* (as recognized by classical economists; Sylos Labini, 1957, pp. 52-53). Furthermore, it is ontologically based on differences.

1.1. Hayek: Competition as a discovery process

The passage from O'Driscoll and Rizzo (1985) reported above is in line with the critics of the neoclassical vision of competition developed by Nobel laureate F.A. von Hayek (1946, p. 105), who was writing that «what [economists] have been discussing in recent years under the name of 'competition' is not the same thing as what is thus called in ordinary language». In fact, the Austrian economist explained, «what the theory of perfect competition discusses has little claim to be called 'competition' at all», because «this theory throughout assumes that state of affairs already to exist which, according to the truer view of the older theory, the process of competition tends to bring about (or to approximate) and that, if the state of affairs assumed by the theory of perfect competition ever existed, it would not only deprive of their scope all the activities which the verb 'to compete' describes but would make them virtually impossible» (Hayek, 1946, p. 105). A couple of decades later, Hayek (1968, p. 9) was further stressing that «for some 40 to 50 years [economists] have investigated competition primarily under assumptions which, if they were actually true, would make competition completely useless and uninteresting», adding that «*wherever* we make use of competition, this can only be justified by our

71 For a complete overview of various theories of the market, see Mitchell (2014).

not knowing the essential circumstances that determine the behaviour of the competitors».

The problem of knowledge is essential in this regard: in the process of competition, different economic agents are trying to achieve completely separate plans, and therefore it would be absurd to think that they possess the same *data* (Hayek, 1946, p. 106). The point is that, with the assumptions of perfect competition, both buyers and sellers are supposed to be already fully informed about consumers tastes and preferences (sellers) and different products available in the market (buyers); instead, according to a "realistic" vision of competition, those data, those pieces of information, constitute precisely what needs to be discovered through the process of competition; they are a dynamically emergent outcome rather than a datum.

Therefore, for Hayek (1946, pp. 115-116) competition is «essentially a process of the formation of opinion: by spreading information, it creates the unity and coherence of the economic system which we presuppose when we think of it as one market. It creates the views people have about what is best and cheapest, and it is because of it that people know at least as much about possibilities and opportunities as they in fact do. It is thus a process which involves a continuous change in the data and whose significance must therefore be completely missed by any theory which treats these data as a constant».

In a nutshell, Hayek (1968) defined competition as a discovery procedure, which means a process through which sellers and buyers discover each other, generating an emergent order characterized by the search for mutual consistency of plans.

1.2. Kirzner: Competition as an (entrepreneurial) process

Hayek's vision was further developed by Israel M. Kirzner (1973), according to whom the neoclassical static view of competition is not the proper paradigm to analyse the competitive process. Kirzner's starting point is a «dissatisfaction with the usual emphasis on *equilibrium analysis*» and the «attempt to replace this emphasis by a fuller understanding of the operation of the market as a *process*» (Kirzner, 1973, p. 1). The American economist tried to «look to price theory to help us understand how the decisions of individual participants in the market interact to generate the market forces which compel *changes* in prices, in outputs, and in methods of production and the allocation of resources. [...] The efficiency of the price system, in this approach, does not depend upon the optimality (or absence of it) of the resource allocation pattern at equilibrium; rather, it depends on the degree of success with which market forces can be relied upon to generate spontaneous corrections in the allocation patterns prevailing at times of disequilibrium» (Kirzner, 1973, pp. 6-7).

In line with the criticism I am developing here, for Kirzner it is not possible to refer to competition as a state of affairs, and therefore his attempt was to develop an organic theory of the market as an economic *process* (Kirzner, 1997, p. 61). Consumers, entrepreneur-producers and resource owners are the players in the market; the latter, in turn, is where their interacting decisions, during any period of time, take place. Every player has his own content of (limited) knowledge, tastes and expectations. Depending on their knowledge, tastes and expectations, the players set up their action decisions, or plans. Since, in order to carry out their plans, individuals need to interact, it is only through interaction and though the flow of time that that content of information will be modified and, eventually a revision of decisions can happen.

> During the given period of time, exposure to the decisions of others communicates some of the information these decision-makers originally lacked. If they find that their plans cannot be carried out, this teaches them that their anticipations concerning the decisions of others were overly optimistic. Or they may learn that their undue pessimism has caused them to pass up attractive market opportunities. This newly acquired information concerning the plans of others can be expected to generate, for the succeeding period of time, *a revised set of decisions* (Kirzner, 1973, p. 10).

As defined by Kirzner (1973, p. 10), then, the market process is built up by «this series of systematic changes in the interconnected network of market decisions». Therefore, it is not possible to conceive of a market process in the realm of perfect knowledge. The process arises precisely because of the initial ignorance of market participants and the natural uncertainty of human action. And the process can only happen during the flow of *real time*. With no market ignorance and no review of plans, there is no process at all. This is therefore how Kirzner (1973, p. 12) explained the *competitive nature* of such a process: since from one period of market ignorance to the next ignorance has been somewhat reduced, market participants realize that not only should they implement more attractive opportunities but also that such attractiveness needs to be judged in comparison with the opportunities offered by competitors. When the incentive to offer more attractive opportunities stops, the competitive process stops, too. There is no more room for competition at all in a situation of market equilibrium, such as the one that the neoclassical theory of perfect competition describes.

In the description of such a process, almost incidentally and initially imagining a fictional world in which market participants are unable to learn from their experience, Kirzner (1973, p. 14) introduces a special group of individuals who «*are* able to perceive opportunities for entrepreneurial profits; that is, they are able to see where a good can be sold at a price higher than that for which it can be bought». These are *entrepreneurs*, who «immediately notice profit opportunities *that exist because of the initial ignorance of the original market participants*» (Kirzner, 1973, p. 14). Of course, to describe the real market process, it is not necessary to divide the actors into two rigid groups: one that cannot learn from experience and the other one (entrepreneurial) which instead can. It is indeed realistic to introduce the entrepreneurial aspect as an element of the activities of each market participant. It follows that the market process is essentially entrepreneurial (Kirzner, 1973, p. 15): since *entrepreneurship* is *alertness* to profit opportunities deriving from market ignorance, and the market process is the set of plans revisions which follow the modification of knowledge, the two concepts are intrinsically bound.

1.3. Schumpeter: Entrepreneurship, innovation and the *competition that matters*

Before Hayek and Kirzner, Schumpeter (1942, p. 78) observed that «[n]either Marshall and Wicksell nor the classics saw that perfect competition is the exception and that even if it were the rule there would be much less reason for congratulation than one might think». The Austrian economist observed that indeed the conditions of perfect competition are fulfilled only in some agriculture mass production, while «as regards practically all the finished products and services of industry and trade, it is clear that every grocer, every filling station, every manufacturer of gloves or shaving cream or handsaws has a small and precarious market of his own which he tries—must try—to build up and to keep by price strategy, quality strategy—"product differentiation"—and advertising. Thus, we get a completely different pattern which there seems to be no reason to expect to yield the results of perfect competition and which fits much better into the monopolistic schema. In these cases we speak of Monopolistic Competition» (Schumpeter, 1942, p. 79). For Schumpeter, monopolistic competition and oligopolies are the new forms of capitalism.

Schumpeter's vision of competition cannot be disjointed, but rather should be derived from its approach to entrepreneurship, innovation and creative destruction. As is well known, for the Austrian economist, the key analytical point is the concept of economic development: a «spontaneous and discontinuous change in the channels of the flow, disturbance of equilibrium, which forever alters and displaces the equilibrium state previously existing» (Schumpeter, 1911, p. 64).

Such changes, moreover, «are not forced upon [economic life] from without but arise by its own initiative, from within», thanks to the introduction of *new combinations* (innovations), which Schumpeter (1911, p. 66) lists under five types: new goods, new methods of production, new markets, new sources of supply of raw materials and industry reorganizations.

If new combinations are the essence of economic development, in order to exercise their disruptive function in economic life, they require what Schumpeter (1911, p. 74) calls the «fundamental phenomenon of economic development». In fact, if the carrying out of new combinations can be called *enterprise*, «the individuals whose function it is to carry them out [are called] "entrepreneurs"». When changes and innovations happen, normal individuals need guidance and, because of the need for such guidance, «the carrying out of new combinations is a special function, and the privilege of a type of people who are much less numerous than all those who have the "objective" possibility of doing it». Entrepreneurs are the special type of persons, with a special behaviour, able to exercise such a guidance[72].

In a nutshell, innovations are changes in the economic system. Entrepreneurs who introduce innovations belong to a special human type because such changes cannot be faced and managed by normal individuals. After innovations are introduced, businessmen face the struggle to make the innovation win against 'the old way' to do things, against social hostility. In this struggle, it is not the invention that characterized the entrepreneur but his leadership, his ability to master the new situation, and his ability to impose innovations in the

72 For clarifications about the link between entrepreneurship and leadership, see Ferlito (2015).

otherwise repetitive economic life. This is the reason why Schumpeter (1911, p. 88) stressed that it «is not part of his function to "find" or to "create" new possibilities. They are always present, abundantly accumulated by all sorts of people». While many people see things, the entrepreneur does them.

In such a scenario, disruptive entrepreneurs fight what can be defined as the *competition that matters*. Schumpeter is openly critical of the traditional concept of competition, and it is against it that he clarifies what competition really means, moving away from the simple struggle over prices with which it is often associated.

> The first thing to go is the traditional conception of the *modus operandi* of competition. Economists are at long last emerging from the stage in which price competition was all they saw. [...]. But in capitalist reality as distinguished from its textbook picture, it is not that kind of competition which counts but the competition from the new commodity, the new technology, the new source of supply, the new type of organization (the largest-scale unit of control for instance)—competition which commands a decisive cost or quality advantage and which strikes not at the margins of the profits and the outputs of the existing firms but at their foundations and their very lives. This kind of competition is as much more effective than the other as a bombardment is in comparison with forcing a door, and so much more important that it becomes a matter of comparative indifference whether competition in the ordinary sense functions more or less promptly; the powerful lever that in the long run expands output and brings down prices is in any case made of other stuff (Schumpeter, 1942, pp. 84-85).

Here we go: competition, for Schumpeter, is not the fight over prices between identical firms producing the same thing, but rather the new combination fighting against the old way of doing things. Such a concept cannot but be dynamic, and indicating a process, rather than a state of affairs.

2. Competition and entrepreneurship

One of the key insights that emerges from the works of Kirzner and Schumpeter is that competition cannot be separated from the exercise of entrepreneurship. After all, who actually plays the game of competition? While it is easy to recognize that entrepreneurs are the driving force of economic life, it is surprisingly difficult to find an adequate discussion of entrepreneurship in contemporary economics textbooks.

Modern microeconomics offers sophisticated theories of the firm, typically portraying enterprises as profit maximizers or cost minimizers. It also classifies market structures according to the number of firms operating within them. Yet these frameworks often overlook a fundamental fact: at the very core of every firm lies the entrepreneur—or, at least, the entrepreneurial function. Contemporary theory, in this sense, introduces us to numerous "masks" of the entrepreneur without ever revealing the true face behind them.

Textbook economics thus tends to dehumanize the market process, reducing it to impersonal mechanisms and equilibrium conditions. Yet, as already noted, it is impossible to conceive a market process without the purposeful actions and choices of individuals. As Mises (1949a, pp. 258–259) observed:

> The forces determining the – continually changing – state of the market are the value judgements of these individuals and their actions are directed by these value judgments. [...] the market process is entirely the resultant of human actions. Every market phenomena can be traced back to definite choices of the members of the market society.
>
> The market process is the adjustment of the individual actions of the various members of the market society to the requirements of mutual cooperation.

Market prices exercise the role of the polar star in such a process, but this is another, although fundamental, story, which I cannot expand here.

2.1. Schumpeter and his entrepreneur-innovator

As we have seen, for Schumpeter, *new combinations* (innovations) are the main driver of competition and, thus, economic development, thanks to funds provided by bankers. However, new combinations and credit alone are insufficient for the emergence of economic development. A further element is necessary, which Schumpeter (1911, p. 74) called the «fundamental phenomenon of economic development». In fact, if developing new combinations can be called "enterprise", then «the individuals whose function it is to carry them out [are called] 'entrepreneurs'» (Schumpeter, 1911, p. 74). It was at this point that Schumpeter started to develop his famous entrepreneur theory.

But why «is the carrying out of new combinations a special process and the object of a special kind of 'function'» (Schumpeter, 1911, p. 79), called the entrepreneurial function? According to Schumpeter, in the realm of circular flow, economic agents are able to promptly and rationally act and react to given circumstances that repeat themselves over time. *Normal* individuals can face such an environment. But when changes and innovations happen, normal individuals need *guidance* (Schumpeter, 1911, p. 79). Because of the need for such guidance, «the carrying out of new combinations is a special function, and the privilege of a type of people who are much less numerous than all those who have the 'objective' possibility of doing it» (Schumpeter, 1911, p. 81). Entrepreneurs are the special type of persons with a special behaviour who are able to exercise such guidance.

There is another crucial aspect that can be misunderstood, which Schumpeter (1911, pp. 84-91) discussed at length: *leadership*. Calling *innovation* the introduction of new combinations, the Schumpeterian entrepreneur is rightly identified as an *innovator*. The word is not free from ambiguity and misunderstandings. Though scholars have often clarified that innovation is not necessarily a new invention, the risk is high of identifying the entrepreneurial function with the invention of something new. However, an entrepreneur is not an inventor (Schumpeter, 1947, p. 152). The entrepreneur is a special type not simply because he carries out new combinations, but also because, in doing so, he masters a development process that is a process of change. By introducing new combinations into the economic system, entrepreneurs demonstrate that they are capable of acting where normal individuals stop.

According to Schumpeter (1911, pp. 84-87), moving outside the boundaries of the circular flow is difficult and requires special individuals for three kinds of reasons:

> First, outside these accustomed channels, the individual is without those data for his decisions and those rules of conduct, which are usually very accurately known to him within them. Of course, he must still foresee and estimate on the basis of his experience. But many things must remain uncertain; still others are only ascertainable within wide limits, and some can perhaps only be "guessed." [...]
>
> Here, the success of everything depends on intuition. [...]
>
> As this first point lies in the task, so the second lies in the psyche of the businessman himself. It is not only objectively more difficult to do something new than what is familiar and tested by experience, but the individual feels reluctance towards it and would do so even if the objective difficulties did not exist. [...]

> The third point consists of the reaction of the social environment against one who wishes to do something new. [...]
>
> There is leadership *only* for these reasons.

These features need to be further emphasized. Innovation is a change in the economic system (Schumpeter, 1935, p. 4). Because such changes are difficult for regular people to handle and manage, the entrepreneur who introduces innovations is a special type. In carrying out new combinations, entrepreneurs move the system out of the equilibrium state; additionally, after innovations are introduced, businessmen face the struggle of making the innovation win against "the old way" of doing things, against social hostility. In this struggle, it is not the invention that characterizes the entrepreneur, but his *leadership* and his ability to master the new situation. This is the reason why Schumpeter (1911, p. 88) stressed that it «is not part of his [the entrepreneur's] function to 'find' or to 'create' new possibilities. They are always present, abundantly accumulated by all sorts of people».

While many people see things, the leader *does* things. It is therefore «more by will than by intellect that the leaders fulfil their function, more by 'authority,' 'personal weight,' and so forth than by original ideas» (Schumpeter, 1911, p. 88).

2.2. Kirzner: An entrepreneur's alertness to profit opportunities

It is only after a brief introduction of the concept of entrepreneurship in the realm of the market process that Kirzner moves on to detail his perspective on the entrepreneur. The first important note he brought out is that entrepreneurship is related to human action and is therefore potentially present in each individual (Kirzner, 1973, p. 31). In particular, as Kirzner developed the market process notion in opposition to an equilibrium approach, the author contrasted entrepreneurial activity with economizing and maximizing functions. «[...] It is my position that this analytical vision of economizing, maximizing, or efficiency-intent individual market participants is, in significant respects, misleadingly incomplete. It has led to a view of the market as made up of a multitude of economizing individuals, each making his decisions with respect to *given* series of ends and means. [...] A multitude of economizing individuals each choosing with respect to given ends and means cannot, without the introduction of further exogenous elements, generate a market process (which involves systematically *changing* series of means available to market participants)» (Kirzner, 1973, pp. 32-33).

The important point raised by Kirzner is that, in such an analytical framework in which ends and means are given, there is no room to study *how* ends and means are decided (see Chapter 1 in this book). To overcome the economizing notion, he went back to Mises's concept of *human action*. It is necessary to quote Kirzner's words in full:

> [...] Instead of economizing, I maintain, it will prove extremely helpful to emphasize the broader Misesian notion of *human action*. As developed by Mises, the concept of *homo agens* is capable of all that can be achieved by using the notions of economizing and of the drive for efficiency. But the human-action concept, unlike that of allocation and economizing, does not confine decision-maker (or the economic analysis of his decisions) to a framework of *given* ends and means. Human action, in the sense developed by Mises, involves courses of action taken by the human being "to remove uneasiness" and to make himself "better off." Being broader than the notion of economizing, the concept of human action does not restrict analysis of the decision to the allocation problem posed by the juxtaposition of scarce means and multiple ends. The decision, in the framework of the human-action approach, is not arrived at merely by mechanical computation of the solution to the maximization problem implicit in the configuration of the given ends and means. It reflects not merely the manipulation of given means to correspond faithfully with the hierarchy of given ends, but also *the very perception of the ends–means framework* within which allocation and economizing is to take place (Kirzner, 1973, p. 33).

While Robbins's economizing man can only react in a given way to a strictly defined set of ends and means, Misesian *homo agens* can *also* identify which ends to strive for and which means are available. This is possible because human beings can actually «*imagine* the future, even a non-existent, unknowable future» (Kirzner, 1992, p. 25). Instead, economizing behaviour does not take into account the process of identifying ends and means. It is at this point that Kirzner specifically introduced his famous concept of *alertness* to «possibly newly worthwhile goals and to possibly newly available resources» (Kirzner, 1973, p. 35); such alertness is what he labelled the *entrepreneurial element* in human decision-making. If entrepreneurship is alertness, then the succession of different decisions and their revisions can be seen as a sequence of linked actions, the fruit of the learning process due to alertness (Kirzner, 1973, p. 36). In a way, the concept of alertness is linked with *discovery* and *surprise*: profit opportunities do not "fall from the sky", but neither do entrepreneurs deliberately look for them:

> [...] The profit opportunities created by earlier entrepreneurial error do tend systematically to stimulate subsequent entrepreneurial discovery. The entrepreneurial process so set into motion, is a process tending toward better mutual awareness among market participants. The lure of pure profit in this way sets up the process through which pure profit tends to be competed away. Enhanced mutual awareness, via the entrepreneurial discovery process, is the source of the market's equilibrative properties (Kirzner, 1997, p. 72).

From this, Kirzner derived his concept of the *pure entrepreneur*. For Schumpeter, the action that identifies the pure entrepreneur is to bring out new combinations; for Kirzner (1973, p. 39), he or she is «a decision-maker whose *entire* role arises out of his alertness to hitherto unnoticed opportunities». For both economists, in fact, entrepreneurship is completely independent of the ownership of the means of production. The entrepreneurial function is instead strictly related to a special attitude: introducing new combinations (action) for Schumpeter and alertness (pre-action) for Kirzner. Regarding alertness, however, a clarification becomes necessary: The Kirznerian entrepreneur does *not* possess greater knowledge. On the contrary, alertness is defined as «*the "knowledge" of where to find market data*» (Kirzner, 1973, p. 67). Therefore, the Kirznerian type of entrepreneurship is in no way related to a certain kind of superiority but consists *only* in «"knowing where to look for knowledge" rather than knowledge of substantive market information» (Kirzner, 1973, p. 68); this is the reason why Kirzner did not label this attitude as *knowledge* but *alertness*.

The most distinctive feature of the Kirznerian entrepreneurial function is to move the market from a disequilibrium status towards equilibrium (Kirzner, 1973, pp. 69-75). The starting point of human action, in fact, is always a state of disequilibrium characterized by market ignorance. As already noticed, it is through interaction in the market that knowledge can be transmitted and acquired, bringing out revisions to plans. Entrepreneurial alertness allows such changes to happen, and, therefore, by reducing market ignorance and driving plans towards mutual compatibility, it is an *equilibrating* force. The market approach, in fact, focuses «on the role of knowledge and discovery in the process of market equilibration. In particular, this approach (a) sees equilibration as a systematic process in which market participants acquire more and more accurate and complete *mutual knowledge* of potential demand and supply attitudes, and (b) sees the driving force behind this systematic process in what will be described below as *entrepreneurial discovery*» (Kirzner, 1997, p. 62).

The equilibrating process consists exactly of the acquisition of better mutual information concerning the plans made by different market actors[73]. Profit opportunities only actually exist and are "visible" to entrepreneurial alertness in states of disequilibrium[74]. In this sense, alertness allows discovery, and discovery plays an equilibrating role, reducing market ignorance (Kirzner, 1997, p. 68).

2.3. An entrepreneurial synthesis

In drawing up this synthesis, it is important to first of all repeat that Schumpeter's and Kirzner's entrepreneurial theories both arose in opposition to neoclassical equilibrium theory. What the two economists brought out from such opposition are two analyses of human behaviour driving the economic system in certain directions.

Schumpeter's entrepreneur, a maker and master of change, is a *deus ex machina* for capitalistic economic development. A very specific period of economic history is related to this function: the era of "heroic" leader entrepreneurs characterized the eighteenth, nineteenth and beginning of the twentieth centuries. As historical conditions change through *trustification*, the role of entrepreneurs changes too, while *the responsibility* of forging economic development through "new combinations" shifts to research centres and managers.

Kirznerian entrepreneurship, however, is not conceived as a historical matter or a specific characteristic of "superior people". Rather, it is a general feature of human action, consisting of the possibility of setting up a means–ends framework in order to exploit unnoticed profit opportunities. Under this perspective, everybody is potentially entrepreneurial over time and space. Space and time conditions do not change the general features of entrepreneurship, which has remained

73 In the market economy, the problem of coordination finds a solution in the market process and the key role is played by prices (Kirzner, 1963, p. 38).

74 «[...] mutual knowledge is indeed full of gaps at any given time, yet the market process is understood to provide a systemic set of forces, set in motion by entrepreneurial alertness, which tend to reduce the extent of mutual ignorance. Knowledge is not perfect; but neither is ignorance necessarily invincible. Equilibrium is indeed never attained, yet the market does exhibit powerful tendencies toward it» (Kirzner, 1992, p. 5).

a constant element of human beings' behaviour over centuries. Kirznerian entrepreneurs are not the "prime cause" of economic development; rather, through their alertness, they generate the market process through a process of information exchange and therefore ignorance reduction. Alertness becomes an equilibrating force, helping economic actors make their plans mutually consistent.

My perspective is that *both* entrepreneurial ideas can coexist when looking at a new synthetic approach to entrepreneurship. The source of misunderstanding is believed to be that the two economists labelled different concepts with the same word. The Schumpeterian entrepreneur is not incompatible with the Kirznerian entrepreneur. While there is some agreement with the theory of human action described by Kirzner, it seems too weak to fully explain the essence of entrepreneurship. Kirzner's theory can be the first brick in integrating human action and entrepreneurship theories if the label of the theory as an entrepreneurial theory is renounced to instead be called *alertness theory*. Markets are characterized by ignorance, and economic agents define their sets of ends and means consistently with their expectations and the limited content of their knowledge. In doing so, they trigger the market process and the never-ending processes of information exchange and revising plans. They are alert to profit opportunities, and they learn from experience. The acquisition of new information, arising from the interaction between the subject and the surrounding reality, generates new knowledge via never-ending interpretative processes.

However, among these economic actors, *special types* can actually arise. The introduction of new combinations and the leadership attitudes do not need to be excluded by Kirzner's model. Schumpeter's entrepreneurs arise from Kirznerian alertness, driving the economic system towards *change*. If alertness is a unique state of mind that comes from Mises's idea of purposeful human action, then new combinations can be seen as a subset of alertness. They are a unique type of action that brings something stronger than what was known into the market process in terms of *change*. Similarly, Schumpeterian entrepreneurs are fully consistent with the human action model. They are alert to unnoticed profit opportunities, and they need to set up their end–means frameworks. In doing so, however, the kind of plans and the set of actions they carry out, since they are not theoretically different from all the other kinds of actions, are practically different for the special consequences they bring into the economic system. In fact, such actions introduce radical discontinuities in the way things are done[75].

The disruptive character of Schumpeterian entrepreneurs and the coordinative role as described by Kirzner are, therefore, not entirely inconsistent. Looking at the system from the outside, Schumpeter's entrepreneur shows us the importance of technological change for economic evolution. Kirzner's insights, instead, shed light on the working of the economic system from within (that is, profit opportunities arising from ignorance and alertness as well as the possibility of seizing them) (Kirzner, 1999, p. 16).

It seems that recently Kirzner (1999) became aware of the potential compatibility between the two visions[76]. Kirzner (1999, p. 5) stressed how Schumpeter's view is valid in order to understand «the psychological profile typical of the real-world entrepreneur» and the "creative destruction", which Schumpeter saw as the central and distinguishing feature of the "capitalist" system. Kirzner (1999, p. 12) recognized that alertness requires «boldness, self-confidence, creativity and innovative ability» as described by Schumpeterian entrepreneurship. Moreover, it seems that Kirzner also accepted the special psychological attitude necessary for entrepreneurship typical of Schumpeter's vision[77].

Schumpeterian entrepreneurship characterized by leadership and innovation, can be seen as a special action arising from the Kirznerian concept of alertness as related to the Misesian approach to human action, but brought out by special types of humans, entrepreneurs, and with radical consequences not simply for the market process but for the economic development process.

It can be imagined as an *alertness* or Kirznerian theory in which human beings, as *homo agens*, define their end–means framework and

75 Kirzner (1992, p. 50) probably moved towards my vision, stating that «entrepreneurship exercised in innovative production tents to generate technological progress».

76 Kirzner (2008, p. 8) pointed out that the «merely alert entrepreneur [...] was never intended as alternative to the creative, innovative Schumpeterian entrepreneur».

77 Kirzner (1999, p. 13): «abstract prescience [must] be supported by psychological qualities that encourage one to ignore conventional wisdom, to dismiss the jeers of those deriding what they see as the self-deluded visionary, to disrupt what others have come to see as the comfortable familiarity of the old-fashioned ways of doing things, to ruin rudely and even cruelly the confident expectations of those whose somnolence has led them to expect to continue to make their living as they have for years past».

their plans. Interaction between these *homo agens* defines the market process, which is characterized by ignorance reduction, plans revisions, and coordination. Among such plans, some are *entrepreneurial*, disruptive plans ("new combinations"), brought out by Schumpeterian entrepreneurs and defining economic change.

Figure 6.1: Human Action, alertness and entrepreneurship.

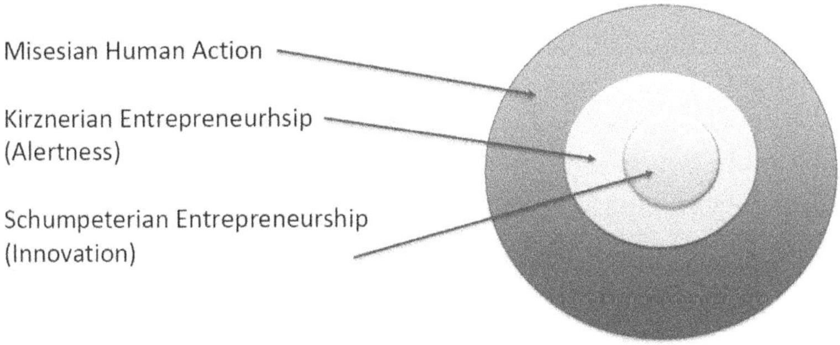

Source: Ferlito (2016, p. 55).

As shown in Figure 5.1, entrepreneurship and alertness are both subsets of human action, but they differ in the unique set of consequences they bring to the economic system – consequences that are only observable *ex post*.

With the help of Horwitz (2019), a final word needs to be spent on how entrepreneurs make their entrepreneurial decisions. How do business owners decide which output to attempt to produce and which goods to combine in the production process in order to eventually obtain the desired output? The main beacons for them are (profit) expectations and the price system. Horwitz (2019, p. 22) explains that the «fundamental challenge of economic production involves answering the twin questions of "what should be produced?" and "how should we produce it?" The first of the two questions relates to consumer preferences: what is that people wish to buy, or might wish to buy if it were available to them? The second question, which is the one that is often overlooked especially by critics of capitalism, is the harder one: if we are to make this product, which combination of inputs should we use to make it such that we use the least valuable inputs possible? This question is what economists mean by "economic efficiency"». How do entrepreneurs compare alternative goods and alternative processes of production to determine if they are creating value rather than destroying it?

Here it is enough to say that what «enables us to engage in these comparisons of value are market prices determined by the exchange of goods and services against money» (Horwitz, 2019, p. 22). Market prices exist thanks to private property, «which enables people to exchange and form markets, which in turn leads to the emergence of market prices» (Horwitz, 2019, p. 22). Market prices are, thus, the objective synthesis of billions of subjective evaluations arising from market interactions; thanks to the guidance provided by prices, which give information about consumer preferences and scarcity, entrepreneurs can effectively decide what to do and how. Similarly, market prices allow to determine if a production process generated or destroyed value, thanks to the comparison between outlays and receipts; as Horwitz (2019, p. 23) put it, «[m]onetary calculation of profits and losses provides producers with ex post feedback about the wisdom of their past choices that, without market prices, would be unavailable».

Considering that these decisions and production processes happen in a context of uncertainty generated by the passage of time and by the limited content of information available to each individual, the role of entrepreneurial choices appears even more important (Horwitz, 2019, p. 24). Successes and failures become an important signal for the entire economic community.

3. From competition to concentration

With the help of Schumpeter, Hayek and Kirzner, I tried to:

- Dismantle the idea of perfect competition, intended as a state of affairs where competition is indeed absent;

- Replace it with the idea of a dynamic process unfolding in real time and therefore characterized by the unending emergence of novelty;

- Identify the competition process as a struggle between opposing forces (new versus old in the Schumpeterian vision, alertness versus non-alertness in Kirzner);

- Place entrepreneurship at the root of the competition process, so as to stress that the process itself is not abstract but rather made of the interactions between decisions taken by living human beings.

By identifying competition as a process – alive, organic and active in historical time - characterized by the struggle between competing choices made by living human beings, it is possible to appreciate the Nietzschean nature of the process itself:

> if it be a living and not a dying organisation [...] will have to be the incarnated Will to Power, it will endeavour to grow, to gain ground, attract to itself and acquire ascendency—not owing to any morality or immorality, but because it *lives*, and because life *is* precisely Will to Power. [...] "Exploitation" does not belong to a depraved, or imperfect and primitive society: it belongs to the nature of the living being as a primary organic function; it is a consequence of the intrinsic Will to Power, which is precisely the Will to Life (Nietzsche, 1886, p. 200).

In short, as I always try to explain to my students, an entrepreneur does not enter the market with the aim of becoming one among many, of being equal and homogeneous with respect to other entrepreneurs. On the contrary, the essence of entrepreneurship is precisely the will to power, the desire to get rid of competitors and not to homogenize with them, and the physiological need to conquer growing market shares thanks to winning strategies (Ferlito, 2022a). Disruption, rather than equilibrium, is the essence of market forces at work, as «[n]o agent can enter a market, or extend his range of activity within one by making offers to other agents, without disrupting some market relationship presently existing between them and others [and t]his fact is of course the very essence of competition» (Lachmann, 1986, p. 5).

The natural consequence is that true and not fictional entrepreneurship shapes the market process, generating a dynamic competition in which neither the starting point nor the final outcome can be – in each industry – a fragmented archipelago of firms doing the same thing with no distinguishable features.

On the contrary, the *will to power* at the root of entrepreneurial action can only bring about *concentration* as the natural result of a competitive process understood for what it is and not the fiction that is served up to inert students who, unfortunately, will become professors and continue to teach that fiction.

Schumpeter (1942) reached the same conclusion: the emergence of oligopolistic capitalism as the natural outcome of competition; but he saw this as the end of entrepreneurship. It is very well known that Schumpeter's vision of entrepreneurship evolved over decades. The emphasis on the entrepreneur and his exceptional character, grounded in his will and leadership, gave way to a deeper analysis of the entrepreneurial function (still focused on implementing new combinations) that gradually lost its link to the entrepreneur *as a person*. As he lived through the passage from the "heroic" stage of industrial development hallmarked by individual entrepreneurs to the next stage characterized by the emergence of trusts, new combinations called *innovations* were still present in Schumpeter (1939), and innovations became central to the business cycle analysis. Entrepreneurs were still present, but Schumpeter gradually recognized the declining importance of the entrepreneurial function in the age of trusts. Schumpeter did not renounce his view of entrepreneurs; he simply observed that the general economic scenario was changing: «Already, the volitional aptitudes that made the successful entrepreneur of old are much less necessary and have much less scope than they used to have. It is no chance coincidence that the epoch in which this decrease in importance of the entrepreneurial function first asserted itself is also the epoch in which the social and political position of the *bourgeoisie* first began to display obvious symptoms of weakness and to be attacked with success» (Schumpeter, 1939, p. 109).

Such an observation is a bridge towards what Schumpeter (1942, pp. 131-134) called the *obsolescence of the entrepreneurial function*. Schumpeter (1942, p. 132) observed that the peculiar function of "getting things done", the drive of the personal will, was losing importance for two orders of reasons. On one hand, the task of innovation was becoming the activity of trained specialists; while on the other hand, the social environment was becoming accustomed to economic change and therefore resistance to it was declining. «Now a similar social process—in the last analysis the same social process—undermines the role and, along with the role, the social position of the capitalist entrepreneur. His role, though less glamorous than that of medieval warlords, great or small, also is or was just another form of individual leadership acting by virtue of personal force and personal responsibility for success. His position, like that of warrior classes, is threatened as soon as this function in the social process loses its importance and no less if this is due to the cessation of the social needs it served than if those needs are being served by other, more impersonal, methods» (Schumpeter, 1942, pp. 133-134).

The decline of the entrepreneurial function and entrepreneurs, according to Schumpeter, opened the doors to the end of "capitalism" as we know it. Economic progress becomes depersonalized and automated, while committees and planning offices replace individual action. The result, Schumpeter (1942, p. 134) stressed, may not differ from what Marxist scientists describe as *de facto* socialism.

My perspective is different: it is the innovation process[78] as such, at the core of competitive and entrepreneurial dynamics, which requires concentration to propagate and reproduce itself. The entrepreneurial *will to power*, which sets in motion competition and innovation, generates a capitalist dynamic in which expansion, intended as growth and consolidation, is the key to survival.

> The characteristic feature of the process of industrial concentration is precisely that it creates by no means negligible technological discontinuities. Only large firms can apply certain methods, both technical and organizational, and only large firms can realize certain economies of scale. And the transition from small to large firms is not gradual; there are jumps and the jumps become broader as concentration proceeds (Sylos Labini, 1957, p. 33).

In a nutshell, if innovation is the essential element for economic development to happen (Sylos Labini, 1992, p. 5), concentration is the essential condition for technical progress to emerge.

The great wave of American indigenous innovations, which benefited the rest of the world thanks to adoption and adaptation, started in the 1870s and culminated in the three decades that followed World War II (Phelps, 2013). This is exactly the same period in which the process of industrial concentration began and affirmed itself, making oligopoly not a special case but «the most frequent market form of modern economies» (Sylos Labini, 1957, p. 14)[79]. In fact, we may say that, when innovation spreads quickly, concentration becomes a precondition for further technical progress. When a new technique is rapidly diffusing, the entrepreneur introducing it would have to be careful to gain enough profit before the wider adoption of that technique makes his or her

78 Broadly intended, following Pasinetti (1981, pp. 76-78).

79 Robinson (1933, pp. 307-326) in 1933 was already describing the first half of the 20th century as a world of monopolies.

investment meaningless. Such a phenomenon creates the incentive to introduce innovations that are gradually more difficult to be rapidly adopted and one way to do so is indeed to increase business size and introduce techniques with a higher degree of imitation barrier, thanks to the scale of necessary investments.

Innovation and concentration must therefore walk together (Robinson, 1956, pp. 86-87). In fact, within the realm of concentrated oligopoly, technology «creates external barriers between each group of firms and its potential competitors» (Sylos Labini, 1957, pp. 53-54).

However, the process of industrial concentration «creates by no means negligible technological discontinuities. Only large firms can apply certain methods, both technical and organizational, and only large firms can realize certain economies of scale. And the transition from small to large firms is not gradual; there are jumps and the jumps come broader as concentration proceeds» (Sylos Labini, 1957, p. 35).

Furthermore, it would be misleading to believe that such a process would be in contradiction with free markets and, in particular, with open international trade. Quite the contrary: competition and innovation walked together, in the past decades, with the growing scale of international trade openness, which is often – but misleadingly – labelled as globalization. However, it is not difficult to imagine how access to a wider market – higher demand – can be a powerful incentive for enterprises to grow and for entrepreneurs to get together to win competition on international markets, which is possible only thanks to economies of scale: «growth of the market tends to increase the average size of firms and to lower the price» (Sylos Labini, 1957, p. 62). Furthermore, when the process of concentration begins, demand becomes the main determinant of new investments, as, within a concentrated industry, production activity is very little sensitive to changes in interest rates; profit expectations can be nurtured only by higher demand (Sylos Labini, 1957, p. 165).

Once the process of concentration is set in motion, the technical progress it generates, bringing about increased productivity, can in itself further increase demand thanks to higher incomes (profits and wages) (Sylos Labini, 1957, p. 167), therefore setting in motion a virtuous cycle:

Figure 6.2: Entrepreneurship, competition and concentration.

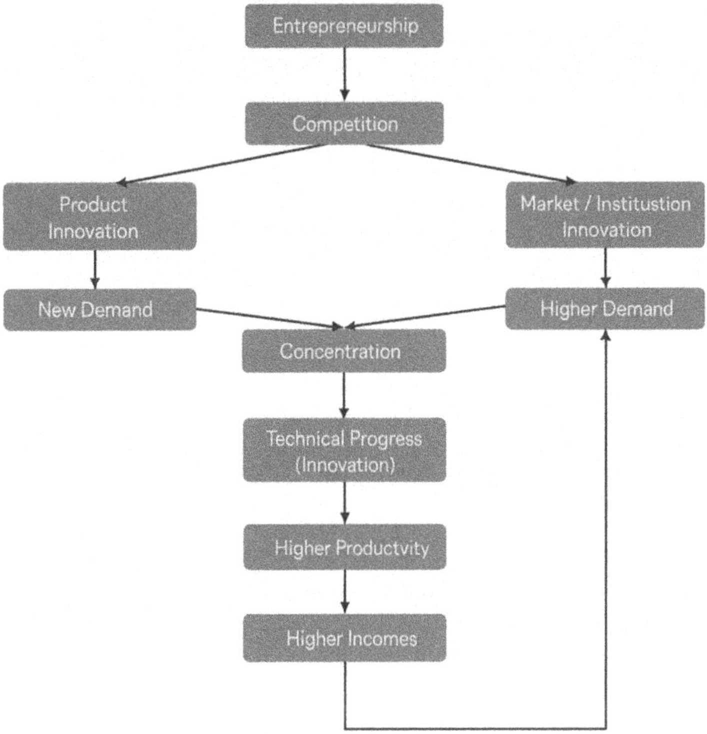

Concentration is a necessary condition for technical progress also because, under an oligopolistic regime, firms can pursue a target of profit maximization with a higher degree of independence: price policy comes to be strictly related to the target of financing new investments (Sylos Labini, 1992, p. 205) and the rate of growth of a firm's production will be proportional to the profit rate of the same firm (Sylos Labini, 1992, p. 215).

In such a scenario, small and medium enterprises are not supposed to disappear; they can constitute a vibrant and supportive ecosystem for bigger firms to thrive. In fact, smaller firms can remain innovative in terms of spirit and ideas, but they may lack the scale and market power to make innovations happen: a cooperative spirit between small and big enterprises can be seen as key for the innovative process to remain vibrant (Sylos Labini, 1993, pp. 270-272).

The same reasoning can be applied to the potentially virtuous cooperation between developed and emerging economies, whereby innovative processes in the former can be stimulated by potential demand in the latter, while an inversion of the direction cannot be excluded a-priori (Sylos Labini, 1984, p. 153).

Finally, the idea that technical progress generates not only higher productivity (as it is natural to believe) but also higher income is supported by the evidence about the inverse relationship between the investment/output ratio (I/Y) and the unemployment rate (u) that can be found, with reference to the cases of the United States and Japan, in Sylos Labini (2004, pp. 59-61). The relationship seems to hold also in the case of Malaysia[80].

Figure 6.3: Gross Fixed Capital Formation (% of GDP) versus Unemployment Rate – Malaysia.

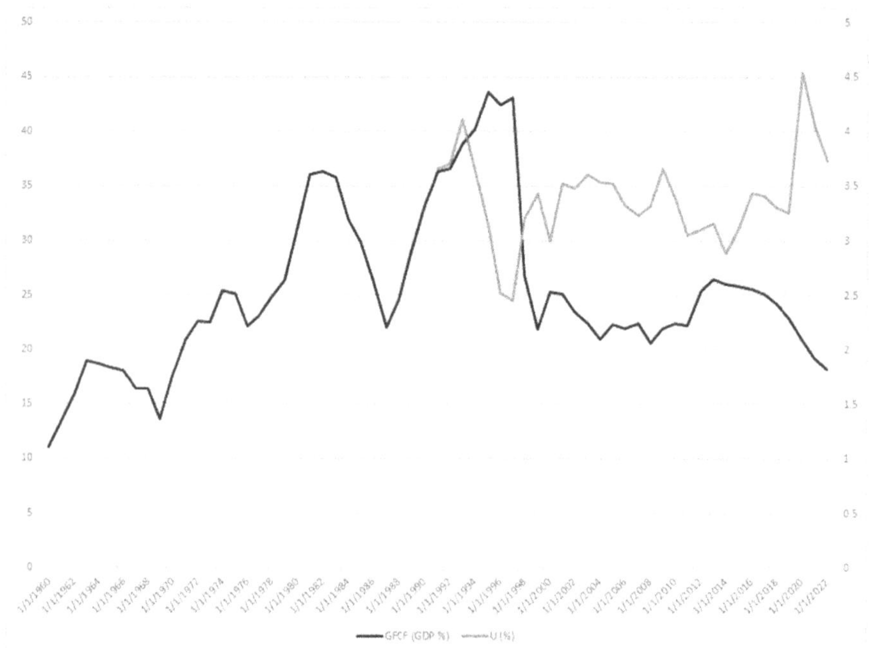

Source: World Bank database.

80 The anomaly of the latest years can be attributed to the special effects produced by the Great Lockdown.

4. Empirical evidence

In a recent work, Brancaccio, Giammetti and Lucarelli (2022, pp. 110-112) embraced an approach to measuring concentration based on the ownership of capital. Analysing data on 5,515 listed companies from 71 countries for the period 2001-2016, they identified the *nodes* of these firms, i.e., the different agents participating in the shareholding structure. In 2001, they identified 14,694 nodes related to each other through more than 400,000 ownership links. In 2016, the nodes reached more than 40,000, with more than one million mutual shareholding participations. Such a shareholding network kept increasing until the financial crisis in 2007 and then restarted to grow after 2008.

Similarly, by using Lorenz curves, Brancaccio, Giammetti and Lucarelli (2022, p. 115) showed that the great majority of firms in the sample recorded 80% of *net control* in the hands of around 1% of the shareholders, indicating a high capital concentration.

Another interesting and promising perspective for future research on industrial concentration is the top 50 companies market capitalization as a percentage of the world GDP.

Table 6.1: Top 50 companies market cap as a % of GDP.

Date	Global GDP (USD Trillion)	Global GDP Growth (%)	Top 50 Companies Market Cap as a % of GDP	Growth (%)
31-Dec-90	23.6		4.70%	
31-Dec-00	34.0	44.07%	22.10%	370.21%
31-Dec-10	66.2	94.71%	12.70%	-42.53%
31-Dec-20	84.5	27.64%	27.60%	117.32%

Source: https://www.visualcapitalist.com/top-50-companies-proportion-of-world-gdp/.

As can be seen, the market capitalization of the top 50 firms in the world not only constantly increased, but it did so at a faster pace than GDP growth. The slowing down in 2010 can be attributed, as in the case of Brancaccio, Giammetti and Lucarelli (2022) data, to the effects of the 2007 financial crisis.

Figure 6.4: Top 50 companies market cap as a % of GDP.

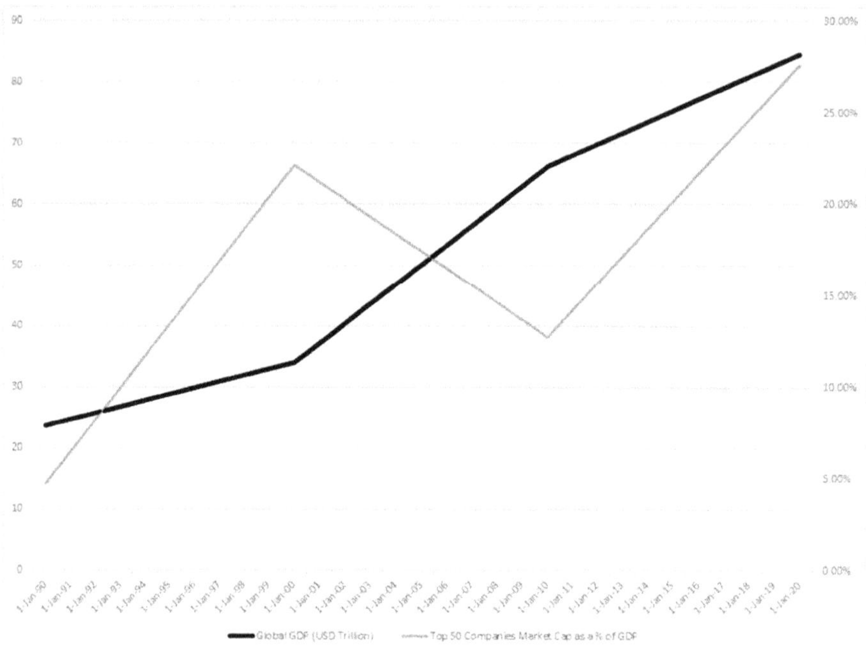

Source: https://www.visualcapitalist.com/top-50-companies-proportion-of-world-gdp/.

The relative share of the top firm in the world also increased. In 1990, the chart was led by IBM, whose market capitalization represented 0.27% of the world's GDP. In 2000, the leader was General Electrics (1.4%), in 2010, Exxon Mobil (0.56%) and in 2020, Apple (2.7%)[81].

The same trend can be observed in the growth of the estimated number of large companies (with more than 250 employees) worldwide during the last two decades.

81 https://www.visualcapitalist.com/top-50-companies-proportion-of-world-gdp/.

Figure 6.5: Estimated number of large companies (250+ employees) worldwide from 2000 to 2021 (in 1,000s).

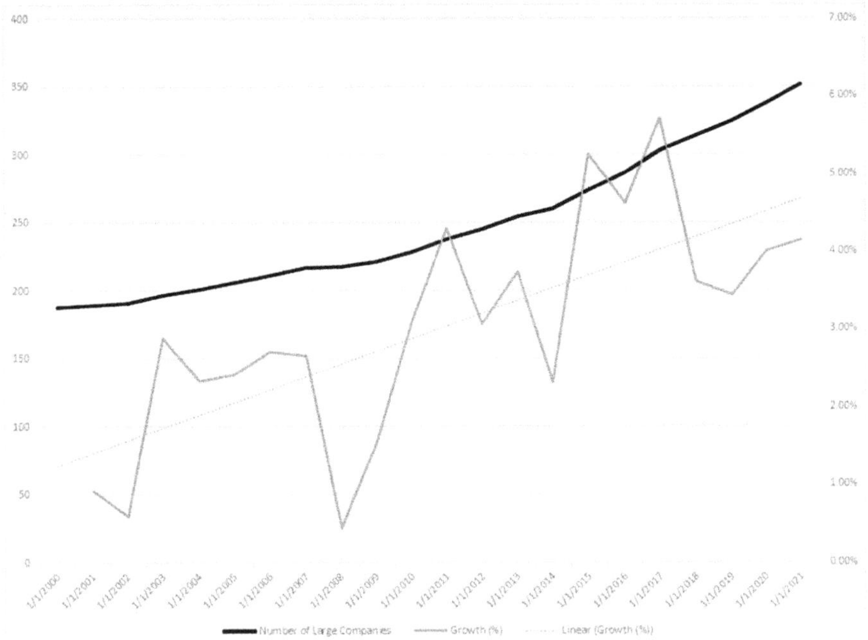

Source: https://www.statista.com/statistics/1261035/large-global-companies/.

Such evidence may seem in contradiction with the declining trend recorded in the HH market concentration index worldwide, which was 0.16 in 1988 and 0.04 in 2020 (World Bank[82]). However, what is interesting to observe, beyond concentration in absolute terms, is the role of big enterprises within a certain economy.

According to World Bank data, formal Small and Medium Enterprises (SMEs) account for 90% of businesses around the world, employing 50% of the workforce but generating 40% of the GDP[83]. This means that, worldwide, 10% of big firms contribute to around 60% of the national product.

82 https://wits.worldbank.org/CountryProfile/en/Country/WLD/StartYear/1988/EndYear/2021/Indicator/HH-MKT-CNCNTRTN-NDX.

83 https://www.worldbank.org/en/topic/smefinance.

Malaysian data is quite in line with the world trend. In fact, 2021 Micro, Small and Medium Enterprises (MSMEs) represented 97.4% of the total number of registered firms, employed around half of the labour force, but generated only 37.36% of the GDP (the data has remained quite stable over the past decade). This means that the remaining 2.6% of businesses – the big ones – generated 62.64% of it! (DOSM, 2022).

The situation is different in Indonesia, where the informal sector still plays a very important role in the national economy. In the archipelago, MSMEs represent 99.9% of the business population, employ almost 97% of the workforce and generate 61% of the GDP (Bank Indonesia[84] and OECD[85]).

Conclusion

The main aim of this chapter has been to dismantle the conventional notion of perfect competition—understood as a static state in which competition is, in fact, absent. Unfortunately, this is still how the concept is typically presented to economics students.

Drawing on the insights of Schumpeter, Hayek, and Kirzner, I have sought to replace that static vision with the idea of competition as a dynamic, real-time process characterized by the continual emergence of novelty. The market process is thus conceived as an open-ended, evolutionary system whose outcomes cannot be predicted in advance. Competition, in this sense, is best understood as a process of tension and struggle between opposing forces—the new versus the old in Schumpeter's framework, or alertness versus non-alertness in Kirzner's.

Moreover, competition is not an impersonal mechanism. At its core lies entrepreneurship, reminding us that the process is not abstract but rooted in the concrete actions, decisions, and interpretations of living human beings who respond to the signals transmitted through market prices.

The entrepreneurial drive that fuels competition must, by its very nature, possess what might be called a Nietzschean spirit: a will to power that propels growth and renewal. This dynamic gives rise to a virtuous

84 https://www.bi.go.id/en/bi-institute/BI-Epsilon/Pages/Tantangan-Digitalisasi-UMKM-Berbasis-Budaya.aspx.

85 https://www.oecd-ilibrary.org/sites/13753156-en/index.html?itemId=/content/component/13753156-en.

cycle of market expansion, technological progress, productivity gains, higher incomes, and greater demand—a pattern clearly discernible throughout the work of Paolo Sylos Labini.

From this perspective, oligopolistic capitalism emerges as the natural outcome of the competitive process—not because, as Schumpeter suggested, the entrepreneurial function becomes exhausted, but because concentration is the very condition that allows entrepreneurship to survive and flourish.

This trend is evident not only in the rising market capitalization and number of large firms that have accompanied globalization, but also in the dominant role such corporations play in modern economies: they constitute roughly 10 percent of all businesses, yet account for about 60 percent of global GDP.

References

Baranzini, M. and Marangoni, G. (1995), *Macro e Microeconomia. Teoria e Applicazioni*, Padua, Cedam.

Brancaccio, E., Giammetti, R. and Lucarelli, S. (2022), *La guerra capitalista. Competizione, centralizzazione, nuovo conflitto imperialista*, Milan-Udine, Mimesis.

DOSM (2022), *Micro, Small & Medium Enterprises (MSMES) Performance 2021*, Putrajaya, Department of Statistics Malaysia.

Ferlito, C. (2015), *Entrepreneurship: State of grace or human action? Schumpeter's leadership vs Kirzner's alertness*, «European Journal of Economic and Social Systems», 1-2, pp. 11-36.

Ferlito, C. (2016), *Hermeneutics of Capital. A Post-Austrian Theory for a Kaleidic World*, Hauppauge (NY), Novinka.

Ferlito, C. (2022), *Diamo a Marx quel che è di Marx*, «Rubrics», 5 December, https://www.rubrics.it/diamo-a-marx-quel-che-e-di-marx/.

Hayek, F.A. von (1946), *The meaning of competition*, in *The Collected Works of F.A. Hayek*, Volume xv: *The market and other orders*, Chicago, The University of Chicago Press, 2014, pp. 105-116.

Hayek, F.A. von (1968), *Competition as a discovery procedure*, «Quarterly Journal of Austrian Economics», 5, 3, 2022, pp. 9-23.

Horwitz, S. (2019), *Ludwig Lachmann as a Theorist of Entrepreneurship*, «Studies in Logic, Grammar and Rethoric», 57, 70, pp. 19-40.

Kirzner, I.M. (1963), *Market theory and the price system*, Princeton, Toronto, New York, and London, D. van Nostrand.

Kirzner, I.M. (1973), *Competition and Entrepreneurship*, Chicago, University of Chicago Press.

Kirzner, I.M. (1992), *The Meaning of market process: Essays in the development of modern Austrian economics*, London and New York, Routledge.

Kirzner I.M. (1997), *Entrepreneurial Discovery and the Competitive Market Process: An Austrian Approach*, «Journal of Economic Literature», xxxv, pp. 60-85.

Kirzner, I.M. (1999), *Creativity and/or alertness: A Reconsideration of the Schumpeterian entrepreneur*, «The Review of Austrian Economics», 11, pp. 5-17.

Kirzner, I.M. (2008), *The alert and creative entrepreneur: A clarification*, IFN working paper no. 760, Stockholm, Research Institute of Industrial Economics.

Lachmann, L.M. (1986), *The Market as an Economic Process*, Arlington, Mercatus Center at George Mason University, 2020.

Mises, L. von (1949), *Human Action*, New Haven, Yale University Press.

Mitchell, R.E. (2014), *Economists' Assumptions about Markets. From Adam Smith to Joseph Schumpeter*, Santa Barbara, Denver and Oxford, Praeger.

Nietzsche, F. (1886), *Beyond Good and Evil: Prelude to a Philosophy of the Future*, New York, The Modern Library, 1927.

O'Driscoll, G.P., Jr. and Rizzo, M.J. (1985), *The economics of time and ignorance. Austrian Economics Re-Examined*, London and New York, Routledge, 2015.

Pasinetti, L.L. (1981), *Dinamica struttuale e sviluppo economico. Un'indagine teorica sui mutamenti nella ricchezza delle nazioni*, Turin, UTET, 1984.

Phelps, E. (2013), *Mass Flourishing. How Grassroots Innovation Created Jobs, Challenge, and Change*, Princeton, Princeton University Press.

Robinson, J. (1933), *The Economics of Imperfect Competition*, New York, St Martin's Press, 1969.

Robinson, J. (1956), *The Accumulation of Capital*, London, Palgrave Macmillan, 2013.

Schumpeter, J.A. (1911), *The Theory of Economic Development*, New Brunswick and London, Transaction Publishers, 1983.

Schumpeter, J.A. (1935), *The analysis of economic change*, «The Review of Economics and Statistics», 17, 4, pp. 2-10.

Schumpeter, J.A. (1939), *Business Cycles. A Theoretical, Historical, and Statistical Analysis of the Capitalist Process*, 2 vols., Chevy Chase & Mansfield Centre, Bartleby's Book & Martino Publishing, 2005.

Schumpeter, J.A. (1942), *Capitalism, Socialism and Democracy*, London and New York, Routledge, 2003.

Schumpeter, J.A. (1947), *The creative response in economic history*, «The Journal of Economic History», 7, 2, pp. 149-159.

Sylos Labini, P. (1957), *Oligopoly and Technical Progress*, Cambridge, Harvard University Press, 1962.

Sylos Labini, P. (1984), *Le forze dello sviluppo e del declino*, Rome-Bari, Laterza.

Sylos Labini, P. (1992), *Elementi di dinamica economica*, Rome-Bari, Laterza.

Sylos Labini, P. (1993), *Progresso tecnico e sviluppo ciclico*, Rome-Bari, Laterza.

Sylos Labini, P. (2004), *Torniamo ai classici. Produttività del lavoro, progresso tecnico e sviluppo economico*, Rome-Bari, Laterza.

Varian, H.R. (2007), *Microeconomia*, Venice, Cafoscarina.

CHAPTER 7

Products, Processes and Policies (PPP): A Neo-Schumpeterian Approach to Innovation[86]

Introduction

Innovation has long been recognized as a cornerstone of economic progress, yet its meaning, drivers, and mechanisms remain the subject of continuous debate. From Adam Smith's early reflections on the forces of economic growth to the contemporary insights of Philippe Aghion, Richard Nelson and Edmund Phelps, scholars have sought to explain how new ideas emerge, diffuse, and transform societies. At the centre of this intellectual tradition stands Joseph Schumpeter, whose theory of economic development framed innovation not as an incremental improvement within an existing equilibrium, but as a disruptive, endogenous process that reshapes the very structure of the economy.

Schumpeter's seminal contribution was to define economic development as the result of "new combinations" — novel goods, methods of production, markets, sources of supply, or industrial organizations — introduced by entrepreneurs and made possible through the creation of credit. This "trinomial" of innovation, entrepreneurship, and finance reframed the understanding of competition, replacing the static notion of price rivalry with a dynamic process of *creative destruction*. In this vision, competition is the struggle of the new against the established, a force that simultaneously dismantles outdated structures and lays the foundation for future growth.

While the Schumpeterian framework remains highly influential, the contemporary global economy presents new challenges and opportunities that call for a broader perspective. Modern innovation ecosystems extend far beyond the traditional bank–entrepreneur dyad, encompassing networks of venture capitalists, institutional investors, research foundations, and public policy interventions. Moreover, the role of governance, institutional quality, and strategic policymaking has become increasingly central in determining

86 Originally published as C. Ferlito (2025), *Products, Processes and Policies (PPP): CME's Neo-Schumpeterian Approach to Innovation*, «CME Policy Brief», 8, Subang Jaya, Center for Market Education.

whether entrepreneurial energy and financial resources translate into transformative outcomes.

This chapter emerges from the practical policy work of the Center for Market Education across several Asian economies, where the interplay between innovation, institutions, and development is not merely theoretical but deeply consequential. The present chapter also serves as a theoretical introduction to our innovation policy case studies presented in previous works on Malaysia and Indonesia, as well as in forthcoming studies on India and Bangladesh. This chapter was also intended as the theoretical foundation for the quantitative analyses of our proposed pro-innovation policies, as presented in Desfiandi and Banjaransari (forthcoming).

Building on Schumpeter's trinomial, we propose an expanded framework — the PPP model: Products, Processes, and Policies. The first two dimensions align with Schumpeter's original categories of new combinations, while the third explicitly acknowledges the pivotal role of policy. In our view, policies can act either as catalysts that enable innovation or as innovations in their own right. Yet, crucially, no policy can replace the market's role as the ultimate arbiter of success.

By revisiting Schumpeter's insights through the lens of contemporary innovation ecosystems and our PPP approach, this chapter seeks to serve as theoretical introduction to our different papers where we bridge classical theory and current policy debates. In doing so, it underscores that while entrepreneurship and finance remain indispensable drivers of creative destruction, the institutional and policy environment can decisively shape whether investments yield mere activity or genuine innovation.

1. The trinomial of Schumpeterian innovations: New combinations, new men, new money

Schumpeter's theory of innovation and entrepreneurship is so well-known that it is worth briefly restating its core concepts—both to follow in Schumpeter's footsteps and to liberate his ideas from common clichés.

To begin with, Schumpeter's concept of entrepreneurship must be understood within his broader vision of economic development. In constructing his theory, Schumpeter introduced innovations and the entrepreneurial figure only after explaining what development entails, how it differs from the circular flow (and the place of static theory), the emergence of innovation, and the role of bankers. The entire first part of Chapter 2 in Schumpeter (1911a) is dedicated to defining economic development and explaining why it cannot be grasped using the tools of circular flow analysis. As Schumpeter (1911a, p. 64) writes, «[d]evelopment in our sense is a distinct phenomenon, entirely foreign to what may be observed in the circular flow or in the tendency towards equilibrium. It is spontaneous and discontinuous change in the channels of the flow, disturbance of equilibrium, which forever alters and displaces the equilibrium state previously existing».

The first point is, that, that economic development is a *disruptive phenomenon*, a *transformative process*: economic development is the disruption or departure from an existing equilibrium state. Such transformations, moreover, «are not forced upon [economic life] from without but arise by its own initiative, from within» (Schumpeter, 1911a, p. 63). For Schumpeter, therefore, development such a process is an endogenous one.

Economic development – an endogenous disruption process – arises thanks to the introduction in the economic system of what Schumpeter calls "new combinations", the first of the three elements of the Schumpeterian innovation trinomial: new combinations are the *form* taken by innovations. At this regard Schumpeter lists five possible forms through which new combinations manifest themselves: «(1) The introduction of new goods—i.e., something with which consumers are not yet familiar—or a new quality of goods. (2) The introduction of a new method of production, that is one not yet tested by experience in the branch of manufacture concerned, which by no means has to be founded on a new, scientific discovery and can also exist as a new way of handling a commodity commercially. (3) The opening of a new market, that is a market into which the particular branch of manufacture into which the country in question has not previously entered, whether or not this market had existed before. (4) The conquest of a new source of supply of raw materials or semi-finished goods, again irrespective of whether this source already exists or whether it has first to be created. (5) The carrying out of the new organization of any industry, such as the creation of a monopoly position (for example through trustification) or the breaking up of a monopoly position» (Schumpeter, 1911a, p. 66). New combinations, therefore, are at the heart of economic development.

New combinations, however, do not fall from the sky. They require the intervention of the second and third element of the trinomial. The second element, which Schumpeter (1911a, p. 74) called the «fundamental phenomenon of economic development», is typically associated with Schumpeterian theory: entrepreneurship. While the act of developing new combinations may be called "enterprise", «the individuals whose function it is to carry them out [are called] 'entrepreneurs'» (Schumpeter, 1911a, p. 74). It is at this stage that Schumpeter begins elaborating his famous theory of the entrepreneur.

This leads to a central question: why «is the carrying out of new combinations a special process and the object of a special kind of 'function'» (Schumpeter, 1911a, p. 79), known as the entrepreneurial function? In Schumpeter's view, within the circular flow – or the *normal* static economic flow, economic agents are equipped to act and react rationally in recurring circumstances. Ordinary individuals can navigate such an environment. But when innovation occurs—when circumstances deviate from the norm—ordinary individuals need leadership (Schumpeter, 1911a, p. 79). This need for guidance means that «the carrying out of new combinations is a special function, and the privilege of a type of people who are much less numerous than all those who have the 'objective' possibility of doing it» (Schumpeter, 1911a, p. 81). Entrepreneurs are thus a special type of person, exhibiting distinctive behaviours and capacities.

Another crucial and often misunderstood element is leadership—a topic Schumpeter (1911a, pp. 84-91) explored extensively. Since innovating means introducing new combinations, the Schumpeterian entrepreneur is naturally viewed as an innovator. However, the term "innovation" can be misleading. Although scholars often clarify that innovation is not necessarily invention, there is a persistent risk of conflating entrepreneurship with inventiveness. But Schumpeter was adamant: the entrepreneur is not an inventor (Schumpeter, 1947, p. 152). What defines the entrepreneur is not merely the act of developing new combinations, but the ability to lead a transformative process. Entrepreneurs push the economic system beyond its existing boundaries, demonstrating the capacity to act where others hesitate.

Schumpeter (1911a, pp. 84-87) identified three reasons why moving beyond the circular flow demands exceptional individuals:

> First, outside these accustomed channels the individual is without those data for his decisions and those rules of conduct which are usually very accurately known to him within them. Of course, he must still foresee and

> estimate on the basis of his experience. But many things must remain uncertain, still others are only ascertainable within wide limits, some can perhaps only be "guessed." [...] Here the success of everything depends upon intuition. [...] As this first point lies in the task, so the second lies in the psyche of the businessman himself. It is not only objectively more difficult to do something new than what is familiar and tested by experience, but the individual feels reluctance to it and would do so even if the objective difficulties did not exist. [...] The third point consists in the reaction of the social environment against one who wishes to do something new. [...] There is leadership only for these reasons.

These traits must be underscored. Innovation constitutes a transformation of the economic system (Schumpeter, 1935, p. 4), and entrepreneurs are special because such changes cannot be managed by ordinary actors. By implementing new combinations, entrepreneurs drive the system away from equilibrium—and once innovation is introduced, they must also battle entrenched resistance. What defines them is not invention, but leadership—the ability to master and advance the new. As Schumpeter (1911a, p. 88) emphasized, it «is not part of his [the entrepreneur's] function to 'find' or to 'create' new possibilities. They are always present, abundantly accumulated by all sorts of people».

Many may observe opportunities, but the entrepreneur acts on them. Thus, «more by will than by intellect [...] leaders fulfill their function, more by 'authority,' 'personal weight,' and so forth than by original ideas» (Schumpeter, 1911a, p. 88). Economic leadership is fundamentally distinct from invention. Schumpeter had emphasized this even more strongly in the first edition of *Theorie* (Schumpeter, 1911b, p. 123):

> You can always have the new combinations, but it is the act and the force to act that is indispensable and decisive. [...] The decisive moment is therefore energy and not merely the 'insight.' The latter is much more frequent, without leading to even the most simple act. What matters is the disposition to act. It is the ability to subjugate others and to utilize them for this purposes, in order to prevail that leads to successful deeds—even without particularly brilliant intelligence.

The third critical element of the innovation trinomial is credit. As Schumpeter (1911a, p. 69) explains, «the possessor of wealth, even if it is the greatest combine, must resort to credit if he wishes to carry out a new combination, which cannot like an established business be financed by returns from previous production». This implies that new combinations cannot be financed through existing savings—economic development necessarily involves the creation of debt. Schumpeter considered development unthinkable without what he termed the «creation of purchasing power by banks» (Schumpeter, 1911a, p. 73), even while acknowledging that this process triggers the boom-and-bust cycle. One of Schumpeter's most powerful assertions is that the entrepreneur's role is meaningless without the banker—who is at least equally essential to the implementation of new combinations. Schumpeter (1911a, p. 74) stated this emphatically: «The banker, therefore, is not so much primarily a middleman in the commodity "purchasing power" as a producer of this commodity. [...] He makes possible the carrying out of new combinations, authorises people, in the name of society as it were, to form them. He is the ephor of the exchange economy». In modern times, the financial ecosystem that supports innovation extends well beyond the traditional banking system. Aghion et al. (2021, Chapter 12) highlight that this ecosystem—comprising a robust network of research foundations, institutional investors, and venture capitalists—exerts a significant influence on innovation[87].

It becomes clear that entrepreneurs and capitalists are, from a functional perspective, distinct figures: the former initiate new combinations, the latter provide (or create) the purchasing power required.

Figure 7.1: The trinomial of Schumpeterian Innovations.

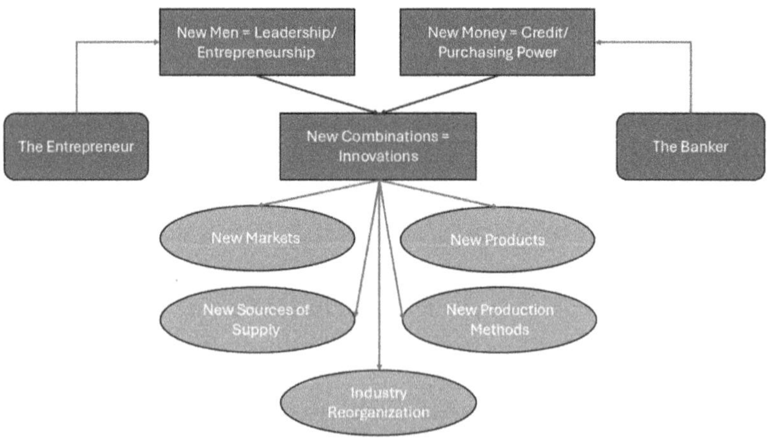

87 See also Kalemli-özcan and Saffie (2023) and Celik (2023).

2. Investment, competition and creative destruction

What emerges from the previous section is that innovation – the key driver behind growth (Nelson, 1996, p. 3) and development (Sylos Labini, 1992, p. 5) – requires both entrepreneurship and money: while money remains sterile if not utilized in the production process, entrepreneurship is merely an empty rebellious impulse without financial means. We can thus introduce a fourth layer—or an element that consolidates the previous reflections: investment. Indeed, upon closer examination, the combination of entrepreneurial initiative and financial resources—when productively employed in the production process, broadly understood—can be identified as investment.

This is why, in CME approach to the topic of innovation, the boundary between innovation and investment may appear rather fluid. Innovation represents the possible—but not inevitable—outcome of a successful union between money creation and the entrepreneurial function, thereby constituting the concrete manifestation of investment. Innovation is *act*, while investment is *potency*[88].

Figure 7.2: Investment and innovations as potency and act.

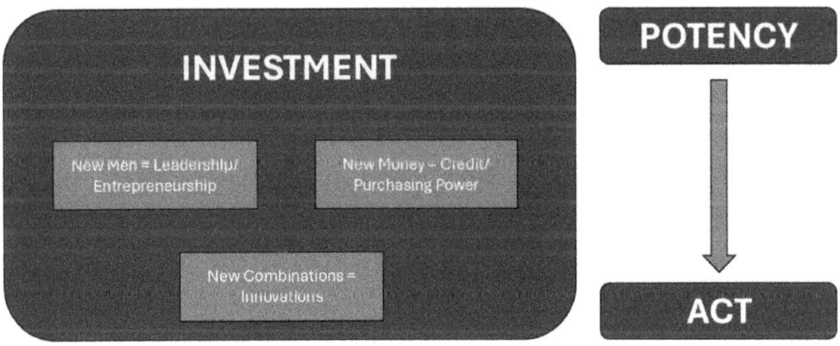

Here the "innovation box" is a subset within the broader domain of investment. The critical distinction lies in the *transition from potency to act*, which occurs only when an investment passes the "market test", that is, when entrepreneurial creativity and financial initiative succeed in meeting genuine human needs within the discipline of market validation, and bring into economic life a genuine novelty.

88 Investment is potency in the sense that *in potentia esse* means being in ability, being in possibility, or being-able-to-be. The passage from potency to act – from investment to innovation – is moving from *possible* to *actual being* (Stein, 1950, p. 36).

This transition mirrors Edith Stein's Aristotelian-Thomistic distinction between *potentia* and *actus*, reinterpreted phenomenologically. For Stein, *potency* is not mere potentiality but a structured openness to form, an orientation toward fulfilment that demands actualization through encounter with being. Applied to economics, investment represents the *potentia*—the anticipatory openness of capital and entrepreneurial imagination toward future realization. Innovation, by contrast, represents the *actus*—the manifestation of that inner orientation once meaning is actualized in a concrete product, process, or institutional transformation (as we shall see).

In this sense, the entrepreneur plays a role analogous to the *personal subject* in Stein's ontology: the one who mediates between potentiality and actuality, translating latent possibilities into realized forms through intentional, meaning-bearing action. The hermeneutical process that precedes innovation—interpreting opportunities, allocating capital, and projecting expectations—reflects precisely the interpretative movement through which the subject "extracts" meaning from reality, rather than arbitrarily imposing it.

Thus, the relationship between investment and innovation, understood through Stein's lens, embodies the movement of being from potential toward fulfilment, where human creativity acts as the mediating principle. Investment is the horizon of *possibility* (the openness of capital and imagination), while innovation is the *event of realization*, the point at which meaning crystallizes into form. Hermeneutics, in Emilio Betti's sense, secures the objectivity of this process: innovation is not a purely subjective creation but the discovery and actualization of meanings already latent in the structures of the world, brought to light through entrepreneurial interpretation and market verification.

However, innovation and investment do not occur in isolation. Rather, they unfold through a dynamic struggle within what can be described as *the competition that matters*. Schumpeter is explicitly critical of the traditional concept of competition, and it is in contrast to this conventional view that he redefines the true meaning of competition—distancing it from the simplistic notion of a price war to which it is often reduced (Ferlito, 2024).

> The first thing to go is the traditional conception of the *modus operandi* of competition. Economists are at long last emerging from the stage in which price competition was all they saw. [...]. But in capitalist reality as

> distinguished from its textbook picture, it is not that kind of competition which counts but the competition from the new commodity, the new technology, the new source of supply, the new type of organization (the largest-scale unit of control for instance)—competition which commands a decisive cost or quality advantage and which strikes not at the margins of the profits and the outputs of the existing firms but at their foundations and their very lives. This kind of competition is as much more effective than the other as a bombardment is in comparison with forcing a door, and so much more important that it becomes a matter of comparative indifference whether competition in the ordinary sense functions more or less promptly; the powerful lever that in the long run expands output and brings down prices is in any case made of other stuff (Schumpeter, 1942, pp. 84-85).

For Schumpeter, competition is not a price war among identical firms producing the same goods, but rather the struggle of new combinations against established ways of doing things. This concept is inherently dynamic, pointing to an ongoing process rather than a static condition.

This process gives rise to what Schumpeter famously termed *creative destruction*, «the process by which new innovations continually emerge and render existing technologies obsolete, new firms continually arrive to compete with existing firms, and new jobs and activities arise and replace existing jobs and activities» (Aghion et al., 2021, p. 1): when a new approach successfully emerges and displaces the old, a part of the existing economic order is permanently lost and replaced by innovation[89]. This, for Schumpeter, is the driving force of capitalism, the true essence of competition—not a battle among equals over prices, but a dynamic clash between the new and the old. The entrepreneur does not enter the market to become just another player among many, equal and homogeneous with others. On the contrary, entrepreneurship is driven by a *will to power*—a desire to overcome competitors, not to blend in with them—and by a natural impulse to capture increasing market share through superior strategies (Ferlito, 2022 and 2024). In a nutshell, disruptive entrepreneurs aim at dominant positions (Aghion and Howitt, 1982, p. 349).

89 Schumpeter's concept of creative destruction, articulated between the publication of his seminal works in 1911 and 1942, was incorporated into modern endogenous growth theory as the central driving force of economic development only with the publication of Aghion and Howitt (1982), although such an insight was already recognized by Schumpeter at the beginning of the twentieth century.

Disruption, not equilibrium, defines the essence of market forces within the context of creative destruction. Technological advancement is an evolutionary process bringing the economy in a continuing state of disequilibrium (Nelson, 1996, p. 3). As Lachmann (1986, p. 5) observed, «[n]o agent can enter a market, or extend his range of activity within one by making offers to other agents, without disrupting some market relationship presently existing between them and others. This fact is of course the very essence of competition» (Lachmann, 1986, p. 5). It becomes evident, therefore, that innovation is not determined by the prevailing market structure; rather, the causality runs in the opposite direction. Innovators, by surpassing incumbent competitors and pre-empting the entry of imitators, actively construct their own dominant—albeit transitory—position within the industry (Nelson and Winter, 1982, p. 281).

The natural consequence is that a genuine, as opposed to fictional, competitive process cannot result—either at the outset or in its final stage—in a fragmented archipelago of firms all doing the same thing without distinctive features. Rather, the will to power that lies at the heart of entrepreneurial action inevitably leads to concentration[90], the natural outcome of a competitive process properly understood[91]—not the fiction passed on to passive students who, sadly, go on to become professors and perpetuate that same fiction (Ferlito, 2024).

Once initiated, the process becomes self-reinforcing. Technical progress not only generates industrial concentration, but concentration itself becomes a prerequisite for further innovation. When innovation spreads rapidly, concentration is necessary to sustain additional technical progress. In cases where a new technique diffuses quickly, the entrepreneur introducing it must secure sufficient profit before widespread adoption renders the initial investment obsolete. This

90 At this regard, our analysis is consistent with the creative destruction paradigm developed by Aghion et al. (2021).

91 In this regard, the pioneering work of Paolo Sylos Labini, who studied under Schumpeter at Harvard during 1948–1950 (Ferlito, 2011), deserves recognition. Building on the foundations laid by his teacher in *Capitalism, Socialism and Democracy* (1942), Sylos Labini (1957) emphasized not only that oligopolies represent the most prevalent form of industrial organization, but also that advances in industrial concentration are a necessary precondition for innovation to occur. It is also noteworthy to observe the parallel with the conclusions reached during the same period by Joan Robinson (1956).

dynamic creates an incentive to develop innovations that are increasingly resistant to rapid imitation, a goal often achieved by expanding firm size and adopting techniques with higher barriers to replication, largely due to the scale of required investments.

Innovation and concentration, therefore, must advance together (Robinson, 1956, pp. 86–87). Indeed, within a concentrated oligopolistic structure, technology «creates external barriers between each group of firms and its potential competitors» (Sylos Labini, 1957, pp. 53–54). At the same time, the process of industrial concentration «creates by no means negligible technological discontinuities. Only large firms can apply certain methods, both technical and organizational, and only large firms can realize certain economies of scale. And the transition from small to large firms is not gradual; there are jumps and the jumps come broader as concentration proceeds» (Sylos Labini, 1957, p. 35).

Concentration is also essential for technical progress because, under oligopolistic conditions, firms can pursue profit maximization with greater independence. Price policy becomes closely tied to financing new investments (Sylos Labini, 1992, p. 205), and the growth rate of a firm's production is proportional to its profit rate (Sylos Labini, 1992, p. 215). This does not imply that small and medium-sized enterprises (SMEs) vanish; rather, they can form a dynamic and supportive ecosystem that allows larger firms to flourish. While smaller firms often retain an innovative spirit and generate new ideas, they may lack the scale and market power to bring these innovations to fruition. A cooperative relationship between small and large enterprises thus emerges as a crucial factor in sustaining a vibrant innovation process (Sylos Labini, 1993, pp. 270–272).

These theoretical insights are corroborated by Aghion et al. (2005), who demonstrate an inverted-U relationship between innovation and industrial concentration. Their findings confirm Sylos Labini's view that concentration is indeed a prerequisite for innovation[92]. However, once concentration reaches a certain threshold, dominant firms tend to preserve their position not through continued innovation but through political patronage (Baslandze, 2023; Bombardini et al., 2023).

---

92 Bykova (2017), for instance, examined the relationship between innovation and concentration in Russia, providing further evidence in support of the inverted-U relationship. See also Symeonidis (1996).

The inherently destructive nature of truly innovative competition, the natural tendency toward concentration, and the cumulative power of innovation are key features of a paradigm in which creative destruction is seen as the foundation of economic growth (Aghion et al., 2021, p. 15).

At the same time, this paradigm transcends the false dichotomy between macroeconomics and microeconomics, aligning more closely with Erik Lindahl's (1919) perspective. According to Lindahl, microeconomics examines individual choices, while macroeconomics addresses the outcomes of the social interactions generated by those choices. As Wagner (2020, p. vii) observes, «[m]icro denotes the individual entities whose actions and interactions generate the phenomena we designate as macro». Within Schumpeter's framework of creative destruction, entrepreneurs and bankers are the individual actors generating micro-level phenomena—innovations—whose consequences, however, manifest at the macro level as economic growth and, though beyond the scope of this discussion, business cycles.

3. The PPP approach as an extension of the Schumpeterian trinomial

These previous reflections lead us to the concluding point of the present chapter: the crucial role of institutions and policymaking in fostering innovation. The recognition of innovation as a key driver of development[93] has long been established in economic thought—from Adam Smith (1776)[94] to more recent contributions by Phelps (2013)[95], with Schumpeter serving as a pivotal figure in between (Sylos Labini, 2004). Within this intellectual tradition, stretching from Smith to Phelps, institutions[96] and culture are acknowledged as essential preconditions for the emergence of innovation.

In recent years, the Center for Market Education, with the support of the Tholos Foundation, has been actively publishing policy papers

93 Innovation is also recognized as the main source of economic convergence (Peters and Zilibotti, 2023, p. 476).

94 According to Adam Smith, economic development is a consequence of the division of labour, which in turn depends on the extension of the market. But, indeed, both division of labour and the enlargement of the market can be considered innovations (or *new combinations*) in Schumpeterian terms.

95 See also Phelps et al. (2020).

96 For an overview of the literature on the relationship between institutions and growth, see Nelson (2005).

and briefs exploring the relationship between policy solutions and innovation across various Asian countries[97].

The idea for this chapter emerged from the realization that, while working on specific country cases, we were—at least partially unconsciously—developing our own approach to the topic of innovation. We later labelled this approach as the PPP model: Products, Processes, and Policies.

Upon further reflection on how our perspective has evolved within the broader policy debate, we recognized that our approach can be seen as an extension of the Schumpeterian trinomial. Indeed, our first two *P*s—products and processes—clearly correspond to the first two examples of new combinations identified by the Austrian economist: new products and new methods of production. However, we also believe that, from a broader perspective, Schumpeter's remaining examples—new markets, new sources of supply, and new forms of industrial organization—can likewise be categorized under the notion of new processes. These do not necessarily alter the product itself, but rather the way in which production and economic activity are organized.

Acknowledging the pivotal role that institutions play in economic development—and placing policy-making among key institutional arrangements—we introduced a third P: Policies. In our framework, policies play a dual role in relation to innovation:

- Policies as catalysts: They can either hinder or facilitate innovation, depending on their design and implementation.
- Policies as innovations themselves: Innovative policy solutions can represent a novel way of addressing challenges, not merely by influencing other actors, but by embodying innovation in their own right.

Looking back at our previous publications, we can identify examples that reflect this framework. For instance, fiscal reform initiatives and the application of the harm reduction principle fall under the first category, where policies serve as catalysts for innovation. On the other hand, proposals such as the entrepreneurial rail model applied to urban mobility and development (Ferlito and Rambey, 2024) can be

97 See, in particular, Ferlito and Shamsunahar (2023), Banjaransari (2024), Kabir et al. (2025), Basu (forthcoming), Ferlito et al. (2025).

considered innovations in themselves—entirely new ways of shaping reality through policy[98].

The importance of institutional arrangements is evidenced, among other factors, by the strong correlation observed between countries' scores in the Global Innovation Index (GII) and their performance in other internationally recognized benchmarks, such as the International Property Rights Index (IPRI) [99], the International Trade Barrier Index (TBI)[100], and the Index of Economic Freedom[101].

For instance, the log-to-log correlation between the IPRI and the GII reaches 86.42%.

Figure 7.3: Log-to-log correlation between IPRI and GII.

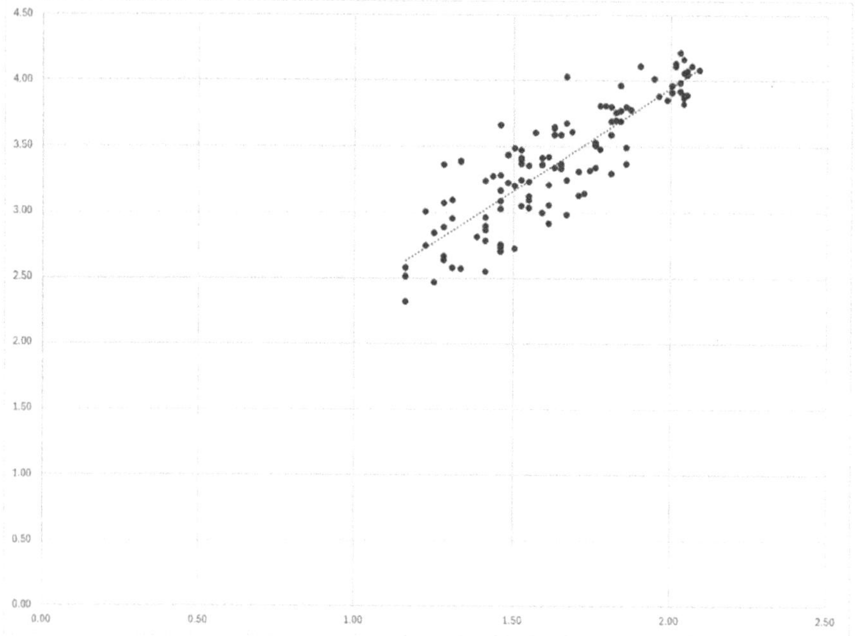

Source: Our re-elaborations on data from IPRI and GII.

98 A comprehensive volume on the relationships between policy and creative destruction is Akcigit and Van Reenen (2023). Several intellectual stimuli can be found also in Aghion at al. (2021).

99 Developed by the Property Rights Alliance: https://internationalpropertyrightsindex.org/.

100 Developed by the Tholos Foundation: https://www.tradebarrierindex.org/.

101 Developed by the Heritage Foundation: https://www.heritage.org/index/.

Similarly, the log-to-log correlation between the Global Innovation Index and the protection of intellectual property—one of the subcomponents of the IPRI—amounts to 84.41%. In this regard, it is important to emphasize that intellectual property (IP) protection can serve as both a stimulus and a barrier to innovation. Therefore, IP policies should be complemented by measures that ensure open market entry, allowing incumbent firms to be challenged[102]. Such competitive pressure provides an additional incentive for firms to remain innovative and competitive (Aghion et al., 2021, p. 63).

Figure 7.4: Log-to-log correlation between Intellectual Property and GII.

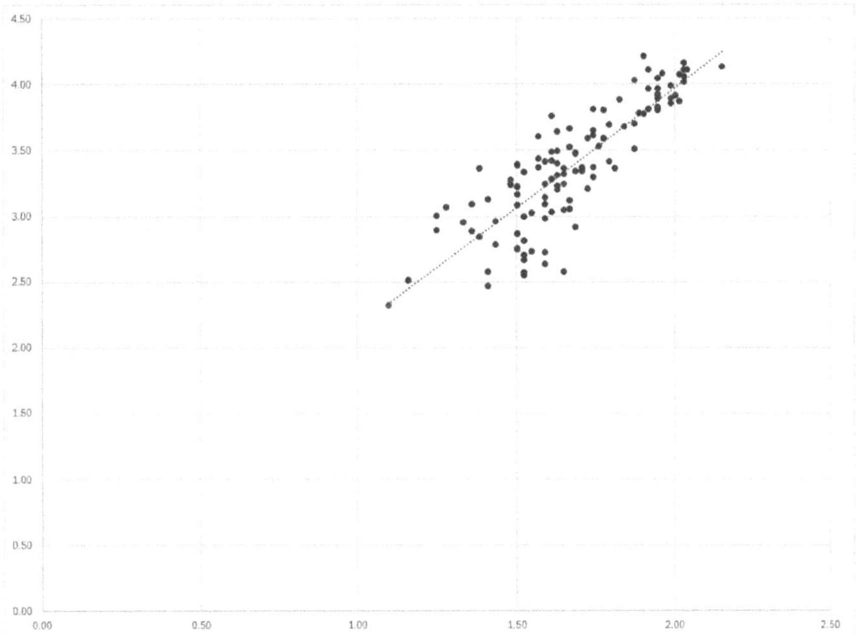

Source: Our re-elaborations on data from IPRI and GII.

With respect to international trade, our analysis shows that innovation is negatively correlated (log-to-log: –54.36%) with countries' scores in the International Trade Barrier Index. This indicates that higher levels of trade restrictions—both tariff and non-tariff barriers—are associated with lower innovation capacity.

102 In example, by strictly limiting the patent scope to what the "inventor" did (Nelson, 1996, p. 143).

Figure 7.5: Log-to-log correlation between TBI and GII.

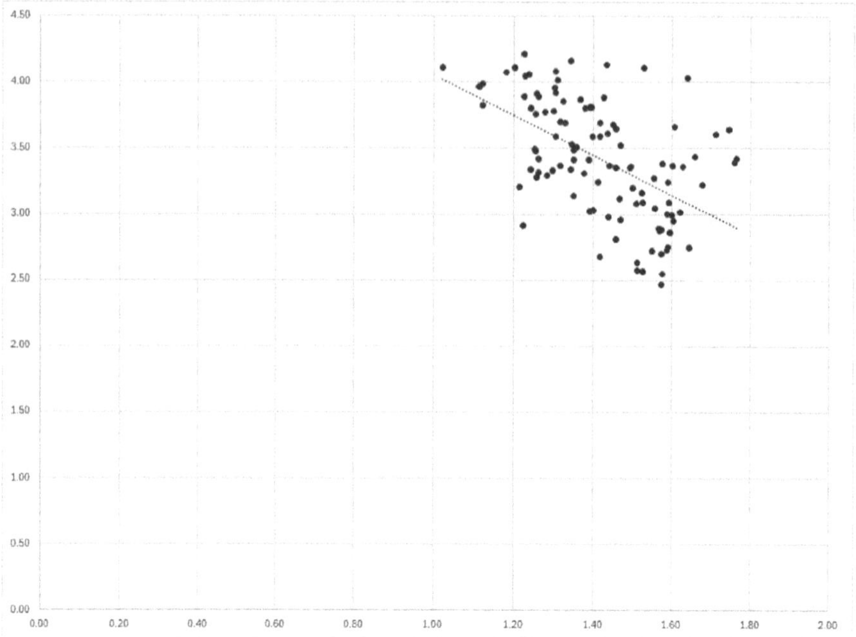

Source: Our re-elaborations on data from TBI and GII.

Similarly, a log-to-log correlation close to 72% is found between innovation and economic freedom as measured by the Heritage Foundation.

Figure 7.6: Log-to-log correlation between Index of Economic Freedom and GII.

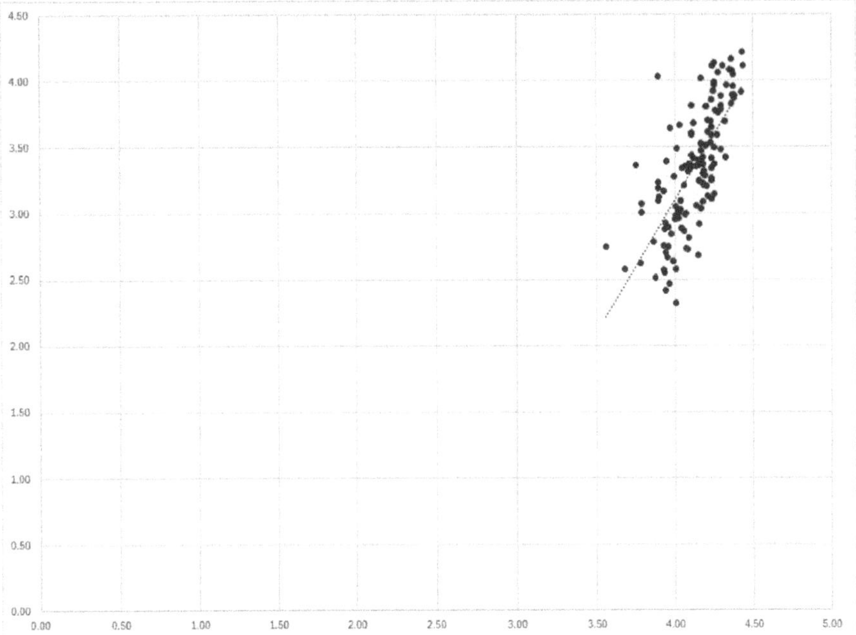

Source: Our re-elaborations on data from IEF and GII.

Such evidence, demonstrating the relationship between innovation and institutions, is employed by Desfiandi and Banjaransari (forthcoming) to formulate a set of policy recommendations consistently identified as conducive to innovation. As will be shown in their paper, and as suggested by the present analysis, pro-innovation policies must be grounded in the protection of property rights, the safeguarding of intellectual property, the reduction of trade barriers, and the expansion of economic freedom (and, at a certain extent, the favouring of industrial concentration). A more detailed discussion of these policies, however, lies beyond the scope of this introductory work.

In conclusion, the trinomial of Schumpeterian innovations can then be revised as follows.

Figure 7.7: The trinomial of Schumpeterian innovations revisited.

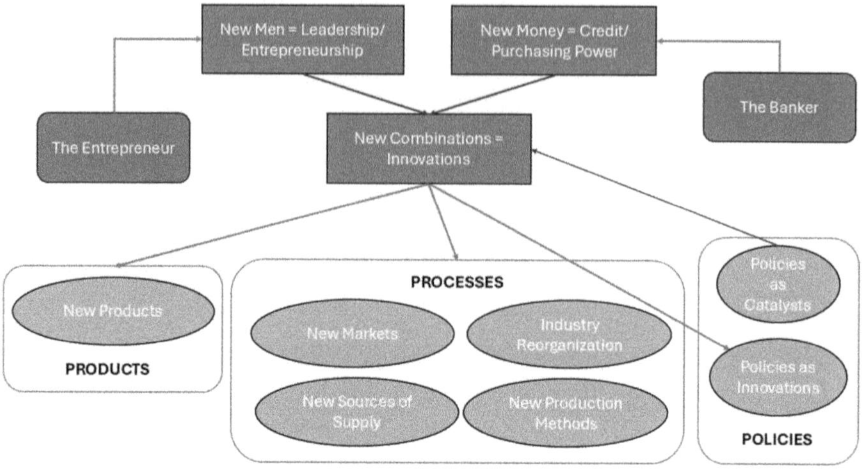

4. Important clarifications

In conclusion, a few important clarifications are necessary.

First, as illustrated in Figure 7.2, not all investments lead to innovation. We have depicted the "innovation box" as a subset of the investment domain to highlight that while all innovations stem from investments, not every investment results in innovation.

Second, although contemporary literature on creative destruction emphasizes the role of innovation in driving economic growth, it often overlooks the essential interplay between entrepreneurship and money creation—both of which are crucial for the creative destruction process to unfold. For this reason, we found it necessary to return to Schumpeter's original formulation, which clearly underscores that the second and third components of his trinomial—entrepreneurship and credit—must not be forgotten or dismissed. Furthermore, it must be acknowledged that these phenomena cannot be understood in abstract terms but must always be grounded in individual decision-making. Even within an era characterized by oligopolistic capitalism and large corporations, agency remains rooted in the choices of individuals. Entrepreneurial and financial decisions are exercised by persons, and the decision-making process therefore retains an inherently personal dimension that cannot be regarded as impersonal. Indeed, «innovation [...] comes from the dynamism of the people», guided by a set of value which comprises "individualism", vitalism and self-expression (Phelps, 2023, p. 18).

Third, our approach diverges from the current literature in the importance we assign to the role of policies. While several authors suggest that policies can directly generate innovation, we maintain that policy can serve only as a facilitator—unless it constitutes an innovation in itself. Regardless of how supportive the institutional framework may be, the ultimate success of an investment and its transformation into innovation—the transition from potency to act—is determined by the market test[103]. In the long run, no product can survive unless it earns the favour of consumers. Policies can assist the process of creative destruction[104] – in example, by supporting a revival of the values which supported the great wave of innovations of the past 200 years (Phelps, 2023, p. 19) – but they cannot substitute for the market mechanism.

Concluding remarks

This chapter has revisited Schumpeter's trinomial of innovation—new combinations, entrepreneurship, and credit—and extended it into the Center for Market Education's PPP framework: Products, Processes, and Policies. By reconnecting Schumpeter's insights with contemporary debates on innovation and institutional design, we have emphasized that innovation is not an abstract or automatic outcome, but rather the result of entrepreneurial initiative supported by financial resources, and shaped decisively by the institutional and policy environment.

103 In this respect, our position is simultaneously consonant with and divergent from the critiques advanced by economists such as Roland (2023, p. 521), who observes that «innovation and entrepreneurship are by far not at the heart of the economics teaching curriculum, which still mostly emphasizes resource allocation and price theory. This is a pity, because Schumpeter's vision of capitalism is probably more relevant to understanding the dynamics of economic systems like capitalism and socialism, compared to mainstream price theory, which still forms the basics of economics education». We concur that entrepreneurs, entrepreneurship, and innovation ought to assume a central place within economic analysis (Ferlito, 2020). Nevertheless, it is only through a rigorous understanding of price theory that one can grasp why innovation results in enduring processes of creative destruction, as its permanence is secured solely through the competitive test of the market.

104 In certain instances, public policies may act as impediments to the process of creative destruction. Such measures are often the outcome of lobbying efforts by incumbent firms, which aim to safeguard their dominant position through preferential regulations and political protection, rather than contributing to the advancement of the innovation frontier (Baslandze, 2023; Bombardini et al., 2023).

The analysis has shown that institutions matter profoundly. Strong protection of property rights, the safeguarding of intellectual property, the reduction of trade barriers, and the expansion of economic freedom are all consistently correlated with higher levels of innovation capacity. Policies, however, cannot replace the market test; they can only facilitate innovation or, in some cases, embody innovation themselves. Ultimately, investment must pass through the discipline of the market, where consumers determine which initiatives endure.

At the same time, we have stressed that entrepreneurship and finance remain inherently personal phenomena. Even within oligopolistic capitalism, innovation originates from individual decision-making and leadership, underscoring the centrality of human agency in the process of creative destruction.

The reflections presented here should be read as an introduction to a broader research agenda. Building upon this theoretical foundation, forthcoming works will offer quantitative analyses and country-specific case studies—covering Malaysia, Indonesia, India, and Bangladesh—that apply the PPP framework to concrete policy contexts. In this way, the present chapter serves not as a conclusion, but as the starting point of a wider effort to bridge economic theory and policy practice, with the ultimate goal of fostering environments where innovation can flourish as the true driver of sustainable development.

However, there is more. Although the reasoning presented here can still be considered embryonic, we have tried to stress how economic innovation manifests the ontological rhythm of potency and act, uniting phenomenological essence and hermeneutical discovery—the same dynamic through which, for Edith Stein, finite beings participate in the continuous unfolding of being itself.

References

Aghion, P., Antonin, C. and Bunel, S. (2021), *The Power of Creative Destruction. Economic Upheaval and the Wealth of Nations*, Cambridge and London, The Belknap Press of Harvard University Press.

Aghion, P., Bloom, N., Blundell, R., Griffith, R. and Howitt, P. (2005), *Competition and Innovation: An Inverted-U Relationship*, «The Quarterly Journal of Economics», 120, 2, pp. 701-728.

Aghion, P. and Howitt, P. (1982), *A Model of Growth Through Creative Destruction*, «Econometrica», 60, 2, pp. 323-351.

Akcigit, U. and Van Reenen, J. (Eds.) (2023), *The Economics of Creative Destruction. New Research on Themes from Aghion and Howitt*, Cambridge and London, Harvard University Press.

Banjaransari, A. (Ed.) (2024), *Sebuah Agenda Inovasi untuk Pemerintah Indonesia*, Washington, DC, and Jakarta, Tholos Foundation and Center for Market Education Indonesia.

Baslandze, S. (2023), *Barriers to Creative Destruction*, in Akcigit and Van Reenen (Eds.) (2023), pp. 558-584.

Basu, P. (forthcoming), *An Innovation Policy Agenda for India*, «CME Policy Paper», 9, Subang Jaya, Center for Market Education.

Bombardini, M., Cutinelli-Rendina, O. and Trebbi, F. (2023), *Lobbying behind the Frontier*, in Akcigit and Van Reenen (Eds.) (2023), pp. 533-557.

Bykova, A.A. (2017), *The Impact of Industry's Concentration on Innovation: Evidence from Russia*, «Journal of Corporate Finance Research», 11, 1, pp. 37-49.

Celik, M.A. (2023), *Creative Destruction, Finance, and Firm Dynamics*, in Akcigit and Van Reenen (Eds.) (2023), pp. 611-637.

Desfiandi, A. and Banjaransari, A. (forthcoming), *The Quantitative Impact of CME PPP Approach to Innovation*, «CME Policy Paper», 10, Subang Jaya, Center for Market Education.

Ferlito, C. (2011), *Sylos Labini's Unpublished Notes on Schumpeter's* Business Cycles, «The Quarterly Journal of Austrian Economics», 14, 1, pp. 88-129.

Ferlito, C. (2020), *The Entrepreneur: "One, No One and One Hundred Thousand"*, «CME EduPaper», 2, Subang Jaya, Center for Market Education.

Ferlito, C. (2022), *Diamo a Marx quel che è di Marx*, «Rubrics», 5 December, https://www.rubrics.it/diamo-a-marx-quel-che-e-dimarx/.

Ferlito, C. (2024), *Competition, Innovation and Concentration. A Nietzschean Essay in Honour of Paolo Sylos Labini*, «CME EduPaper», 9, Subang Jaya, Center for Market Education.

Ferlito, C., Foo, P. and Bin Sazuki, F. (2025), *Indirect Taxation and Innovation: An ASEAN Framework*, «CME Policy Brief», 7, Subang Jaya, Center for Market Education.

Ferlito, C. and Rambey, C. (2024), *Peran Real Estat Dalam Inovasi Pembangunan Perkotaan*, in Banjaransari (2024), pp. 18-31.

Ferlito, C. and Shamsunahar, I. (2023), *Harm Reduction, Healthcare Savings and Economic Growth: A Strategy for Malaysia*, «CME Policy Paper», 6, Subang Jaya, Center for Market Education.

Kabir, S., Kabir, M. and Ferlito, C. (2025), *An Innovation Policy Agenda for Bangladesh*, «CME Policy Paper», 8, Subang Jaya, Center for Market Education.

Kalemli-Özcan, Ş and Saffie, F. (2023), *Finance and Growth. Firm Heterogeneity and Creative Destruction*, in Akcigit and Van Reenen (Eds.) (2023), pp. 587-610.

Lachmann, L.M. (1986), *The Market as an Economic Process*, Arlington, Mercatus Center at George Mason University, 2020.

Lindahl, E. (1919), *Studies in the Theory of Capital and Income*, London, Allen & Unwin, 1939.

Nelson, R.R. (1996), *The Sources of Economic Growth*, Cambridge and London, Harvard University Press.

Nelson, R.R. (2005), *Technology, Institutions and Economic Growth*, Cambridge and London, Harvard University Press.

Nelson, R.R. and Winter, S.G. (1982), *An Evolutionary Theory of Economic Change*, Cambridge and London, The Belknap Press of Harvard University Press.

Peters, M. and Zilibotti, F. (2023), *Creative Destruction, Distance to Frontier, and Economic Development*, in Akcigit and Van Reenen (Eds.) (2023), pp. 475-519.

Phelps, E. (2013), *Mass Flourishing. How Grassroots Innovation Created Jobs, Challenge, and Change*. Princeton, Princeton University Press.

Phelps, E. (2023), *Innovation and Growth Policy*, in Akcigit and Van Reenen (Eds.) (2023), pp. 17-19.

Phelps, E., Bojilov, R., Teck Hoon, H. and Zoega, G. (2020), *Dynamism. The Values That Drive Innovation, Job Satisfaction, and Economic Growth*, Cambridge, Harvard University Press.

Robinson, J. (1956), *The Accumulation of Capital*, London, Palgrave Macmillan, 2013.

Roland, G. (2023), *Socialism, Capitalism, State Capitalism, and Innovation*, in Akcigit and Van Reenen (Eds.) (2023), pp. 520-532.

Schumpeter, J.A. (1911a), *The Theory of Economic Development: An Inquiry into Profits, Capital, Credit, Interest, and the Business Cycle*, New Brunswick and London, Transaction Publishers, 1983.

Schumpeter, J.A. (1911b), *The Theory of Economic Development (1911): The Fundamental Phenomenon of Economic Development*, in M.C. Becker, K. Thorbjørn and R. Swedberg, (Eds.), *The Entrepreneur: Classic Texts by Joseph Schumpeter*, Stanford, Stanford University Press, 2011, pp. 79-154.

Schumpeter, J.A. (1935), *The Analysis of Economic Change*, «The Review of Economics and Statistics», 17, 4, pp. 2-10.

Schumpeter, J.A. (1942), *Capitalism, Socialism and Democracy*, London and New York, Routledge, 2003.

Schumpeter, J.A. (1947), *The Creative Response in Economic History*, «The Journal of Economic History», 7, 2, pp. 149-159.

Smith, A. (1776), *An Inquiry into the Nature and Causes of the Wealth of Nations*, London, W. Strahan and T. Cadell.

Stein, E. (1950), *The Complete Works*, Volume 12: *Finite and Eternal Being: An Attempt to Ascend to the Meaning of Being*, Washington, DC, ICS Publications, 2024.

Sylos Labini, P. (1957), *Oligopoly and Technical Progress*, Cambridge, Harvard University Press, 1962.

Sylos Labini, P. (1992), *Elementi di dinamica economica*, Rome and Bari, Laterza.

Sylos Labini, P. (1993), *Progresso tecnico e sviluppo ciclico*, Rome and Bari, Laterza.

Sylos Labini, P. (2004), *Torniamo ai classici. Produttività del lavoro, progresso tecnico e sviluppo economico*, Rome and Bari, Laterza.

Symeonidis, G. (1996), *Innovation, Firm Size and Market Structure: Schumpeterian Hypothesis and Some New Themes*, «OECD Economics Department Working Papers», 161, Paris, Organisation for Economic Co-operation and Development.

Wagner, R.E. (2020), *Macroeconomics as Systems Theory. Transcending the Micro-Macro Dichotomy*, London, Palgrave Macmillan.

General Conclusion: Toward an Interpretative Economics

This volume has sought to rediscover economics as an interpretative science — a discipline rooted in meaning rather than measurement, in understanding rather than prediction. Across its chapters, a unifying conviction has emerged: that the economy is not a mechanical system governed by fixed laws, but a living process of human interpretation, imagination, and coordination through time.

From the redefinition of economics as a science of meaning, to the exploration of capital as a hermeneutical construct, to the renewed understanding of business cycles, money, and entrepreneurship, these essays have aimed to build a coherent intellectual architecture grounded in *verstehen*. Each part contributes to a single argument: that human action — and the markets it generates — cannot be reduced to equations without losing their essence.

In *capital theory*, this approach reveals capital as a dynamic web of expectations and plans, constantly reshaped by entrepreneurs who interpret and reinterpret the world around them. In *monetary theory*, it uncovers the limits of control and the dangers of mistaking measurement for understanding — reminding us that money, credit, and interest are not neutral instruments but expressions of trust and anticipation. And in *innovation and entrepreneurship*, it presents markets as arenas of discovery where creative minds continuously redefine what is possible.

The Austrian and Schumpeterian traditions converge here as a philosophy of openness — of reason understood as dialogue with reality, and of markets seen as evolving orders of meaning. The role of the economist, therefore, is not to predict the future or engineer equilibrium, but to interpret the ongoing conversation between human purposes and the constraints of time.

To reimagine economics in this way is not only an academic endeavour but a moral and civilizational one. In a world increasingly ruled by algorithms and data, the call to re-humanize economics is also a call to safeguard freedom, creativity, and responsibility. Economics must once again become a *science of human flourishing* — attentive to the drama of choice, error, and learning that defines life in society.

If the essays collected here succeed in showing that rigor and humanity, analysis and meaning, can coexist in the same intellectual framework, then this long effort will have achieved its goal. For at its deepest level, the study of economics is an act of interpretation — an attempt to understand not just how people allocate resources, but how they pursue purpose, construct value, and make sense of the world as a field of intelligible meaning rather than as a domain of mechanical necessity.

Emphasizing the hermeneutical nature of economics does not mean surrendering to nihilism or to the arbitrariness of interpretation. On the contrary, it recognizes that the interpretative act is the privileged means through which the human mind encounters *Sein* and discloses the *Wesen* of things. Interpretation, as Emilio Betti reminds us, is not the creation of meaning *ex nihilo*, but the attentive reception of the meaning already inscribed in reality and offered to human understanding.

Thus, the radical subjectivism inherent in hermeneutics is not a descent into solipsism, but the affirmation that subjectivity is the *locus* where being reveals itself. In this light, hermeneutics and phenomenology are not opposing methods but complementary paths: the former describes the movement of consciousness reaching toward meaning, while the latter grounds that movement in the ontological conviction that reality is meaningful in itself. To approach economics hermeneutically is therefore to affirm that markets, choices, and institutions are not mere aggregates of impulses or data, but manifestations of a living order of meaning through which *Sein* becomes intelligible in human action. In the dialogue between interpretation and essence, between the flux of understanding and the stability of being, the economist finds the true vocation of his science: to illuminate the dynamic encounter between human spirit and the world it seeks to comprehend.

Epilogue

As these reflections draw to a close, they also mark the completion of a personal intellectual cycle. The ideas developed across these pages are the result of a journey that began more than two decades ago, driven by a fascination with the living process of the market and the restless creativity of human action. Bringing these essays together is not merely an act of synthesis but an act of gratitude — toward the thinkers who inspired me, the experiences that shaped my understanding, and the enduring dialogue between theory and life.

If there is a legacy to be drawn from these years of study and writing, it lies in the hope that younger minds will take up this interpretative spirit — curious, critical, and humble before the complexity of reality. For economics, like life itself, flourishes only when it remains open to surprise, interpretation, and renewal.

www.ingramcontent.com/pod-product-compliance
Ingram Content Group UK Ltd.
Pitfield, Milton Keynes, MK11 3LW, UK
UKHW020126290926
15471UKWH00003B/307

9 781946 374349